To my parents, who taught me how to be Jewish;
to my husband, who helped me be a Jewish economist;
and to my children, from whom I learned what it is all about.

Contents

Tables and Figures   ix

Acknowledgments   xi

Part I: Jews as Religious Consumers

1   Introduction   3

2   The Economic Context   25

Part II: Investing in Judaism

3   The Cost of Being Jewish in America   53

4   Jewish Education and Human Capital   72

Part III: Constraints and Incentives in American Jewish Life

5   Jewish Families in America   105

6   American Jewish Immigrants   127

Part IV: Exchange and Change in American Judaism

7   Israel and American Judaism   161

8   Whither American Judaism?   180

Key Acronyms   205

Glossary of English Terms   207

Glossary of Hebrew and Yiddish Terms   211

Notes   215

References   219

Index   225

Judaism in Transition

How Economic Choices Shape Religious Tradition

Carmel U. Chiswick

STANFORD ECONOMICS AND FINANCE

An Imprint of Stanford University Press

Stanford, California

Stanford University Press
Stanford, California

Special discounts for bulk quantities of titles in the Stanford Economics and
Finance imprint are available to corporations, professional associations, and
other organizations. For details and discount information, contact the
special sales department of Stanford University Press. Tel: (650) 736-1782,
Fax: (650) 736-1784

Printed in the United States of America on acid-free, archival-quality paper

Library of Congress Cataloging-in-Publication Data

Chiswick, Carmel U., author.
  Judaism in transition: how economic choices shape religious tradition /
Carmel U. Chiswick.
    pages cm
  Includes bibliographical references and index.
    ISBN 978-0-8047-7604-2 (cloth: alk. paper) — ISBN 978-0-8047-7605-9
(pbk.: alk. paper)
    1. Judaism—Economic aspects—United States. 2. Jews—United States—
Economic conditions. I. Title.
    BM205.C495 2014
    296.0973—dc23

                                                            2013047799

ISBN 978-0-8047-9141-0 (electronic)

Typeset by Thompson Type in 11/13.5 Adobe Garamond

Tables and Figures

Tables

4.1. The Major Jewish Holidays   88

8.1. Economic Principles Used in this Book   181

Figures

1.1. Jewish Population by Metropolitan Area, 2000   4

2.1. Highest Degree Attained by Sex, Jews and
     non-Jews, 2000   34

2.2. Occupations of Jewish Men, 1948 and 2000   39

2.3. Occupations of Married Jewish Couples, 2000   41

2.4. Median Earnings by Education and Sex, 2000,
     Non-Hispanic Whites, Ages 25–64   44

5.1. Average Number of Children by Mother's
     Year of Birth   114

6.1. Changing Occupations of American Jewish Men,
     1900–2000   135

6.2. Advanced Degrees Earned by Age and Sex,
     Jews and Non-Jews, 2000   138

Acknowledgments

THIS BOOK OWES ITS CREATION to the inspiration and encouragement from many teachers, colleagues, and students over the years. From Professors Gary S. Becker and Jonathan R. T. Hughes I learned that any interesting subject is worth studying from an economic perspective. From Professors Laurence R. Iannaccone, Barry R. Chiswick, and Evelyn L. Lehrer I learned that religion is an interesting subject for which economics provides important insights. Professors Rela Mintz Geffen, Sergio DellaPergola, Chaim Waxman, and the late Tikva Lecker (z"l) encouraged me to apply my economic tools to the study of American Judaism. Rabbi Allan Kensky and Emily Solow encouraged me to share my work with the Jewish community. The project also benefited enormously from the encouragement and editorial advice of Margo Beth Fleming and comments from reviewers who read the manuscript, in whole or in part. Finally, and most importantly, this book could not have happened without the wholehearted support of Barry Chiswick, my husband, mentor, and assistant par excellence.

Judaism in Transition

PART I

Jews as Religious Consumers

1

Introduction

I GREW UP IN A TIME AND PLACE WHERE Americans looked askance at anyone who was "different." Never mind that everyone around us might be considered "different" by others; our family belonged to a very small Jewish minority in a sea of middle-American Christians. We did not attend the nearby Methodist church; we did not decorate our house with colored lights at Christmastime; and we stayed home from work and school during our religious holidays in the fall. Our neighbors were polite, and I never saw anything like outright anti-Semitism, but there was a clear social distance between us. My parents countered this by developing friendships with other Jewish families, enrolling me in a Jewish after-school program, celebrating Jewish holidays at home, and instilling in me a strong pride in our Jewish heritage. They believed, and I believe with them, that America's diversity makes it great, and that even people who practice a small minority religion like ours can be equal participants in every other aspect of American life.

Judaism is one of the world's great religions, enduring and evolving for thousands of years. It spun off two other great religions, Christianity after the first 1,200 years (approximately) of Judaism and Islam more than half a millennium later. Yet the people practicing this ancient religion have always been a minuscule fraction of the world's population. Today's Jewish population numbers only about 13 million in a world of

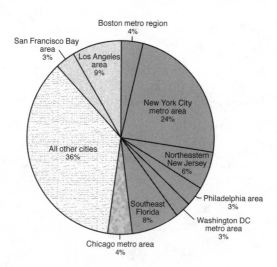

FIGURE 1.1. *Jewish population by metropolitan area, 2000.*
SOURCE: Computed from Schwartz and Scheckner (2001), Table 3:
pp. 262–277.

over 7 billion people, fewer than two Jews for every thousand people in
the world. The only country in which Jews are numerically important
today is Israel, where about 40 percent of the world's Jews constitute
about 80 percent of the population. About the same number live in the
United States, a bit less than 2 percent of the U.S. population. The remaining 20 percent of world Jewry is scattered among many countries in
small communities, each a tiny fraction of the total population in their
respective countries.

In part because they are such a small minority, Jews typically prefer
to live in places where they can join other Jews to form a community. The
chart in Figure 1.1 indicates that nearly two-thirds of the American Jewish population live in and around nine large cities, mostly in the Northeast corridor from Boston to Washington (40 percent), in Florida and
California (20 percent), and in Chicago (4 percent). Within the urban
Northeast, three-fourths of all Jews live in the New York metropolitan
area or nearby New Jersey. Yet because Jews are such a small proportion
of the U.S. population, not even the largest Jewish community makes up
more than a small fraction of the local population.

Jews share with other small religious minorities a concern with preserving their way of life amid the seductions of a very attractive larger society. No wonder, then, that American Jews have pioneered new forms of Jewish observance, clearly influenced by the democracy and religious pluralism that lie at the foundation of the American experience. Despite their minority status in the United States, however, American Jews are one of the two largest Jewish communities in the world, rivaled only by Israel itself. This means that Americans play a dominant role within world Jewry, especially in the Diaspora (that is, outside of Israel). The religious observance of Jews in the United States is thus an important factor in the evolution of modern Judaism, and American Judaism is a crucial determinant of the shape in which Jewish civilization will be passed on to future generations.

Economics, Religion, and American Judaism

Economics is one of the social sciences, all of which are disciplines that use the scientific method—involving observation, theorizing, and empirical testing of hypotheses—to study some aspect of human behavior. The aspect of human behavior that is the subject of economic inquiry is how we act when we can't afford to have everything that we want. The technical term for this is *scarcity*. Some people are so wealthy that they seem to be able to buy anything, but most of us are not, and we have to learn to live within our income. We can raise that income by working longer or harder, by investing wisely, or by receiving a lucky windfall, but for the most part we are limited in these opportunities. Our income is an important determinant of our lifestyle, and our lifestyle choices affect our spending patterns, behavior that is at the heart of the study of economics.

Although the behavior of the very rich may seem to be free of the problems of scarcity, this applies only to their ability to purchase goods and services in the market. Like the rest of us, their time is limited to twenty-four hours a day, seven days a week, 365 days a year (mostly), and a finite life span. In addition, they share with us a desire for the many things that money can't buy, love being the most popular example. Other examples are family life and religious faith. These are what economists call *self-produced* (or sometimes *home-produced*) goods because each individual has to direct his or her own time and effort into the process of "making" such a good. Money can be used to buy things that enrich this process or make it easier, but love, family relationships, and religious expression cannot be bought with money alone, no matter how much they are desired.

This book on the economics of Judaism is about how scarcity affects the religious behavior of ordinary American Jews and their families. By "ordinary," I mean the majority of Jews who view religion as one aspect of life but not necessarily their main interest. My primary concern is with people whose lifestyle choices do not make religion a central focus and who choose occupations outside of the religious community, effectively excluding the clergy and members of various ultra-Orthodox sectlike groups. Most of us "ordinary" Americans spend both money and time on our religious observance, but many of us also wish we had more time and/or money to spend. By viewing religion as one of the self-produced goods that must compete with other items in a larger consumption pattern, economics provides important insights into many aspects of religious observance at the grassroots level.

My own research on the economics of religious observance has focused on American Judaism, in part because it is the religious community to which I belong and with which I am most familiar. Understanding the economic context for decision making has helped me understand myself, my family, and my community. Although Judaism is well studied by many historians and other social scientists, it has rarely been studied by economists and almost never with the modern approaches developed by economists in the last half-century. The present book is intended to fill this void in studies of American Judaism.

This book also begins to fill a void in the literature on the Economics of Religion, where references to Judaism are few in number, typically perfunctory, and often misinformed. Just as economic studies of other religious groups give us insights into Jewish behaviors, Judaism provides comparisons and contrasts that broaden the context for looking at the religious behaviors of non-Jews. By bringing the Economics of Religion to Judaism, and Judaism to the Economics of Religion, I hope to explain some of the puzzles raised by others regardless of their own religion (or lack thereof) and professional background.

Individuals as Agents of Social Change

When it comes to religion—any religion—it is probably safe to say that nobody is perfect. Each religion prescribes certain behaviors and proscribes others, providing adherents with guidelines to distinguish between right and wrong, moral and immoral, appropriate and inappropriate attitudes and actions. Judaism is no exception, with rules of observance that run the gamut from very broad (for example, "love God") to very specific (such as, "eat meat only from certain parts of certain animals slaughtered in a certain way and never in the same meal as milk or dairy products"). Although one might wish to follow every rule in order to be a "good" Jew, people often have difficulty doing so. Some observances seem more important than others, and some are difficult to fit into a contemporary lifestyle. Because people make choices during the course of their everyday lives that are not always consistent with the teachings of their religion, religious leaders always seem to be exhorting them to mend their ways.

This book is about economics, so it will not delve into the substance of Jewish law, nor will it question its validity as a guide to good behavior. What interests us here is how economic incentives affect decisions about time and money—how prices and incomes influence whether a law or custom is generally observed or broken, whether it is viewed as central or peripheral, whether it is perceived to be relevant or outdated, and therefore whether it persists as part of the culture. We can approach this problem by thinking of costs and benefits associated with each religious observance or each group of religious observances. Costs can be direct or indirect. Direct costs include the time and money spent on an observance, as well as any psychological discomfort that may be entailed. For example, the direct cost of following the Jewish dietary laws includes not only the extra cost of kosher meat but also the inconvenience of limiting food preparation to kosher kitchens, thereby ruling out nearly all time-saving restaurants and fast-food establishments. Indirect costs occur when religious observance makes it more difficult to acquire an education, to succeed in business, or to live in peace with one's neighbors. Observant Jews incur such costs when they forgo professional meetings that are scheduled on Saturday or on Jewish holy days, for example, or when business is conducted informally over lunch in a nonkosher restaurant.

Our expectation (hypothesis) would be that expensive rules would be obeyed only if the benefits were seen to be large, while low-benefit rules might be obeyed only if their cost is low. Much of what follows in this book will be directed at better understanding how the full cost of Jewish observance affects the religious behavior of American Jews.

There is a famous cartoon that depicts a large crowd of people racing off to one side of the frame with a politician running anxiously behind them. Its caption has the politician saying, "I have to catch up with them—I am their leader." Although the cartoon is intended as a wry comment on the workings of democracy, it is more generally applicable to many kinds of fundamental social change. The combined actions of individuals, each making decisions perceived as being in their own best interest, can lead to changes in social norms that may or may not conform to those espoused by their designated leaders. As is well known, true sovereignty requires the consent of the governed.

It is ultimately the individual Jew who decides how much Judaism contributes to his or her well-being, how much time and effort to devote to Jewish observance, and how important this is when selecting a marriage partner. It is the individual family that decides whether to attend the synagogue service, how to celebrate each holiday, and how much Jewish education to seek for its children. Although synagogue officials may worry about budgets, and communal institutions may scurry to raise funds, they know that participation is affected not only by the income of their community members but also by the costs—direct and indirect, both time and money—of the services that they offer relative to the benefits they provide. Focusing on how economic incentives affect the everyday decisions of ordinary American Jews provides insights into both the nature of American Jewish religious observance and the nature of Judaism as an evolving part of American culture.

Persistence and Change in Religious Judaism

To say that Judaism is an ancient religion is to imply that modern Judaism is somehow the same as the religion of our ancestors in antiquity. Yet Judaism is far from static, changing with the times and socioeconomic environment almost from its inception more than 3,000 years ago. This apparent paradox is possible because religious Judaism combines a Great Tradition, common to all Jews everywhere, with Small Traditions specific to a particular time and place. The Great Tradition comes from antiquity and effectively defines a religious group as Jewish. A Small Tradition is Jewish in the sense that it implements the Great Tradition in ways that resonate to Jews living in a specific cultural context. Whereas the Great Tradition determines the substance and content of religious Judaism, a Small Tradition implements it and complements it with music, visual art, custom, and cuisine. It is "small" only in the sense that it need not be shared by Jews living elsewhere, but some—like the Ashkenazi and the Sephardi traditions that are part of today's American Jewish heritage—extend over large geographical areas and last for centuries.

Economic forces have little effect on Judaism's Great Tradition, which remains fairly stable as it has for millennia. In contrast, economic forces are a very important influence for a Small Tradition, especially one that is new and in a state of flux. The Small Tradition most familiar to Americans is Ashkenazi Judaism, the religious culture of Jews in most of Western and Eastern Europe since about the tenth century, from the Middle Ages until the present. The second most important in the United States is Sephardi Judaism, the religious culture developed by the Jews of medieval Spain and spread with their exile in 1492 throughout the rest of the Mediterranean basin, to the Moslem world, and to the Americas. American Jewish immigrants came primarily from the Sephardi tradition until the middle of the nineteenth century, but the overwhelming majority of today's American Jews are the descendents of more recent immigrations of Jews with Ashkenazi traditions.

American economic conditions in the twentieth century were very different from those of the medieval Muslim world in which Sephardi Judaism flourished and from the medieval European world that gave rise to Ashkenazi Judaism. It should be no surprise, then, that we are witnessing the emergence of a new American Small Tradition, neither Ashkenazi nor Sephardi, although clearly influenced by both. Students of Jewish history and geography typically attribute Small Tradition differences in matters of observance to cultural differences in the societies where Jews are found, but differences in the economic environment are rarely considered as a separate influence on behavior. By examining various ways in which the American economic environment has shaped the religious observance and communal institutions of American Jewry, we gain insights into our history as well as the processes that affect our own lives today. The American Jewish experience can also provide useful insights for other religions, in the United States and elsewhere, whose members are facing similar economic incentives.

Persistent: Judaism's Great Tradition in America

The Great Tradition of Judaism is rooted in the Hebrew Scriptures. Especially fundamental are the first five books of Scripture, known in Hebrew as Torah, in English as the Five Books of Moses, and in Greek as the Pentateuch, the first five books of Christianity's Old Testament. The Torah contains stories of Creation and the early history of the Jewish people, it designates the most important religious holidays, and it prescribes laws pertaining to religious ritual, social organization, and everyday life. Conceptually, the Torah is a gift from God to the Jewish People as a whole, and its original Hebrew language can never be altered. Physically, the Torah is a parchment scroll onto which the original Hebrew words have been hand copied by a scribe specialized in this task. The Torah has been translated into many languages, but it is sacred only in its original Hebrew. It is read aloud on an annual cycle as a central part of the synagogue service, especially on the Sabbath and on Festivals.

Although the Torah's laws are timeless, the social setting in which they are followed is constantly changing. The challenge has always been, as it is today, to understand the eternal essence of the Torah so that it will not be lost in the course of changing circumstances. Over the millennia a very large body of literature has been amassed for this purpose. In antiquity, this took the form of an oral tradition preserved among sages who gathered for that purpose, probably beginning as early as the second century BCE but codified in written form as the *Mishna* in about 200 CE. The oral tradition continued with newer commentaries and interpretations, a selection of which (called the *Gemara*) were codified in the sixth century to augment the Mishna. The Mishna and the Gemara together are known as the Talmud. In subsequent centuries the written word came to displace oral traditions, but Torah laws continued to require new explanations whenever Jews tried to implement them in a new social or economic environment. Some of the most influential of these later commentaries typically appear as marginal notes on each page of Talmud while others, written from medieval times up until the present day, are published as separate codes of Jewish law. The Talmud itself is now part of Judaism's Great Tradition, although some of its passages reflect the various Small Traditions in which they arose and no longer resonate today.

In addition to Torah, the Hebrew Scriptures include books of the Prophets and an anthology of Writings. (The Hebrew acronym for these three sections is *Tanakh*, the Jewish name for the books in Christianity's Old Testament.) *Prophets* is a collection of books either by or about named individuals (for example, Jeremiah, Isaiah) or continuing the story of the Jewish people in the Land of Israel (such as Chronicles I and II) and concerning itself with changes in national life and religious practices. *Writings* is a collection of literary works, an anthology that includes the book of Psalms (that is, hymns), the book of Proverbs, and a number of self-contained literary works (for example, the books of Ruth, Esther, Daniel, Job, Lamentations, Ecclesiastes). Unlike the Torah, which is understood conceptually as a gift directly from God to the Jewish People, books of the Prophets and the Writings are understood to have been created by their authors who, even if divinely inspired, were nevertheless unambiguously human. These books all belong to the Great Tradition, and portions of them are often read aloud on relevant occasions during the synagogue service.

Judaism's Great Tradition includes a number of holidays and related observances derived directly from the Hebrew Scriptures. Torah itself specifies that the seventh day of the week shall be set aside for Shabbat, a day on which no creation is to take place. This is a day of rest in which Jews and their live-in employees refrain from the productive activities of the six previous days, whether they be associated with earning a living or household chores. Torah also specifies observance of Rosh Hashanah (the Jewish New Year) and Yom Kippur (the Day of Atonement) in the autumn. There are also the three festivals of Pesach (Passover), Shavuot (the Feast of Weeks or Pentecost), and Sukkot (the Feast of Tabernacles), sometimes referred to as the "Pilgrimage Festivals" because in antiquity they required a pilgrimage to the Temple in Jerusalem. The specific dates for these holidays are identified on the ancient Jewish calendar, a lunar calendar where days begin and end at sunset and where a "leap-month" is added every few years on a set schedule to preserve the seasonal incidence of holidays. Later additions to the Great Tradition calendar commemorate subsequent events, the most familiar to Americans being Chanukah (associated with the book of Maccabees) and Purim (with the book of Esther).

Finally, no survey of Judaism's Great Tradition would be complete without mentioning the Torah's instructions affecting everyday life. Some of these have to do with social behavior and ethics, like the proscriptions against murder, theft, false witness, and incest, and can be applied to non-Jews as well as Jews. Others are applied to Jews alone, like tsitsit (wearing a fringed garment as a reminder of one's ritual obligations), mezuzah (posting on the doorposts of one's house the Torah passage affirming the uniqueness of one God), tefillin (binding this same Torah passage to one's forehead and arm during weekday morning prayers), and brit milah (ritual circumcision of infant males).

Torah also presents the dietary laws by which Jews have been identified for millennia. These laws, collectively known as kashrut, apply only to animal products (meat and dairy) and specify which animals are permitted (that is, kosher) and how they are to be slaughtered. (Americans of all religions enjoy kosher-style delicatessen, meats prepared with recipes brought to the United States by Ashkenazi Jewish immigrants, but these are not ritually kosher unless they were slaughtered appropriately and isolated from all dairy products, including cheese.) Jews are permitted to eat most vertebrate fish and most fowl (except carrion-eaters), but among land animals they are restricted to ruminants (that is, grazing animals that chew their cud) with cloven hooves. Milk and dairy products are acceptable only if they come from a kosher animal and may never be eaten with any meat except fish. Various authorities specializing in these laws stamp their logo on a product's box or label to attest that its contents are in fact kosher.

While not all American Jews today are punctilious in their observance of these Torah-based laws, they are part of the Great Tradition that unites us and defines us as Jews. Torah is read in every synagogue, regardless of ideology, and Jewish education takes place in Hebrew schools because that is the language of religious ritual. Jewish calendars give the dates of all the holidays, although most American Jews observe some more diligently than others. Despite the exceptions inevitable in a society that encourages idiosyncratic religious practice, nearly all American Jewish men wear a tallit (fringed prayer shawl) in the synagogue; most American Jewish homes have a mezuzah on their doorposts; and Jewish boys are circumcised on the eighth day after birth. All of these practices fulfill obligations specified in Torah and are understood as part of the Great Tradition. Observance of the dietary laws is much more problematic, however. Some American Jews observe kashrut strictly; others observe it partially, while still others ignore it entirely. We will have more to say on this subject later on in this book.

Fading: The Ashkenazi Small Tradition

The old Small Tradition most familiar to Americans is Ashkenazi, the Jewish culture of immigrants who arrived from Germany in the mid-nineteenth century or from Eastern Europe and Russia during the years of mass migration, 1881–1924, from whom most of today's American Jews are descended. Ashkenazi Jewish culture extends well beyond the religious realm, effectively defining Judaism as an ethnicity in a multicultural environment. Yet it is an important aspect of the religious comfort zone for many American Jews, and this is its primary interest here. If the words of synagogue ritual draw heavily on the Hebrew Great Tradition, their melodies depend on the Ashkenazi Small Tradition. The synagogue's Torah scroll is part of the Great Tradition, but the design of its cover depends on the Small Tradition. Judaism's Great Tradition says that the Sabbath and holidays (which, it will be recalled, begin at sundown) are to be welcomed with a festive meal, but the cuisine itself depends on the Small Tradition.

The mother tongue of Ashkenazi Jewry was Yiddish, a Germanic language but with a large influence from Hebrew and from the Slavic languages of Eastern Europe and Russia. The broad secular culture developed in this language is called *Yiddishkeit*. Most of the Jewish immigrants to America spoke Yiddish, which they often translated as "Jewish" because *yid* is the Yiddish word for Jew. The children of these immigrants learned to speak English as their first language, however, and few of their grandchildren acquired any fluency in Yiddish. The most common Yiddish words that made their way into the American vernacular came from occupations in which Jewish immigrants concentrated, especially occupations in entertainment and in the garment industry, and from the few Ashkenazi culinary treats that became part of America's ethnic cuisine. It is worth noting, however, that few Hebrew words have entered into American English, presumably reflecting the fact that Jews rarely interacted with their non-Jewish neighbors and colleagues when it came to religious matters.

Although Hebrew was always used in old-country synagogues and in religious ritual, Yiddish was the language that dealt with everyday matters that might come within the purview of Ashkenazi Jewish observance. Most important, it was the language of the kitchen, where women's religious responsibilities were dominant. An important aspect of holiday observance, foods contribute to the texture of religious experience. The Great Tradition laws of kashrut would determine whether a food was *fleishig* (meat), *milchig* (dairy), or *pareve* (neutral, so it could be eaten in a meal with either meat or dairy products), but the recipes associated with each holiday would be distinctively Ashkenazi. In American Jewish homes the holiday of Hanukah is celebrated with *latkes* (potato pancakes); Purim is celebrated with *hamentashen* (triangular pastries filled with poppy seeds, prunes, or other sweet fruit pastes); and it is customary to serve honey cake on Rosh Hashanah. Many festive meals begin with chicken soup, with or without matza balls, and/or gefilte fish (literally, stuffed fish, but in America usually just the stuffing mixture shaped into patties). Passover, an eight-day holiday in which no form of leavening (including bread and most cakes) may be eaten, has whole cookbooks devoted to it and is especially associated with recipes made with matza (unleavened bread eaten as part of the Pesach ritual) and nuts.

Jewish immigrants from Russia and Eastern Europe came from an environment in which all Jews were Ashkenazi and all Ashkenazi were Jews. Although scholars might know the difference between Great and Small Traditions, the distinction was not necessarily familiar to ordinary people. The immigrant community in America, largely bereft of its old-country religious leadership, often confused its Small Tradition for the Great Tradition, taking Ashkenazi synagogue customs as being the "authentic" or "traditional" essence of Judaism or engaging in (secular) political activities as equivalent to Jewish religious expression. The confusion was compounded by the emergence of a new Small Tradition that—for lack of a better term—may be called American. Although the Ashkenazi tradition remains an important part of the American Jewish heritage, most Jews today practice in the new American tradition that is also influencing Judaism elsewhere by a process popularly described as "Americanization."

A New Small Tradition in the Making

The American Small Tradition actually has its roots in the European Enlightenment, but for various reasons—not least of which was the destruction of European Jewry during the Holocaust—it has developed most vigorously in the United States. As a new subculture it is still in the process of formation. Some of its new traditions are proposed by the religious leadership and accepted by the laity, such as the contemporary celebrations—both religious and secular—of a Bar Mitzvah (for a boy) or Bat Mitzvah (for a girl) ceremony when a young person reaches the age of thirteen years. Some customs are adaptations by the clergy to their congregants' habits, as in the scheduling of evening synagogue services at a fixed time instead of at sundown. Other new customs required an interaction between laity and clergy, as when lay pressure for egalitarianism in the synagogue eventually led to the acceptance of women in most non-Orthodox synagogues as full participants in ritual. Whether spontaneous or imposed, however, any such change is part of a trial-and-error process that must stand the test of time. Innovations stand or fall on their success in preserving the Great Tradition and transmitting it from one generation to the next. It is this issue that is at the heart of today's controversy over religious intermarriages between Jews and non-Jews, about which there will be more in a later chapter.

While the American Small Tradition is still in formation, some of its characteristics are already clear. For example, its language is English, the mother tongue of nearly all American Jews. Few American Jews know more than a few words of Yiddish, and these tend to be nostalgic references rather than a living language. In contrast, there are a great many books written in English on Jewish subjects, including serious works on religious themes. Today's Jewish cuisine reflects American kitchen habits, relying on prepared foods and modern appliances that do not require long hours in the kitchen. As with the Yiddish language, American Jews retain a fondness for a few Ashkenazi dishes associated with holidays or comfort foods—one thinks of gefilte fish, matza ball soup, lox and bagels—but their everyday diet is more likely to rely on recipes for hamburger, pizza, tuna fish, and Chinese carryout. In fact, American Jews enjoy the cuisine of many ethnic groups, and Jewish cookbooks adapt recipes for Italian, French, Chinese, Japanese, or Thai dishes to conform to the laws of kashrut.

American Judaism from an Economic Perspective

Like much applied research, my work in this area grew out of my own personal experience as a "typical" American Jew of my generation. Like many Jewish girls in the late twentieth century I went to college, earned an advanced degree, and became a "career woman." I married a Jewish man whose education and career were similar to my own, and we had two children who are now adults. My husband and I began our marriage as urbanites, living and working in a big city. As new parents we moved to the suburbs and commuted to our jobs as professors in a large urban university. We joined a Conservative synagogue near our home, but our participation had to compete with many other demands of work and family life, so our attendance was irregular and invariably accompanied by some degree of parent–child tension. Our children attended a Conservative Jewish day school through the eighth grade and the local public high school for grades nine through twelve; they were both Bar Mitzvah at age thirteen and left home at age eighteen to attend a liberal arts college in the big city of their choice.

Like other parents in our community, our lives could be thought of as one great big balancing act. We faced constant trade-offs between work and leisure; between our roles as individuals, as partners, as parents, and as the adult children of our own aging parents who lived far away in other cities. We faced trade-offs between time spent on household chores or on true leisure, between time spent in solitude or with others, between family life or participation in the outside community either together or individually, between our careers and everything else. Our religious life as Jews also had a place in this complex pattern. Frequently we had to explicitly make room for our Jewish observance, choosing to spend time in the synagogue or to celebrate a religious holiday at home to the exclusion of all other activities. Sometimes we sought ways to blend our Jewish and secular activities, reducing conflict between the two or even developing mutual complementarities so that they enriched each other. And sometimes we ended up choosing the secular over the religious, resolving a potential conflict by simply not observing a Jewish religious obligation. Our lives were so full of possibilities that there were not enough hours in the day for everything that we wanted to do.

Because my husband and I are both labor economists, we study—and teach about—dealing with scarcity when resources are limited and there are many desirable ways to spend them. Labor economics focuses especially on the allocation of time, the ultimate scarce resource with which every human being is endowed. Studies of time allocation provide important insights into how economic choices affect decisions about marriage, divorce, fertility, childrearing, education, health, migration, and now religion. Our familiarity with this research affected the way in which we understood our own lives, providing a larger context for our immediate choices and a jargon that was convenient shorthand for discussion of everyday problems. Perhaps inevitably this affected the way in which we communicated with our children as well as with each other, so that the economic way of articulating time allocation issues became second nature to everyone in our family. Like everyone else, budgeting time was a constant preoccupation for us; unlike most other families, we invariably found that an economic perspective provided helpful insights that made our decisions a bit easier.

When Lifestyles Collide

Just how helpful our economic perspective had become, and how different we were from most other families in this respect, was brought home to us by an unsettling experience that occurred when our younger child was in fourth grade and our older was a freshman at the local public high school. As part of its Jewish education program, our son's Jewish day school was sponsoring a weekend retreat for the families of fourth graders. The retreat was to take place at a highly subsidized rate in a resort located about four hours' drive from home. That Friday the fourth graders and their teachers were dismissed from school at noon, giving them plenty of time to reach the retreat before the Sabbath would begin at sunset, about 6:00 pm at that time of year. This was a very exciting opportunity that we all looked forward to, and our fourth grader was happily involved with his classmates making intricate weekend plans for their time together.

Although the school schedule had been altered to avoid conflict with the retreat, the other members of our families had no such accommodation. Some of the parents simply stayed home from work on Friday, and others worked for only half of the day, using their vacation leave so they would be able to arrive at the retreat before sundown. Others felt unable to do this for a variety of reasons and opted out of the weekend entirely. We made a carpool arrangement with another family so that one parent would leave early with the younger children and the other parent would leave later with our high-school student whose classes didn't end until 4:00 pm. This solution appealed to us because we could work most of a full day and because it reinforced our principle that high-school students could not skip afternoon classes short of an emergency.

Viewed as a time-allocation problem, this arrangement was a straightforward resolution of competing goals. Some of us would miss the first two hours of the Sabbath observance but would be full participants in the remaining twenty-two hours of this special day and could experience the rest of this weekend as an intact family unit embedded in a joyous community. We decided that the value of the extra two hours spent at work or at school was greater than the value of an extra two hours added to the weekend retreat or even an extra two hours of Sabbath observance. This choice is actually very common in the American Jewish community; in fact, most synagogues schedule "late" Friday night services well after sundown in the winter so that their congregants have time to get home after a full day's work.

Unfortunately for us, the organizers of our weekend did not see things this way. Although they repeatedly offered us additional discounts on the already-low price of the retreat, they felt that it was essential for all of us to attend during the full twenty-four hours of the Sabbath. Clearly, they did not understand the nature of full costs: It was not the scarcity of money that caused our problems but rather the scarcity of time. We were told that other parents who could not take off from work were staying behind, and high-school students were making other arrangements for the weekend. (This was my first insight that a "family" activity in the Jewish community was typically oriented to young children and rarely included teenagers.) If we couldn't arrive before sundown, we were asked not to come at all.

This imposed a new constraint on our time-allocation problem, and the families in our proposed carpool had to revise their decisions accordingly. The other family chose to split itself, the mother participating in the retreat with the younger child and the father remaining at home with their high-school student. Because my husband was to be out of town that weekend, our fourth-grader had to choose between going to the retreat with the other family or staying at home with his older brother and me. Although he was clearly torn and very disappointed at missing his special weekend, he ultimately decided that family togetherness was too important a part of the Sabbath experience for him to just leave behind. Young as he was, he already understood that a religious observance is multidimensional and that its full cost includes the value of alternative uses of time.

Getting from There to Here

This experience was a blip in the lives of our children, but it turned out to be a major event in my life as an economist. Although I knew that economics was an important underpinning of all time-allocation decisions, the other parents I spoke with did not think about them as economic problems. They could articulate their financial budget problems and their time-allocation problems, but they often failed to connect them as part of the same decision. It seemed to me that this placed them under greater stress than necessary, and they often felt guilty about making choices that to us were legitimate trade-offs. A similar lack of appreciation for economic factors characterized Jewish professionals, whether in communal organizations or the clergy, leading to an unfortunate disconnect between their notion of a "good" Jewish decision and the time-constrained choices made by ordinary American Jews. In short, I decided that what my American Jewish community could use was a good dose of labor economics. That's why I began to think seriously about the influence of economic incentives on our Jewish religious observance.

Many years have passed since then, and I am only now actually writing this book. In the meantime I have had a great deal of experience with my various balancing acts, all of which both delayed and enriched this enterprise. I started by writing research papers applying the fundamentals of the Economics of Religion—at that time a new and exciting subfield of economics—to American Judaism. I organized scholarly conferences in the United States and in Israel to attract more economists into the study of religion and other issues important to the Jewish community. My husband's research on the economic experience of American Jews as an ethnic/religious group was very influential and further stimulated my thoughts. I also began to speak to Jews in my community about how economics could help them understand the trade-offs in their own religious lives. I spoke to groups of American Jews about themselves and to groups of Israeli Jews wanting to better understand their American counterparts. Every one of these activities and speaking engagements required me to focus on issues of direct interest to my audience and gave me feedback that proved valuable for my own understanding of those issues.

As a result, this book is a distillation of my research, my community interactions, and my own life as seen from an economic perspective. It is not intended as the final word on this subject but rather as a stimulus to further thinking about the nature and consequences of our Jewish lifestyle choices, religious and otherwise. These choices are made by all of us, and I hope that the reader will find them recognizable even without any prior knowledge of economics per se. The primary goal of this book is to provide insights into American Judaism as it is practiced today, so as to focus attention on some of the most important trade-offs one faces as an American Jew. In the process, I hope to show how economic circumstances have helped to shape a distinctive American Jewish religious culture.

A secondary goal is to serve as a guide to thinking about comparable issues for other religious groups. Just as learning about economic influences on other religions has given me a new perspective on the nature of American Judaism, so I hope that learning about economic influences on Judaism will stimulate useful insights on other religions in the United States and elsewhere. Some of these other religions, like Judaism, are identified with a specific ethnic group, although others cross ethnic boundaries. Some non-Jewish religions, like Judaism, arrive in the United States with immigrants and change over time as the immigrants assimilate into the American economy. These are but two examples of comparability that allow the Jewish experience to shed light on how economic influences affect other religious groups. If in the process the reader learns something about the economic way of thinking, or acquires some of the intellectual tools that economists find so useful, then my ambitions as a teacher will also be gratified.

Plan of the Book

This book is organized in four parts. Part I introduces the subject and provides some background on the economic circumstances of American Jews. Part II shows how economic concepts can provide a useful perspective for looking at American Judaism. Part III uses this perspective to look at how economic decisions enter into important aspects of American Jewish behavior. Part IV concludes by considering some implications of this economic analysis for the future of the American Jewish community.

Part I: Jews As Religious Consumers

After this brief introductory chapter, Chapter Two describes the economic situation of American Jews in the year 2000, at the turn of the twenty-first century. Most of us think we know what we mean when we say that someone is Jewish, but in fact the community is very diverse, many of our stereotypes are obsolete, and not all stereotypes were ever based on fact to begin with. Chapter Two looks briefly at some of the different ways Jews identify themselves and chooses a definition suitable for the purpose at hand. It then presents statistical data on the education, occupation, and incomes of American Jews. This provides a general portrait of the Jewish community, as well as the economic circumstances in which Jewish individuals and families live and allocate their scarce resources.

Part II: Investing in Judaism

The full price of any consumption good is the sum of its money price and the value of time spent consuming that good. The cost of any time-intensive Jewish religious observance is therefore heavily influenced by the value of a consumer's scarce time. Chapter Three develops these ideas and discusses how to estimate the value of time. It argues that the main American synagogue movements—especially the Reform, Conservative, and Reconstructionist—gained traction among ordinary Jews because they provided time-saving (and thus cheaper) alternatives for religious expression. The chapter concludes with new insights into the relationship between the education and incomes of American Jews and the growth of these synagogue movements.

Another basic principle of modern labor economics is the role of human capital, by which is meant any skill or knowledge that is learned, whether purposely (for example, in school) or not (for example, by life experience), whether from parents, teachers, peers, or society at large. Whereas Chapter Two looks at investments in the secular education of American Jews, especially subjects related to the labor market and occupational skills, Chapter Four considers religious education as an investment in Jewish human capital.

Jewish knowledge and skills greatly enhance the religious experience obtained by attending synagogue services or performing religious rituals at home. Most Jewish youth in America spend at least several years in formal religious schooling, usually at their local synagogue, and many attend Jewish camps or take trips to Israel. Many Jewish holiday observances are also educational opportunities, teaching some aspect of Jewish history and reinforcing themes of identity and community. This Jewish human capital has many synergies with the secular human capital shared by all Americans, but there are also some differences that potentially conflict. Chapter Four ends with several examples of how Judaism has dealt with such incompatibilities, now and in the past, by adapting holiday observances while still keeping Judaism's Great Tradition.

Part III: Constraints and Incentives in American Jewish Life

Chapter Five applies economic concepts to patterns of family formation and Jewish family life in the United States. It begins with marriage, a partnership contract preceded by a search process often described as a "dating market" or even a "marriage market." Next come children and the basic economic forces that affect a couple's decisions about how many to have, when to have them, and how to raise them. In a final section, this chapter shows how the overall effect of family decisions made by individuals guided by their own economic incentives are changing the very structure of Jewish communal life with implications for the practice of Judaism in the twenty-first century.

Although Jews have been in the United States for more than 350 years, the roots of today's American Jewish community lie mainly with immigrants from Russia and Eastern Europe who arrived in a great wave between 1881 and 1924. At one point these immigrants and their families made up over 95 percent of all American Jews, and like most immigrants they worked hard adjusting to the economic conditions of their new country. Chapter Six uses the economic tools developed in earlier chapters to focus on the economic adjustment of these Jewish immigrants and their children. It also looks at the Jewish institutions built by and for the immigrant community. Drawing on recent research on the economics of immigration and on immigrant religions, this perspective provides insights on how the immigrant experience shaped the American Jewish heritage well beyond the immigrant generation itself.

Part IV: Exchange and Change in American Judaism

Two major events outside of the United States—the Nazi Holocaust that destroyed most of European Jewry and the founding of the State of Israel in 1948—had a big impact on American Jews and Jewish observance in the United States. Israeli Jews differ from American

Jews in their economic circumstances and in their political status as a religious majority, giving rise to Israeli Jewish religious observance and institutions that differ from those in the United States. The two Jewish communities communicate with each other, however, and exchange resources in ways that are mutually beneficial. Chapter Seven explores how Israel's existence as a Jewish state altered the economic incentives faced by American Jews. It then considers some ways in which Judaism in Israel has profoundly influenced American Jewish education, religious observance, and communal institutions.

The final chapter uses an economic perspective to see where American Judaism is headed, at least for the next few decades. Chapter Eight begins with a brief review of the economic principles used and the topics considered in this book. It looks at how economic conditions have changed in the United States, comparing the twentieth-century past with the twenty-first-century future, and considers the implications of this change for the American Jewish community. It then looks at how the new economic context affects Judaism and Jewish observance, selecting for closer examination some recent trends that look especially promising. The economic perspective provides insights into the vibrancy and creativity that characterizes American Judaism, and this book ends by summarizing the case that Americans are contributing a new Small Tradition to the long history of Jewish religious civilization.

2

The Economic Context

IT USED TO BE EASY TO PORTRAY THE ECONOMIC LIFE of American Jewry. Early in the twentieth century Jews became stereotyped as Yiddish-speaking Ashkenazi immigrants in New York City, living in Jewish neighborhoods on Manhattan's Lower East Side and working in the garment industry. Of course there was more diversity than this description suggests, but even so you would not have been very far off the mark. Similar immigrant Jewish communities existed in cities like Chicago, Boston, and Baltimore, although they were much smaller than the one in New York. Jewish immigrants worked in many different industries, often as laborers but also as workers in retail enterprises or as self-employed entrepreneurs. There were also important communities of Jews who were *not* immigrants. In Cincinnati, for example, descendents of an earlier wave of Ashkenazi immigrants from Germany were at the center of what had just been established as the American version of Reform Judaism. The descendents of even earlier Sephardi immigrants from Spain and its American colonies formed communities in places like Providence, Atlanta, and New Orleans. Most of these nonimmigrant Jews were well educated by the standards of the day and worked either in the professions or in retailing, often as owners of shops—some of which would grow into major department stores. And there were already Jewish communities in West Coast cities like San Francisco, Seattle, and Portland, with even smaller groups of Jews scattered throughout the Midwest and the Great Plains.

Today, a full century later, American Jews are much more diverse in their residential patterns. As we saw in Figure 1.1, the New York and northern New Jersey metropolitan areas now account for only 40 percent of the Jewish population. Almost the same number of people live in small Jewish communities in many cities, sometimes even in places with too few Jews to sustain a synagogue. American Jews also show much greater diversity in their choice of occupation. Although only 2 percent of the U.S. population is Jewish, it is probably safe to say that there are at least some Jews in nearly every occupation. An up-to-date portrait of the economic life of American Jewry must relinquish the old stereotypes and focus on the characteristics that affect the occupations and earnings of today's Jews, the economic context in which American Jews now live their everyday lives.

The most fundamental of these characteristics is education, by which we usually mean the secular (nonreligious) studies acquired in American schools. (Jewish education is also critically important, so much so that it will be the focus of an entire chapter later in this book.) Education takes many forms, but the knowledge and skills acquired with formal schooling are closely related to a person's choice of occupation and to his or her productivity in the adult labor force. From this perspective, education is an investment that increases future earnings by raising one's skill level, by qualifying one for an occupation with higher earnings potential, or both. One hundred years ago, low-income American Jews saw a secular education as their ticket to upward mobility. Today, the stereotypical American Jew is often described as highly educated. This chapter presents the evidence on which this characterization is grounded.

For most people, the first feature that comes to mind when I refer to the economic context of American Jewry is the income of a typical Jewish family. Of course this is important, and later in this chapter we will look at this subject in some detail. Before doing so, however, we will look more closely at the occupational distribution of American Jews. A person's occupation can be viewed as a "bridge" by means of which a person's skills—typically acquired through education—are converted into earnings. But this is only part of the story. Most of us spend a large chunk of our waking hours at work, and our occupational title can be thought of as a shorthand name for what we actually do during those hours. Our occupation is part of our identity as adults, and our experiences at work help shape who we are when we come home at night. Just as the skills we bring to the workplace make us more efficient in our jobs, the skills we learn at work can be applied in our roles as consumers, parents, and Jews. The work lives of American Jews are an important part of their economic context, and this chapter will pay special attention to this subject.

It is clear that we can no longer portray the economic life of American Jewry with the easy generalizations of the past. Instead, we need to find some new generalizations that are appropriate for today. When economists want to describe a group characterized by much diversity, they feel most comfortable if they can ground it on a statistical portrait that takes account of that diversity. This chapter will summarize the statistical evidence on educational attainment, occupational distribution, and family incomes of American Jews. But the way in which we understand the meaning of these statistics will be affected by the nature of the data from which they have been computed. We thus begin with a brief discussion of the data available for painting a statistical portrait of the economic context of American Jewry.

The Data

The U.S. Census Bureau carries out a census of the population and its characteristics every ten years, and since 2000 it has conducted a monthly American Community Survey. From these we can learn a great deal about changes in the education, occupation, and residential patterns of the American people. As a matter of policy, however, it does not ask questions about religion—in fact, any response that might reveal a person's religion is suppressed before the data are made public. For the early decades of the twentieth century it is possible to piece together information on the occupations of Yiddish-speaking Russian immigrant men and their sons, and this seems to provide good insights into the characteristics of Jews during that period. With each passing decade, however, Yiddish-speaking immigrants become less and less representative of American Jewry.

Fortunately there are several recent surveys of American Jews that can be used to paint a more up-to-date portrait, one taken in 1990, one in 2000, and another in 2000–2001. Each of these surveys is based on interviews with a nationwide random sample of Jewish households—that is, of people in households in which at least one adult member is Jewish. We will draw heavily on the information provided by these surveys, which will be described in the following pages in more detail.

A survey of American Jews faces two major obstacles before it can even begin. The first obstacle is that there is so much diversity among Jews, and Jews are similar in so many ways to non-Jews, that it is sometimes difficult to decide whether a specific person should be counted as part of the Jewish population. The second obstacle is that Jews are such a small proportion of the population, and they are so widely scattered geographically, that it is both difficult and expensive to find a sample large enough to provide solid information about the Jewish population as a whole. We begin, therefore, with a consideration of these problems and how they were addressed in the data on which we will depend.

Identifying Jews

As any scientist knows, the first step in measuring a phenomenon is to define it. Defining a person as Jewish is not such an easy task. Jewish religious law views anyone born of a Jewish mother to be Jewish, especially if that person is raised as a Jew, but regardless of his or her degree of religious observance as long as no other religion is formally adopted. Judaism is not only a religion, however, because "Jewish"—often implicitly assumed to be "Ashkenazi"—is also an ethnicity. In a less pluralistic society there would be little, if any, difference between the two: Everyone of Jewish ethnicity would practice Judaism, and religious Judaism would place one in that ethnicity. In our world today, however, it is possible for a person to identify as Jewish ethnically without practicing Judaism as a religion. Some people in this category even report their religion as something else—for example, Jewish Buddhists, secular or atheistic Jews—and others report having two religions—for example, "half" Jewish and "half" Protestant.

Whether such persons should be classified as Jewish depends entirely on what we are trying to measure. For example, if we wish to learn about the characteristics of people who think of themselves as Jewish in any way then of course all ethnic Jews or "half" Jews should be included. If we wish to study the process of assimilation into the American religious mainstream, we certainly want to include anyone of Jewish ancestry, regardless of his or her current identity. All three of the surveys of American Jewry taken in 1990 and 2000 were designed to include Jews of the very broadest definition, with enough information so that the sample can be narrowed to the definition most appropriate for any particular investigation.

Because this book is concerned with how the economic environment affects Jewish religious behavior, it is most appropriate to define Jews as people who claim Judaism as their religion. That is, we should focus on the characteristics of people who answer the question "What is your religion?" by simply responding "Judaism" without qualifying it as shared with some other religion. Unfortunately, it is rare that survey information can be found that distinguishes this group from nonreligious people who self-identify as Jews. When the choices are Protestant, Catholic, Jewish, Other, or None, most Jews by any definition will choose "Jewish," although some people whose religious observance is very weak may choose "None." Religious identity is usually reported simply as "Jewish" without probing for any more detail. It is even rarer that questions about ethnicity include "Jewish" as an option, and even if they did we would be no closer to sorting out which Jews have Judaism as their sole religion and which Jews view themselves as "secular" but not "religious." Any statistic that purports to describe "Jews" must be affected by the ambiguity of who is considered to be a Jew.

Although this technicality may seem a bit arcane, it has been the source of no small controversy in the American Jewish community. The biggest furor surrounding the 1990 National Jewish Population Survey was over a single statistic: the rate of religious intermarriage, computed as the percent of Jews whose spouse was not Jewish. The original report of that survey estimated the intermarriage rate—that is, the proportion of Jews who married non-Jews—at 52 percent for Jews married during the most recent five years, 1985 through 1990. This rate was based on a broad definition of Jews that included everyone with at least one Jewish parent, even those who were raised with some other religion and those who did not currently claim Judaism. It was soon pointed out, however, that what people were really interested in was the intermarriage rate of people who were raised as Jews or who considered themselves to be Jews by religion. Using this slightly more limited definition gave an estimate of about 42 percent—still high enough to be considered important for the future of the community, but somewhat less dramatic than the original estimate.

The subject of this book is how individual choices about Jewish religious observance influence the development of American Judaism and its religious institutions. For the most part, this influence comes from people who consider Judaism to be their religion. Jews who identify themselves otherwise—whether as secular Jews or ethnic Jews with no religion—are an important part of today's Jewish community, but they are rarely active in synagogue life and their effect on religious observance is indirect at best. Unless explicitly noted otherwise, all the statistics presented in this chapter are limited to those survey respondents who clearly identified Judaism as their religion.

Finding Jews

The other major obstacle to developing data on the characteristics of American Jews arises because Jews are not only a very tiny minority, but they are scattered all over the country. It is true that Jews tend to concentrate in a few major metropolitan areas, but it is also true that there are many places in which only a few Jews live. Most surveys of Jews are limited to these larger metropolitan areas and have no information about people in more isolated communities. They also tend to be based on lists of synagogue members and people who donate to various Jewish community organizations, missing the many Jews who are not affiliated at any one time. Community surveys also tend to double-count people who live in more than one place: college students who live away from their parents, for example, or retired "snowbirds" who spend their winters in a warmer climate where they participate in its Jewish community as well as that of their home city.

To learn about the characteristics of American Jewry as a whole in all of its diversity, we need a nationwide random sample of at least several thousand Jewish households. Because Jews are only about 2 percent of the U.S. population, any nationwide random sample of fewer than 10,000 households (which is considered to be a fairly large sample) would have information on only about 200 Jewish households. To identify a random sample of 5,000 Jewish households, we would need the response to "What is your religion?" from a random sample of at least 250,000. This is a large and expensive undertaking! And, like the U.S. Census, most large surveys based on nationwide random samples do not ask questions about religion and so cannot be used to identify Jews.

Fortunately, as already mentioned, there are a few suitable surveys that are now available to us. In 1990 the National Survey of Religious Identity (NSRI) asked a random sample of people in more than 100,000 households about religion (Kosmin 1991). In 2000, the American Religious Identification Survey (ARIS) replicated NSRI with a sample of about 50,000 households (Kosmin et al. 2001), and the National Survey of Religion and Ethnicity (NSRE 2000) was conducted with a somewhat modified methodology, polling a sample of over 174,000 households. Jewish households were identified from these surveys as ones in which one or more adult members said that Judaism was their religion, their ethnicity, or their parentage.

Three Surveys of American Jews

This procedure yielded three nationwide random samples of Jewish households, very broadly defined, that could be surveyed to learn about the characteristics of American Jews. The National Jewish Population Surveys (NJPS 1990 and 2000/01) were conducted with samples obtained from the NSRI and NSRE, respectively, sponsored by the United Jewish Communities and its predecessor organization, the Council of Jewish Federations (Kosmin 1991; Schwartz et al. 2004). The American Jewish Identity Survey (AJIS) was conducted in 2000 using a sample from ARIS, sponsored by The Graduate Center of the City University of New York (Mayer et al. 2001). Data obtained from NJPS 1990 came from a sample of almost 2,500 Jewish households, data from NJPS

2000/01 came from a sample of about 4,500 Jewish households, and data from AJIS came from a sample of 1,668 Jewish households.

The Jewish households included in these surveys were defined as households in which at least one adult member was a Jew, using a broad definition. The members of Jewish households would have included everyone identifying themselves as Jewish by ethnicity or parentage even if not by religion, as well as any non-Jews living in the same household as a Jew. If we want to focus on the characteristics of people who claim Judaism as their religion, our samples will become decidedly smaller. NJPS 1990 estimated that about 64 percent of the adults who were Jewish by this broad definition responded that their religion was Judaism, as compared to 54 percent of the broadly defined Jews in AJIS and about 73 percent of adults in the NJPS 2000/01 sample.[1] Because Jews—even by the broadest definition—are less than 2 percent of the U.S. population, the 2000 U.S. Census provides data on the characteristics of non-Jews to use as a basis of comparison.[2]

Most of the statistics used here to describe the characteristics of American Jews come from a subsample of NJPS 2000/01 limited to people who claim Judaism as their religion. This is a decidedly more restricted definition than the one used in the official report of that survey, which includes people who claim Judaism by ethnicity or parentage but not by religion. Yet the overall picture of American Jewry is generally not affected by this difference. The distinctive features of American Jews with regard to educational attainment and occupational distribution are slightly muted when the broader definition is used, but only slightly. Without impugning the Jewishness of these other Jews, this chapter uses religion as the selection criterion whenever possible in order to focus on the distinctiveness of this community.

It is important to keep in mind that survey respondents may not all mean the same thing when they identify their religion as Judaism. When we talk about "ordinary" American Jews, we usually think of Conservative or Reform Jews because these two synagogue movements dominated American Jewish religious practice during most of the twentieth century. In 2000 some two-thirds of all Jewish adults and 70 percent of adult synagogue members self-identified as either Conservative or Reform.[3] Another 23 percent of the adult synagogue members are Orthodox, but they account for only 10 percent of the Jewish population. Statistics for the Orthodox include both the "Modern Orthodox," who have much in common with members of the Conservative movement, and the smaller ultra-Orthodox groups whose lifestyles are very distinctive. Another one-fourth of all Jewish adults identify themselves as "just Jewish," Jewish with "no denominational preference," or "secular" Jews, but these make up only 5 percent of the synagogue members.

The (Secular) Education of American Jews

American Jews have a reputation for being very well educated. This does not mean that every American Jew has a PhD or a degree in medicine or law, but it is true that over one-third of the Jewish men and one-fifth of the women have an advanced degree (that is, at the master's level or above) in some field. In contrast, only 10 percent of the non-Jewish men and 7 percent of the non-Jewish women had an advanced degree. Among Jews, about 20 percent (21 percent of the men and 19 percent of the women) had a master's-level degree and another 13 percent of the men and 5 percent of the women had a PhD or advanced professional degree.

The bar graph in Figure 2.1 compares the educational attainment of Jewish men and women from the NJPS 2000 survey with the U.S. averages from the 2000 Census.[4] The greatest contrasts between Jews and non-Jews are at the high and low ends of the education spectrum. As we have seen, Jews are about three times more likely than non-Jews to have earned an advanced degree. At the other end of the education spectrum, people who have never completed high school account for 16 percent of the non-Jews but virtually none of the Jews, whether men or women. Overall, non-Jewish men are twice as likely as Jewish men to terminate their formal education after high school, and non-Jewish women are about 50 percent more likely to stop their schooling after high school than Jewish women.

Who Are the Less-Educated Jews?

While it is clear that the Jewish community as a whole is well educated, there is a large minority—32 percent of the men and 46 percent of the women over the age of thirty—who never graduated from college

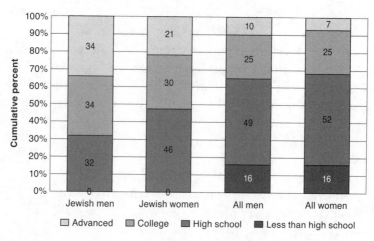

FIGURE 2.1. *Highest degree attained by sex, Jews and non-Jews, 2000 (percent distribution).*

SOURCES: Computed from NJPS 2000/01 for Jews ages 30 and over; U.S. Census of Population, 2000 for all persons ages 25 and over. See Schwartz et al. (2004) and U.S. Bureau of the Census.

or a postsecondary technical school. More than a third of these Jews were born prior to 1935 and thus finished high school before 1953. They would include members of a generation whose schooling may have been disrupted by the Great Depression, World War II, or postwar immigration, and they also include people who continued with less formal types of education. Among the youngest Jews, ages thirty to thirty-four, only 6 percent of the men and 7 percent of the women have no more than a high-school diploma. This suggests that the proportion of Jews without a college degree is largely a generational phenomenon that is likely to decrease even further in the coming decades.

Another 25 percent of the less-educated Jewish men in 2000 were born between 1946 and 1955 and would have graduated from high school between 1964 and 1973. This was a period of great turmoil on college campuses, especially at the major universities where Jewish men were more likely to be found. It was also a time when there were attractive employment opportunities that did not require a college diploma. Some of these dropouts may have returned later to complete their degree, but others—presumably the least successful and the most successful—may never have done so. Women in this less-educated group do not display this pattern, being much more evenly distributed by age, except for the youngest (ages thirty to thirty-four) and oldest (age sixty-five and older) described in the preceding paragraphs.

Another group of Jews with less than a college degree may be those raised in ultra-Orthodox—sometimes described as "devoutly religious"—families where religious studies are valued more highly than a secular education. NJPS 2000 reported this group to be just a tiny fraction of Jewish adults ages twenty-six through sixty-five, nearly all of whom had less than a college education, but with too few survey observations to be meaningful. While the ultra-Orthodox are of interest in their own right, their influence on American Judaism as a whole is limited in part because they remain a small fraction of the Jewish population and in part because they choose to isolate themselves from the rest of the religious community. Data for the Orthodox usually combine the ultra-Orthodox and Modern Orthodox into a single category, within which 35 percent of the adults over age eighteen in 2000 had no more than a high school education.

Who Are the Highly Educated Jews?

As already noted, Jews have a long-standing reputation as a people with an affinity for education. Some of the reasons for this are closely related to the economic decisions of Jewish families, and a later chapter will explore this subject more deeply. For the moment, suffice it to say that the immigrant forebears of today's American Jews were for the most part not very highly educated. They worked hard in low-level occupations, sent their children to the public schools, and made great sacrifices so that their children might acquire a good education. Sons and daughters were both sent to school, although financial hardship often meant that boys would be favored for higher education. For decades, each generation of American Jews—women as well as men—had more schooling than the last one. If today's young Jews are less likely to be more educated than their parents, it is only because so many of the parents of today's young adults have already reached the highest rung of the educational ladder.

The data for Jews in Figure 2.1 pertain only to persons whose religion is reported to be Judaism, excluding those who report more than one religion and those who say they are of Jewish ethnicity but not religion. People in these latter categories tend to have education levels somewhat lower than people who are Jews by religion, closer to (but still higher than) the average for non-Jews. This is particularly striking if we look at the people with advanced degrees. For those born after 1941, the proportion with advanced degrees among men who claim Judaism as their religion exceeds the corresponding proportion for all Jewish men (broadly defined) by 4 to 6 percentage points among older men and by 8 to 9 percentage points among men less than forty-five years of age. The corresponding difference among women was negligible for the older generation but fully 11 to 12 percentage points among women under age forty-five. The proportion of intermarried Jews with advanced degrees is even lower for most cohorts. This suggests that educational attainment is associated with religious behaviors: The looser the attachment of an individual to Judaism per se, the closer his or her educational attainment conforms to the American norm. Some reasons for this will be explored more fully in a later chapter.

Educational Attainment of American Jews

For now, suffice it to note that college graduation is the norm in to-day's American Jewish community, and an advanced degree is respected but not exceptional. Even though the statistics show a substantial minority with less formal schooling, this is not readily apparent to the casual observer. Apart from the ultra-Orthodox, who have voluntarily chosen a lifestyle that eschews high levels of secular schooling, most Jews with low educational attainment are well integrated into the mainstream Jewish community. The elderly with little formal schooling of their own typically have good relationships with children and grandchildren who are highly educated. Women who left college to raise children often participate in informal learning activities, typically belong to families with at least one college graduate, and do not make up a separate stratum in American Jewish society. The American Jewish community is thus aptly described as well educated, comprised mainly of college graduates of whom 50 percent of the men and 40 percent of the women have gone on to earn advanced professional degrees.

Occupational Attainment of American Jews

The occupations of American Jews generally reflect their high education level. According to NJPS 2000/01, some 44 percent of the men identifying Judaism as their religion worked in the professions. For the most part "professional, technical, and kindred" occupations are defined as those for which an advanced degree is a prerequisite; for example, doctors, lawyers, and university professors. Some professions—most notably schoolteachers—may also include people with just a college degree, and others—like entertainers, athletes, or computer whizzes—may not require any university degree at all. Most professionals, however, are in occupations that do require advanced degrees, and most Jews with advanced degrees work in these occupations. Some professionals are self-employed people with a private practice or a small partnership, but most of them are salaried employees working in large firms.

Another 23 percent of these Jewish men work in occupations classified as "managerial." This category includes most businessmen and high-level civil servants, occupations associated with the management of large firms. People in this category are typically paid a salary, although some firms augment this with bonuses for good performance. The owner of a substantial business would be considered "managerial" in these surveys, especially if the business is incorporated and pays him a salary. However, this category does not include owners of very small businesses. For example, a self-employed plumber would be considered a "craftsman," and the owner of a neighborhood boutique would be classified as working in a "sales" occupation.

Taken together, the professional and managerial categories are considered to be "high-level manpower." They are an important part of the white-collar labor force. (The label "white-collar" generally refers to people who work in an office or in a job where one meets customers, in contrast to "blue-collar" workers who work in factories or in other production-related jobs.) The remainder of the white-collar labor force, sometimes referred to as "middle-level manpower," works in clerical or sales occupations. In 2000–2001 only 18 percent of the Jewish men were classified as being in sales occupations, often working for commissions rather than, or in addition to, earning a salary. (Remember, however, that this category does not include many other people in the retail industry whose job might have been classified as managerial.) Another 14 percent of Jewish men work in blue-collar occupations, mostly in crafts and in services. Very few Jews work in occupations associated with farming, fishing, or mining.

Older stereotypes of Jewish occupations are no longer a good description of American Jewish men. Figure 2.2 compares Jewish occupations in 2000 with those prevailing in post-WWII America, half a century earlier.[5] In 1948 nearly 60 percent of the Jewish men worked in high-level white-collar occupations, but about two-thirds of these were in management (that is, business) and only one-third in the professions. By 2000 these proportions had reversed, and two-thirds of the high-level occupations were professional. In 1948 more than half of the Jewish professionals were concentrated in medicine, law, and college and university teaching, while in 2000 these occupations made up only a fourth of the professions.

Jews may have been unusually concentrated in medicine, law, and higher education, and people in these professions may have been a large group within the Jewish community, but Jews have always been greatly outnumbered by non-Jews in each of these professional occupations because Jews are only about 2 percent of the U.S. population. In 1990, for example, when Jewish men were four times as likely as non-Jewish men to be working in these three occupations, only about 8 percent of the men in these occupations were Jewish. In 1948, when Jews were 3.5 times more likely than non-Jews to enter these occupations, Jews would have numbered about 7 percent of the total.

There isn't as much statistical data for women's occupations as for men's because it is only recently that married women, especially those with children, worked outside the home in substantial numbers. Data for recent years, however, suggests a comparable pattern for women. Early in the twentieth century, Jewish immigrant women and their daughters worked in factories, especially in the garment industry as seamstresses or sweatshop laborers. Their occupational choices were greatly influenced by the difficulty they would have faced if they tried to follow a career while raising a family. Although some married women remained in the labor force, most became full-time homemakers with the birth of their

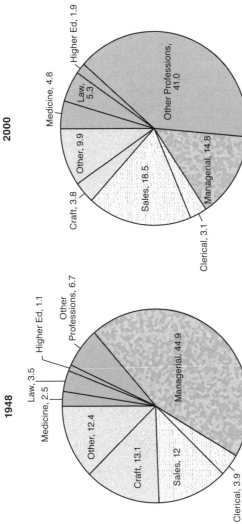

FIGURE 2.2. *Occupations of Jewish men, 1948 and 2000 (percent distribution).*

SOURCES: Computed from B. Chiswick (1999), pp. 68–98, Table 2; and B. Chiswick (2007), pp. 80–111, Table E-1.

NOTE: Based on a broad definition of Jewish men.

first child. They returned to work—often part-time—when their youngest child was in school, sometimes waiting until the children were in high school. As Jewish men established their own businesses, their wives helped out in the office—for example, as employment manager, bookkeeper, receptionist, accountant, or sales representative—sometimes drawing a salary, but more typically as an unpaid partner or assistant. The wives of husbands with larger and more financially stable businesses might work as volunteers or for very low pay in various service agencies of the Jewish community.

Because employment surveys tend to view volunteers and most unpaid family workers as outside of the labor force, we do not have good statistics for this early period on the occupations of Jewish women. By midcentury, however, many Jewish women had some higher education, and public school teaching was the professional occupation most hospitable to women with school-age children. As Jewish women earned advanced degrees in larger numbers, they were able to take advantage of the expansion of professional opportunities for women that came in the later decades of the twentieth century. By 2000, some 79 percent of unmarried Jewish women of working age (twenty-five to sixty-five years old) and 81 percent of the married Jewish women were in the labor force. Most of them were well educated and working in jobs that would be classified as high-level employment.

Two-Career Couples

People with advanced degrees who work in high-level occupations typically view jobs within the context of a career that spans most, if not all, of their working lives. A career requires special attention to long-run goals, building experience and reputation with an eye to future advancement, which is often achieved by transferring from one employer or city to another. The first large generation of Jews with professional careers was largely made up of men married to women without an advanced degree. By now, however, many Jewish adults are in marriages where both spouses are highly educated and have professional careers. This has many implications for family and community life, some of which will be explored more deeply in a later chapter. For now, however, it will be useful just to look at the statistical importance of two-career couples in the Jewish community.

By limiting ourselves to Jewish couples where both spouses identify their religion as Judaism and their age between twenty-six and sixty-five, we are looking at a group with relatively few full-time students and relatively few retirees. We are also looking at the parents of most children under the age of twenty-one. In 2000, both spouses are labor force participants in 80 percent of these Jewish couples. Another 13 percent of these couples have husbands in the labor force and wives classified as "homemakers" at the time of the NJPS survey, but we know that many of these women are only temporarily out of the labor force because of the needs of young children or elderly parents.

Four out of five Jewish couples have both spouses working outside the home, and in half of these couples both spouses work in high-level professional or managerial occupations. The graph in Figure 2.3 provides

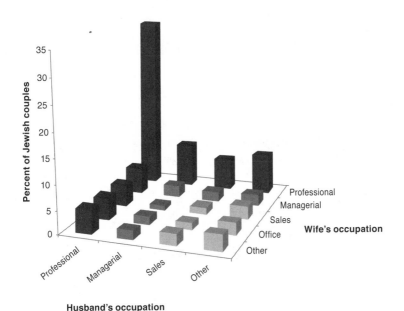

FIGURE 2.3. *Occupations of married Jewish couples, 2000 (both age 25–64 and both with Judaism as religion).*

SOURCE: Computed from NJPS 2000/01. See Schwartz et al. (2004).

a dramatic illustration of the occupational distribution of two-career Jewish couples. In 35 percent of these couples—more than one-third—both have professional careers; in 15 percent one partner has a professional occupation while the other is in management (including owners of large and mid-sized businesses); in another 2 percent both spouses are in managerial occupations. It is clear that in most of these families both spouses have advanced degrees, and both work in high-level occupations with their correspondingly demanding careers.

Another 35 percent of the working couples—more than a third—are ones in which only one spouse has a high-level career. In half of these, the wife is in a high-level occupation while the husband works in sales or has an office job. In the other half, the husband has a high-level career and the wife works in a sales or office-related occupation. (Remember, these statistics are for two-career couples and would not include men in high-level occupations whose wives are full-time homemakers.) Couples in which both partners work outside the home, but neither one has a high-level occupation, make up less than 15 percent of the Jewish working couples.

In summary: Ignoring the fact that some people leave the labor force temporarily during the childrearing or elder-care portion of their life cycle, 80 percent of prime-age American Jewish couples have both spouses in the labor force at any given time. Of these, 35 percent have both spouses in the professions, 15 percent have one in the professions and one in management, and 35 percent have one in the professions and the other in a lower-level occupation. High-level occupations are not only the norm for members of the Jewish community; they are also the norm for today's American Jewish family. This is a topic with many implications to which we shall return later.

Income of Jewish Families

One of the implications for an educated community with many members in professional occupations is that most of its members have upper-middle-class incomes. When NJPS 2000 asked respondents a general question about their family's income level, only 2 percent said they were "wealthy," but more than two-thirds said their incomes were "comfortable" or "very comfortable." As is typical of census or survey questions on income, one-fourth of the families refused to answer a more specific question. Of those that were willing to respond, only 1 percent reported incomes over $500,000, but fully one-fourth reported household incomes of $100,000 or more. While the high nonresponse rate to these questions must be kept in mind, these figures are roughly consistent with the high proportion of Jewish families that have two adult members working in high-level careers.

Although no survey provides information about incomes for a larger fraction of the Jewish population, this section presents an estimate of the average earnings of American Jews based on their occupations and education levels. The U.S. Census 2000 provides information about the average earnings of people ages twenty-five through sixty-five at various education levels and also the earnings of people ages fifteen and over in various occupations. The figures used for our estimates will be median earnings for each category; that is, half the people in this category earn less than the amount indicated, and the other half earns more. (Means, which are computed by adding up everyone's income and dividing by the number of people, are somewhat higher than medians; if we use this concept for our averages the findings would be the same except that average incomes would be higher.)

The procedure used here assumes that Jews and non-Jews in the same occupation and education category earn—on average—approximately the same incomes. There is some evidence that the earnings of Jews may be slightly higher than the average for each of these categories, possibly because they include a disproportionate number of high achievers both in school and in the labor force. On the other hand, there are many examples of Jewish professionals willing to accept low-paying jobs for idealistic reasons. This section takes a conservative approach and assumes that Jews and non-Jews with similar characteristics have approximately the same earnings. We can then use information on the earnings of all Americans to estimate the incomes of Jewish couples in the various categories discussed earlier.

Earnings by Education Level

As we saw earlier, about half of all Jewish men ages twenty-five through sixty-four in 2000, and 40 percent of the women, had advanced professional degrees. Figure 2.4 illustrates the average earnings in 2000

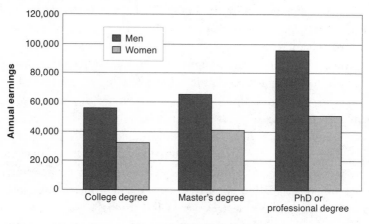

FIGURE 2.4. *Median earnings by education and sex, 2000, non-Hispanic whites, ages 25–64.*

SOURCE: Computed from U.S. Census Bureau, CPS Annual Demographic Survey 2000, March Supplement. PINC-03 Part 90 (males) and Part 155 (females).

of all non-Hispanic whites in this age group, the category that includes nearly all American Jews. For the United States as a whole, the median earnings for people with a PhD or professional degree were $95,660 for men and $50,819 for women. The comparable figures for people with a master's degree (or its equivalent) are $65,445 for men and $41,028 for women. Women tend to earn less than men for various reasons, not only because of discrimination in the labor market but also because they are more likely to choose lower-paid professions, to interrupt their careers when their children are young or when caring for elderly parents, and— importantly for these figures—because they are much more likely to be working in part-time or part-year jobs.

If we assume that Jews have the same median earnings as other non-Hispanic whites with the same level of education, most Jewish families in 2000 probably had incomes over $100,000. Two-career couples in which both partners had a PhD or professional degree would have combined median earnings of $146,500. Those in which only one partner has this level of education and the other has a master's-level degree would average total earnings of $136,688 or $116,264, depending on whether it is the husband or wife who has the higher degree. Couples with one master's degree and one college graduate would average total earnings of $97,773 or $97,043, again depending on which spouse had the higher degree. Using means instead of medians to compute these averages would raise these figures even higher but without changing the basic story.

Whether we compute average earnings based on means or medians, hardly anyone is really average. Actual incomes vary considerably, both over the life cycle and among individuals, and it is important to avoid stereotypes that tend to ignore low-income Jews. Also, as we shall see in a later chapter, high-achieving individuals tend to select other high achievers as marriage partners. This means that many Jewish families will have two above-median earners or two below-median earners. Keeping this in mind, however, it is clear that in the year 2000 the well-educated American Jewish community had a high proportion of families with earnings in six figures.

Earnings by Occupation Category

We can use the same approach to estimate family incomes for people in different occupational categories. Approximately two-thirds of the adult Jewish men in 2000 worked in high-level occupations, and two-thirds of these were in professional occupations. The median earnings of all men in these categories (ages fifteen and over, working full-time and full-year) were $58,363 for professional occupations and $57,164 for managerial occupations (including executives and administrators as well as managers). The comparable figures for women were $39,313 and $36,954, respectively. We saw that four out of five Jewish couples ages twenty-five through sixty-five had two careers in high-level occupations, suggesting combined median earnings of $95,369. If both partners were professionals, their combined median earnings would have averaged $97,682. If one was professional and the other managerial, their earnings would have been $95,317 or $96,483, depending on which spouse was in the professional occupation.

Earnings also vary considerably within the professions. Nearly 10 percent of the Jewish men work in professions classified as "health diagnosing" (for example, medical doctors) or as lawyers and judges. The median earnings of full-time, full-year medical doctors in 2000 was over

$100,000 for men and $86,663 for women, and the comparable figures for lawyers were over $100,000 for men and $76,745 for women. These figures include interns, residents, and newly graduated lawyers under the age of twenty-five, many of whom work long hours and earn relatively low salaries, and they also include people over the age of sixty-five who may be reducing their work load by not seeking new clients. Even so, more than half of the men in these professions have earnings greater than $100,000 per year.

The other profession that Jews enter in relatively large numbers is teaching. The median earnings of postsecondary teachers (mostly in college and university positions) were $61,542 and $43,303 for men and women, respectively, while "other teachers" (mostly kindergarten through twelfth grade in public and private schools) earned a median pay of $39,698 and $34,562, respectively. The earnings differences between men and women are smallest in the "other teachers" category, and many Jewish women have careers in these occupations. Those married to a man working in managerial occupations live in families with combined median earnings of more than $91,726; those married to a college or university professor would live in families with $96,104. Again, it is important to remember that these figures are medians, less than the actual earnings of half of the sample but more than the earnings of the other half. And although teachers typically earn considerably less than professionals in medicine and law, they still tend to be in jobs where median earnings are considerably higher than the national average for all Americans.

Earnings, Income, and Poverty

So far, we have been concentrating our attention on the labor market earnings of Jewish adults, typically as salaries or profits from a small business. Because we have seen that most American Jews are well educated and work in correspondingly well-paid occupations, it is probably safe to say that most of their income comes from these earnings. Yet many families are likely to have other sources of income as well. People with relatively high earnings typically save for the future—for the college education of their children, for example, or for their own retirement—by investing some of their earnings in stocks and bonds, either directly or indirectly by contributing to a pension plan. They are also likely to own their homes, and perhaps also a second home in a different location. People whose parents or grandparents were high earners may also have inherited assets to supplement their own earnings. In addition, many people may benefit from loans or even gifts by relatives with higher incomes.

As a general rule, earnings are not only the largest source of income for most Jewish families but also a somewhat underestimated proxy for their total money income. Families with high earnings also tend to have high nonlabor incomes, and those with low earnings typically have low nonlabor incomes, so the distribution of total income tends to be more unequal than the distribution of earnings. Yet families with low earnings may have income or benefits from other sources that contribute to their well-being. For example, the spouse of a self-employed person may raise the family's income by working in a low-salaried position that provides health insurance coverage for the entire family. Inheritances, gifts, and loans between family members may also help equalize consumption across families with different earnings levels.

This discrepancy between income and earnings make it difficult to measure poverty in the American Jewish community. As a first approximation, poverty is measured as the number of families living in low-earning households, where the actual poverty line is higher the larger the household size. According to NJPS 2000, less than 3 percent of the prime-age American Jews—that is, men and women ages twenty-six to sixty-five who state their religion as Judaism—live in households below the poverty line. Many of these are students or recent graduates beginning their careers in low-paying positions or internships, a temporary "poverty" that is often supported by loans or parental gifts. Others are immigrants who accept low-paying jobs when they first arrive and are not yet settled in their new country. Together these two categories of "temporary" poverty account for at least half of the working poor reported in NJPS 2000.

Low income is much more prevalent among the elderly, and poverty rates for Jews—as for non-Jews—over the age of sixty-five are correspondingly higher. Yet many of the elderly with low incomes have nonearning yet high-valued assets, like an owner-occupied house or condominium. Elderly Jews also may have adult children and grandchildren who support them in other ways, ensuring a lifestyle more comfortable than current money income alone might suggest.

A third group of Jews living below the poverty line is what we call the "voluntary" poor, people who choose a lifestyle that leads them to low-earning occupations. Most noteworthy among these are some ultra-Orthodox groups who emphasize religious education at the expense of secular subjects and who value religious observance at the expense of labor market opportunities. They tend to have large families, and their children acquire few of the skills that command high incomes. Many ultra-Orthodox Jews find work that earns at least a modest living, and some of them receive support from religiously inspired donations or from family members outside the group. Even so, the measured poverty rates are much higher among the ultra-Orthodox than in the rest of the Jewish community.

The Economic Context of American Jewry

This chapter uses statistical evidence to sketch a brief economic portrait of American Jewry. It describes a community in which both men and women tend to acquire very high levels of education. Their education qualifies them for careers in high-level occupations, many of them in the professions, which typically pay salaries that are comfortably high. Some Jews are poor, and others are millionaires. By far the largest majority, however, have incomes that place them squarely in the upper middle class.

Although the primary focus of this chapter has been on income levels, its implications are much broader. Higher education is more than mere career preparation; it affects the way a person perceives him- or herself in relation to others and to the world at large. Education is broadening, making one aware of possibilities and giving one confidence in setting goals. Education also provides problem-solving skills that are useful for many activities unrelated to the labor market. For example, people who are more highly educated tend to be healthier than average; they are less likely to smoke, to be obese, or to have unplanned pregnancies. In part this is because they acquire more health-related information, but it is also because they make better health-related decisions.

A Jewish community that is well educated is also a community of successful problem-solvers who are engaged in many activities and intellectually open to new ideas. Similar observations can be made about the implications of Jewish occupations. Professionals, like managers, are creative problem-solvers—their jobs involve identifying difficulties, diagnosing causes and consequences, analyzing alternative strategies, and coming up with the best solutions. These skills, honed in their educational lives and in their workplace experience, also make them more efficient consumers and carry over to their home lives in important ways.

People in high-level occupations are also characterized by a high degree of technical competence in their respective fields, fields that are sometimes very narrowly defined. The very words *professional* and *professionalism* are used as synonyms for this kind of specialization and technical competence. On a personal level, competence in any one field is an important source of self-esteem. This not only stimulates a desire for competence in other areas, but it provides skills that facilitate its acquisition. On the downside, it makes people less comfortable with situations in which their competence is especially weak. This suggests that a professionally oriented Jewish community would be made of people with multiple skills, people who would respect the superior technical competence of others and who would be uncomfortable in activities where they themselves had little competence.

Consider the implications of this for Jewish family life. Parents who are highly educated would place a high value on education for their children and would build a home environment in which intellectual skills were routinely used. Parents who work in professional occupations would display competence in their own activities and would encourage competence in their children—not only in school but in sports, music, chess, art, and whatever else they might decide to explore. These same values would affect their approach to entertainment, to health care, to relationships with extended family members and friends, and to any other area where skills can be important. In a later chapter we will see how this affects their religious lives as well.

This stylized portrait of the Jewish family, like any stereotype, is surely a caricature. There are dysfunctional Jewish families, and there are professionals whose technical skills do not carry over well into other areas of life. Yet a community characterized by a highly educated membership with a large proportion in high-level occupations has more advantages than just high incomes. The broader implications of education and professionalism are a very important part of the economic context within which Judaism has developed its distinctive path in the United States.

Part II

Investing in Judaism

3

The Cost of Being Jewish in America

MY HUSBAND AND I FACED ONE OF THE MOST WRENCHING arguments of our married life when it was time to enroll our oldest child in kindergarten. Each of us had attended a neighborhood public school in our youth, getting our Jewish education on weekday afternoons and Sunday mornings in a Hebrew school that met near our homes. This was typical for American Jews of our generation because few cities had Jewish day schools during our youth, and few of these were known for the high-quality, secular education that our parents wanted for us. Public schools were associated with Democracy and the American Way, and the parochialism of a private Jewish day school was viewed as limiting and, therefore, undesirable. By interacting with classmates of other religions, Jewish children would become fully integrated into the American mainstream and, at the same time, help dispel whatever invidious Jewish stereotypes the other children might have been exposed to. When my husband and I looked for a house, we considered only locations with an excellent public school within easy walking distance where the children could make friends in the neighborhood. At that point, I assumed that our decisions about education were a foregone conclusion.

My husband, however, had a different perspective. He was especially interested in a Jewish day school located conveniently close to our home. This school belonged to the Solomon Schechter chain (affiliated with the Conservative synagogue movement), whose distinctiveness rests on the way in which secular subjects and Jewish subjects are integrated into a single curriculum. In contrast to my ideological bias toward neighborhood schooling, my husband's bias turned out to be in favor of a Jewish school whenever it provided a high-quality secular education. Whereas I wanted our child to follow my own educational path, he felt that it would be a shame to live so close to such a school and not avail ourselves of the opportunity it offered.

In the end, I agreed that we would start our child in kindergarten at the Jewish day school and reconsider this choice after a year or two of experience. As it turned out, the experience was good in every respect, and both of our children studied there until they were old enough for the public high school. (At that point, any further discussion was moot because at that time Jewish day schools in our area did not go beyond the eighth grade.) Thus we became part of the general American trend toward private alternatives to public schools and part of the American Jewish trend toward day schools as an alternative to the after-school Hebrew programs run by most synagogues.

Trends do not happen in an economic vacuum. Long-run decisions about how to raise Jewish children depend on many factors, including their impact on the family budget. This chapter looks at the budget implications of two such decisions: in which type of Jewish school to enroll one's children and with which synagogue movement to affiliate. The outcomes of these decisions reflect a couple's Jewish lifestyle preferences and are made by individual families. The community also has a stake in them, however, because they affect how Judaism itself is passed on to the next generation. If we want to understand why Jewish families are changing the way they behave, we need to see how changes in the economic environment are having an impact on a family's choices.

The Full Price of Jewish Schooling

Despite the fact that day-school tuition was considerably higher than that of an afternoon Hebrew school, an increasing number of Jewish parents found themselves willing to pay it. This may have reflected a generational shift toward more religious observance or at least toward a greater concern with Jewish education. But that cannot be the whole story. Higher costs usually inhibit demand for a product, so any increase in demand for Jewish day schools would have to be very strong to overcome the deterrent effects of high tuition. Jewish families were behaving as though the cost of Jewish day schools was going down, not up, even though the evidence suggested that tuition charges were higher than ever and still rising. This may seem like a paradox, but it is easily resolved with a bit of modern economics.

Time and Money

The fundamental principle that resolves this paradox is that the money we pay for a consumption item is only part of its full price, and not necessarily the largest part. The other important part is the value of time that we spend in the process of consuming it. This is easy to see, for example, when you consider the time and money spent enjoying an evening at the theater. We spend money on the theater ticket, but we also spend several hours watching the performance, not to mention the time spent traveling to and from the theater. As another example, a doctor's appointment requires not only the fee for an office visit but also the time spent traveling to and from the office, in the waiting room, and with the doctor. In both of these examples, the value of time spent must be added to the money price to obtain the full price of the consumer good or service. We say that an economic good is time intensive if the time spent in its consumption makes up a large portion of its full price.

Returning to my family's education decision, we essentially faced two alternatives. We could send our child to the neighborhood public school, where tuition is essentially free, and supplement this at relatively low financial cost with a three-day-a-week Hebrew-school program at our local synagogue. The other option was the nearby Jewish day school where tuition was substantial (but not excessive) and where there would be no need for a supplemental Hebrew program. Hebrew schools typically meet three days a week, twice at the end of a school day and once on Sunday morning. This means that the children must be transported between the two schools twice a week in the middle of the afternoon, which can be difficult in families with two working parents. It also means that a family that goes to the synagogue on Saturday has no day in which the morning is free for leisure. When I ask other parents why they decided to send their children to a Jewish day school, they often respond that these considerations were crucial. In effect, the high tuition is buying them time—work time during the week (because they don't have to leave early for carpool duty) and family time on Sunday mornings. In contrast, the parents of public-school children typically cite the high day-school tuition as the deciding factor in their choice.

Full Price

The economic concept of *full price* is defined as the sum of the money price of an item plus the value of time spent in its consumption. The money price is typically the same for everyone—the grocery store, for example, charges everyone the same price for a gallon of milk—even though people differ in the size of their total money budget (that is, income level). In contrast, everyone has exactly the same total time budget—twenty-four hours in a day, seven days in a week, and so on—but people vary in the value that they place on their time. The higher the value placed on a consumer's time, the larger is the value of the time component of full price, and the more costly are time-intensive consumption patterns. People with a high value of time look for ways to "save" time, and they tend to complain about activities that "waste" time or even those where they have to "spend too much" time. In contrast, money prices tend to be the deciding factor for people who place a low value on their time because for them the value of time is a smaller fraction of the full price.

To some extent, the different values people place on their time are fundamentally subjective. To evaluate the full price of a good, however, each person has to assign a monetary value to his or her time so that it can be added to—and compared with—the money price of that good. In the simplest case, a worker who is paid by the hour knows that leaving work one hour early—whether to sleep, to go shopping, or to drive a Hebrew-school carpool—involves a reduction in income exactly equal to the hourly wage rate. The wage rate is thus the price that he or she pays for obtaining an extra hour of nonwork time. Modern labor economics has shown that this principle can be generalized for all consumers and for all activities. A person's potential hourly earnings thus provide a good first approximation of the value of an hour spent in any activity.

Because people differ in their wage rates, the cost of time is not the same for everyone. Suppose the parent of one child in our Hebrew-school carpool is a retail clerk earning $10 per hour, while the parent of another child is a lawyer who bills time at $200 per hour. If they each left work two hours early, the clerk would give up only $20 worth of goods and services while the lawyer would give up $400 worth. If they each take turns driving once a week during a thirty-week school year, their foregone purchasing power would come to $600 for the clerk and $12,000 for the lawyer. If carpooling is not feasible and each parent has to drive his or her own child twice a week, the time cost must be multiplied accordingly. Even if they both spend the same amount of time driving the children, the lawyer's time would have to be valued at twenty times more than the clerk's time.

One implication of this is that the full cost of a day-school education relative to that of an after-school Hebrew program is much lower for the lawyer than for the clerk, even if the direct costs of tuition and the time parents spend carpooling are the same for both. Suppose day-school tuition is about $11,000 per year, compared to a modest $1,000 for the Hebrew school. The full cost of Hebrew school includes the value of time for parents driving the carpool, estimated in the preceding paragraphs as two hours per week, or about $1,600 ($1,000 + $600) for the clerk and $13,000 ($1,000 + $12,000) for the lawyer. Because the day school typically ends somewhat later than public school classes and because Jewish education is incorporated into its curriculum, there is no urgent need for midafternoon carpooling. If the day-school schedule permitted the parent to work even one hour longer each week, the cost of time would be cut in half, and the full cost of day school would come to about $11,300 ($11,000 + $300) for the clerk and $17,000 ($11,000 + $6,000) for the lawyer. Thus, even if the clerk and the lawyer faced the same tuition for these two programs, the full cost of day school would be more than six times higher than the cost of a Hebrew school for the clerk (11,300/$1,600 = 7.1) but only 30 percent higher ($17,000/$13,000 = 1.3) for the lawyer. Because a consumer's choice depends on the relative price

of two goods, this suggests that a two-career couple in high-wage occupations would find the Jewish day-school option much less expensive
than would a family with lower wage rates.

The Value of "Leisure" Time

In addition to the after-school sessions, Hebrew schools typically
hold classes on Sunday morning. Day-school parents use their Sunday
mornings for all kinds of activities: sleeping late, reading the Sunday
paper at leisure, enjoying relaxed family time with their children, doing household chores, running errands, participating in community or
synagogue activities, and so on. Each of these activities has value for the
consumer. Because parents who drive their children to school on Sunday
have less time to spend on them, the value of activities that they would
have to give up must be included in the full cost of Hebrew school.

Although most people place a high value on these Sunday morning
activities, I often hear them describe this time as "free." If they mean
that it is discretionary—as in a "free period" in high school—then they
are probably correct. Too often, however, they infer that this time is
costless simply because it does not involve taking time out of paid work.
This is not correct. The true economic cost of an item is the value of
an alternative that you would otherwise have enjoyed, whether it is the
good not purchased or the time not spent in another activity. When you
drive your child to Hebrew school on a Sunday morning, the activities
that you are *not* doing—like sleeping late, lingering over breakfast, and
enjoying the Sunday newspaper—determine the value of your time.

Perhaps surprisingly, the wage rate turns out to be a very good approximation of the value of time spent in these leisure activities because
people allocate their scarce time by the same rule of thumb that they
use to allocate their money budgets. You choose an activity because you
value it more than the alternatives, but you never spend your entire budget on one thing. For example, you may enjoy lolling around on a Sunday morning for an hour or two, but after a while you usually get "tired"
of it. This is because time spent in any activity is subject to the *Law of
Diminishing Returns*, which means that as you spend more and more
time on it the benefit obtained from an additional unit (for example, one
more hour) gets lower and lower.

When you have little time for something, such as interacting with your children, an hour can be so precious that you value it more than any alternatives, such as running errands. You would enjoy spending more time with the children, but eventually the value of an additional hour with them falls to the point where it no longer exceeds the value of an additional hour running errands, and you tell the kids that you've got to get going. This logic is symmetrical: When you have little time to run errands, an hour spent this way is more valuable than it would be in other activities, but at some point an additional hour of errand running is not worth the additional sacrifice of family or leisure time.

It follows that your time-allocation choices lead you to a situation where the value of an additional hour spent in any activity is the same as its value in any other activity. This is what economists call the *marginal value* of time. It does not mean that you get an equal amount of enjoyment out of everything you do, nor does it imply that you spend the same amount of time on every activity. It does mean that when time is managed efficiently, the *last* hour spent has the same value in every activity. This is just common sense, for if an additional hour would be more valuable in one activity than in all the others, you would want to spend more time in that activity. This time-allocation principle applies to all activities, including time spent at work for which the money value of an hour is simply the wage rate. The wage rate is thus a reasonable approximation of the marginal value of time—that is, the money value of the last hour spent—in leisure as well as labor market activities.[1]

The Value of Nonmarket Time

Everyone instinctively budgets his or her time so that its marginal value is the same in all activities, but not everyone has a wage rate that measures it in dollars. Many people enjoy their work or get other kinds of satisfaction from it in addition to their earnings. New workers often start at low wages, putting themselves in a position that leads to higher wages as they gain experience or qualify for a better job. Because these nonmonetary benefits would also be sacrificed by any reduction in hours of work, people in these situations value their time at more than their hourly earnings. Time allocation decisions reflect this higher value, which is underestimated by the market wage rate.

Going to school should be thought of as another kind of job, an age-appropriate occupation for children and youths, which is unpaid but which nevertheless adds market value to a student's future earnings. This is especially evident for older teenagers and adult students. Whether preparing for entrance to higher education or for the job market itself, going to classes and doing homework are activities whose value depends in part on a student's ambitions. Those heading for a high-wage career have more at stake, and thus an incentive to allocate more time and effort to their studies, than those heading for a low-wage career. Children are not actually in the paid labor force, but parents helping prepare them for high-wage professional occupations know that their children's time already has a correspondingly high value. Even parents who themselves are in high-wage occupations may make family time allocation decisions as though a child's time is as valuable as their own.

Full-time housewives constitute another group of workers whose occupation has no market wage but which is nevertheless productive.[2] We could simply assume that a housewife would earn the average wage rate for women in the labor force of her age and education level, and perhaps also in her region and occupation (if she once had one). Alternatively, if a housewife does chores that allow her husband to work longer hours, the value of her extra hours of time can be approximated by the wage rate that he earns. If she drives her children to after-school lessons or makes their homework time more efficient, the value of her time is approximated by the value of their time. From this perspective, a family can be thought of as a single unit that budgets the time of its members so that the marginal value of time in all activities is approximately the same for everyone, including the full-time housewife.

A somewhat different situation applies to people who are not in the labor force because they are retired. Whether their income comes from a pension or from savings accrued in earlier years, typically the result of work in the past, this has no implications for the money value of their time today. This time has value and is budgeted—just like everyone else's—so that the value of the last hour spent is approximately equal for each of their activities. Yet those retirees who do not work in the labor force cannot change their income level by changing the way they spend their time. Because many retirees engage in activities that they "did not have time for" when they were working, we can only suppose that the marginal value of their time is now lower than their former wage rate.

All of these "nonworking" family members—students, housewives, retirees—spend income that does not depend on their own time-allocation decisions. The higher that income, the more goods and services they can buy. No matter how much money they have, however, they never get a bigger time budget than anyone else: twenty-four hours in a day, seven days in a week, fifty-two weeks in a year. Limitations on time affect their ability to enjoy the things that money can buy, and the higher their family's income the more they feel this constraint. Thus, even people who don't themselves earn a wage can have a high value of time, giving them an incentive to purchase time-saving goods and services and to reduce the time-intensity of their nonwork activities.

The Full Price of Hebrew School

Earlier we estimated conservatively that a Hebrew school meeting two afternoons a week would cost $1,000 for tuition plus two hours per week driving a carpool. If we now add another two hours for driving the carpool every other Sunday morning, the cost of time is correspondingly higher: $900 for the $10-an-hour retail clerk and $18,000 for the $200-an-hour lawyer. The full price of an after-school Hebrew program at the synagogue is thus $1,900 for the clerk and $19,000 for the lawyer. In contrast, the full price of a day-school education is still $11,300 and $17,000 respectively, nearly five times higher than the Hebrew school for the clerk but only 10 percent higher for the lawyer. Both parents have a clear choice based on different prices: The full price of day school relative to that of an after-school Hebrew program is much lower for the lawyer than for the clerk.

These two parents have earnings that are plausible, but they are both extreme cases because American Jews generally earn an hourly wage somewhere between $10 and $200. Yet the basic principle that this example illustrates remains valid. As more and more American Jews acquired higher education and moved into high-level careers, the time cost of the three-day-a-week Hebrew schools rose until it came to dominate in the family's budget decision. By the last decades of the twentieth century, when many families had both mothers and fathers in high-wage occupations, the day-school option was becoming more cost effective for many Jewish families.

The growing day-school movement in later decades of the twentieth century coincided with a nationwide renewal of interest in private schooling, but the Jewish day schools grew for other reasons as well. Our immigrant grandparents' educational goal was to help their children realize the promise of America by moving up the socioeconomic ladder. Today's Jewish parents take this for granted, worrying instead about how to enrich their children's American lives by strengthening their Jewish heritage. With this in mind, many parents have felt that day schools provided a better Jewish education than the afternoon Hebrew schools, helped by revisions in the day-school curriculum that significantly improved the quality of general education.

The growth of Jewish day schools has clearly been facilitated and reinforced by the decline in their full price relative to the synagogue-sponsored Hebrew schools. Facing this competition, some Hebrew schools have considered changing their programs from two weekday afternoons to one, reducing their full cost without lowering tuition. Whether this will enable them to compete successfully with the day schools will depend partly on how well they can adapt their curriculum to the shorter classroom time. This economics-driven issue—how to avoid lowering educational standards in a shorter Hebrew school program—is now a major topic of concern among Jewish educators, with important implications for the future of Judaism in the United States.

Prices, Incomes, and Preferences

No matter what the price of a good, rich people can afford to buy more of it than poor people. The Jewish day-school movement may thus be stimulated by rising incomes. A family with supplemental nonlabor income, perhaps gifts from grandparents or perhaps returns from previous investments, finds high money tuitions less intimidating than if they had to finance their children's Jewish education just from their own jobs. Higher income in the community can also translate into scholarships that subsidize the money cost of tuition for low-income families.

People in high-wage occupations experience a double effect, both a high value of time and a high total income, especially pronounced for couples with two professional careers. The high value of time raises the full cost of all time-intensive activities, but high income makes these activities more affordable. Each of these effects alone would make the day-school option more attractive than the Hebrew-school option for high-wage parents. Together they reinforce each other and further increase the demand for day schools. If incomes were to fall, whether from a downturn in the labor market or a drop in the value of nonlabor assets, the incentives to prefer day schools over Hebrew schools would also decline. Indeed, this may be one reason why day-school enrollments stopped growing during the economic slowdown of the early twenty-first century.

Regardless of prices and incomes, some parents prefer sending their children to a day school because they place a higher value on its educational program compared to that of the Hebrew schools. This is a matter of personal preferences and priorities; even families with identical wages and incomes can choose different consumption patterns. Moreover, the higher one's income, the greater the freedom to indulge one's preferences. Whether we're thinking about food, clothing, housing, automobiles, or Jewish education, wealthier families have more options than poorer families and exhibit greater variety in their choices. Our grandparents may have differed in their preferences as much as we do, but today's higher income levels have resulted in a greater variety of Jewish consumption patterns.

Full Price, Income, and Synagogue Affiliation

Family budget decisions take place on two levels. We devise an overall strategy, a more or less explicit long-term plan, when we make general lifestyle choices that reflect the way we want to live. Our day-to-day expenditures of time and money reflect this plan, but we can adjust them somewhat when faced with an unexpected circumstance or to indulge an impulse. For American Jews, deciding whether to affiliate with a Reform, Conservative, or Orthodox synagogue is an important aspect of a Jewish lifestyle choice within which they will conduct their religious observance. Much in the same way that occupational choices affect the family's overall money budget that constrains day-to-day expenditures, so synagogue affiliation provides a framework within which time is allocated to Jewish activities.

The American Synagogue Movements

Economic incentives are determined by the full prices of goods and services, and wage rates are a major determinant of the cost of time-intensive synagogue ritual. As soon as Jewish immigrants arrived in the United States, their wage-earning opportunities rose dramatically above what they had been in Europe. A German Jew arriving in the early decades of the nineteenth century might have started as an itinerant peddler, eventually accumulating enough savings to establish a retail outlet and in the end perhaps a small department store. A Russian Jew arriving at the turn of the twentieth century might have started as a tailor, eventually accumulating enough savings to establish his own firm and perhaps become a manufacturer in the garment industry or open a clothing store. Whatever their occupation, however, Jewish immigrants and their children found America to be a land of opportunity. Coming to America raised wage rates well above what they had been in the old country and thus increased the full cost of time-intensive activities.

Throughout the nineteenth century, American Jews (most of whom were immigrants from Germany prior to the 1880s) experimented with religious reforms that would allow them to remain Jewish without spending as much time as tradition might require. Synagogue services became shorter. Synagogue ritual was altered to accommodate congregants unfamiliar with the Hebrew language, thus greatly reducing the time required for religious education. Some congregations even observed the Sabbath on Sunday instead of Saturday to be more compatible with the prevailing six-day workweek. Home-based Jewish ritual was also affected, with some holiday observances greatly shortened and others simply ignored. In Germany, where economic opportunities for Jews were rising with that country's economic development, Jewish scholars had been developing theological justifications for reforms such as these, and their writings were available to American Jewish reformers. Yet the changes actually introduced varied across communities, suggesting that reforms in American synagogues were a grassroots phenomenon, stimulated by the rising full costs of traditional observance and justified after the fact by German Reform theology.

The American Reform movement was formalized in 1873 as the Union of American Hebrew Congregations (UAHC), a loose association of congregations observing various "reformed" rituals. The founding statement of principles by the UAHC provided theological justification for the reduced-time practices of its member congregations. In reaction, more traditionally minded religious leaders founded the Orthodox Union (OU) in 1898, a similar umbrella organization for synagogues that resisted the radical innovations of Reform Judaism. The Conservative movement broke off from the OU in 1913, as United Synagogue of America (USA) was formed by congregations wanting to reduce the time costs of religious observance but without making the radical changes in theology advocated by UAHC.

These three synagogue movements would dominate American Jewish religious life for the entire twentieth century.[3] Orthodox synagogues appealed to new immigrants because the ritual was familiar, but as wages rose and time became more valuable the upwardly mobile tended to affiliate with Conservative or Reform synagogues. Conservative synagogues were most popular among the adult children of immigrants, many of whom were raised in Orthodox homes and neighborhoods, and Reform congregations tended to be made up of suburban Jews with a very high value of time. All three synagogue movements have experienced change during the course of the twentieth century, a subject to which we will return in a later chapter. For now, we merely observe that twentieth-century American Judaism was effectively defined by these three movements and that religious observance was most time intensive for the Orthodox and least time intensive for the Reform.

Education and Synagogue Affiliation

Whenever the value of time is a large component of the full price of a good, higher-wage people will find it to be relatively more expensive than lower-wage people. If this were the only consideration for choosing a synagogue, we would expect the members of Orthodox congregations to have the lowest wage rates and the members of Reform congregations to have the highest wage rates. People with more education tend to have higher wages, so education would follow a similar pattern: Members of time-intensive Orthodox congregations would have the lowest average education levels, Conservative synagogues would attract members with moderate education levels, and people with high levels of education would affiliate with Reform synagogues. Jews with high wage rates would be tempted to stop attending synagogue entirely, even if they continued to affiliate with—and pay dues to—the synagogue of their choice.

This pattern was clearly apparent by the mid-twentieth century, and many people inferred that higher education undermined a person's interest in religion. Contemporary observers believed that Orthodoxy was an outdated mode of Judaism unsuited to a highly educated American community. Yet by the end of the century we could no longer observe this clear relationship between education and synagogue movements, nor did we still believe that a modern higher education is inherently incompatible with religious sophistication. Indeed, many important Jewish scholars have earned their living in secular occupations that require advanced education. The content of a person's education—what he or she learns in high school, college, or professional school—matters only insofar as it enhances labor market productivity, not because it undermines religious commitment. Wage rates provide the full-price incentives that affect synagogue choice, and if members of a particular synagogue movement tend to have similar levels of education it is more likely to be because they earn their living in occupations with similar wage rates.

Income and Synagogue Affiliation

In contrast with education, which affects synagogue choice only indirectly, family income influences this decision in several ways. As a first principle, the higher a family's money income, the more its members can afford to spend on pretty much anything. Time budgets, however, are fixed for each individual family member. Rich people can buy expensive goods and services, but they can't have any additional time with which to consume them. Rich parents can spend more money on their children, but they can't give them any more time. This is why people with high incomes are more likely to feel time constrained—it's not that they actually have less time than anyone else; it's just that there aren't enough hours in the day for them to enjoy all the things that their money can buy.

High-income people thus have an incentive to find ways to substitute money for time—the higher the income, the stronger the incentive. Working couples hire someone else to do household chores, thus giving them more time for work, family, or leisure activities. Parents pay school tuition to reduce the time they have to spend educating their own children. Synagogues hire professional clergy in part so that their members don't have to devote as much time to prepare for religious services. In general, the wealthier the congregation, the more willing are congregants to pay higher fees to cover these services. This trade-off between time and money shows up in the ranking of synagogue movements by income level: Reform religious practices are the least time intensive but often cost the most money, while Orthodox observance is the most time intensive but relatively inexpensive in terms of money.

We have seen that high wage rates increase the value of time and make each hour of leisure more expensive. Yet high incomes make additional leisure hours more desirable, whether this income comes from wages or from some other source. People whose incomes are derived primarily from wages find these two effects pulling in opposite directions. When both income and wage rates are low, a worker responds to a pay raise by working longer hours because the lost leisure is worth less than the additional things that he or she can buy. When income is high, leisure becomes more valuable, and the law of diminishing returns means that the extra benefit derived from adding more consumer goods is smaller when you already have a lot. For both of these reasons, a high-income worker might respond to a pay raise by working less and enjoying more leisure time.

The idea that American Jewry sorts itself into synagogue movements according to income and education levels seemed obvious in the mid-twentieth century.[4] At that time most Jewish families were upwardly mobile and relied primarily on their jobs for income but had not yet reached the point where leisure was more valuable than their wage. A family with high income was likely to have high wage rates and so face a high value of time, and high wages were typically the consequence of a high level of education. Of the three main synagogue movements,

Reform had the least time-intensive religious observance and tended to attract people with high wage rates, who also had the most education and income. Jews with lower levels of education had lower incomes and avoided the high membership fees of the non-Orthodox synagogues.

For people at the upper end of the wage distribution, however, income may be high enough to shift the decision in favor of leisure. How high does the wage rate have to be before this happens? That depends on the individual, of course, but when income is high the value of an additional hour of leisure can outweigh the monetary gains from an additional hour of work. This can occur even at lower wage rates for workers with additional sources of income such as inheritances or pensions. In today's American Jewish community, where many people are second- and even third-generation high earners, relatively high nonlabor income is not unusual. People invest their savings in stocks and bonds that can be sold for immediate cash and in the meantime yield income to supplement ordinary earnings. Young Jews receive income subsidies and gifts from parents and grandparents and may enjoy an inheritance, or the expectation of inheritance, that further reduces their financial constraints. People with high nonlabor sources of income like these may decide that they can afford to experience a more time-intensive Jewish lifestyle even if its full price is relatively high.

Why Isn't Everyone Reform?

If the association between income and synagogue affiliation characterized American Jews in the middle of the twentieth century, today's Jews with their high education and income levels should overwhelmingly affiliate with Reform synagogues. Yet this is not the case. By the end of the twentieth century sociologists found little or no association between synagogue affiliations and education or income level.[5] At the beginning of the twenty-first century the Reform movement just edges out the Conservative movement in the proportion of synagogue members, with 35 percent and 33 percent, respectively, of the affiliated households. Orthodoxy may have declined substantially in the first half of the twentieth century, and it still accounts for only 10 percent of American Jews, yet it has grown significantly in recent decades and gained new respect among the educated. "Secular" Jews, once associated predominantly with the highly educated, now account for less than 4 percent of the population, and almost 23 percent of all American Jews say they are "just Jewish" but not identified with any synagogue movement. The underlying relationship between education, income, and synagogue affiliation is clearly not as straightforward as it once appeared.

This apparent paradox can be resolved by distinguishing between the effect of wage rates on synagogue choice and the effects of total money income. Earnings determine the value of time and thus affect full prices, inducing a high-wage consumer to substitute money for time-intensive goods. Income determines the size of the budget, affecting the consumer's ability to select goods that suit his or her preferences. If high wage rates have induced less time-intensive forms of American Jewish religious observance, high incomes have encouraged a greater variety of Jewish experience. In the early twentieth century this took the form of a split into the three main synagogue movements. By the later decades of that century these had splintered into a much wider variety of choices. The most formal new movement was Reconstructionist Judaism, an offshoot of the Conservative movement. Other new movements characterized themselves as "nondenominational," "postdenominational," "cultural," "humanistic," or "New-Age" Judaism, to name only a few. The number and size of small, fundamentalist Orthodox movements, some of them decidedly sectlike, grew dramatically. These smaller groups are not united into a single movement, but they are usually referred to as *ultra-Orthodox* to distinguish them from the "modern" Orthodoxy of the formal synagogue movement.

Full prices are still important determinants of synagogue affiliation, but they are much less likely than in the past to differ dramatically from one movement to the next. This factor, together with the generally high incomes in the Jewish community, allows membership decisions to be influenced more heavily by noneconomic factors. People want a synagogue that is conveniently located, where religious practices are congruent with their own preferences, where they find a congenial social environment, and where they will be comfortable with their children's religious training. Just as economic incentives faced by an earlier generation could explain the association among education, income, and synagogue affiliation, the economic incentives faced by today's American Jews can explain why this association is no longer observed.

The Full Price of Religious Observance

Affiliation with a synagogue movement and selection of a Jewish school are both consequences and determinants of a family's Jewish lifestyle choices. These choices are affected by individual preferences, by family traditions, and by friends and neighbors. They are influenced by the family's surroundings, both within the Jewish community and in the general society where they live and work. Economic incentives also influence these choices. Full prices and incomes do not *determine* the outcome, any more than they determine which house one lives in or which clothes one buys. They are an important consideration, however, and we need to appreciate their effects on Jewish observance and lifestyles.

The single most important economic incentive affecting daily behavior is the value of time, because that determines the full price of every activity. People with a high value of time are always tempted to reduce or even avoid time-intensive religious observances regardless of their preferred Jewish lifestyle. Practices regarding the morning prayers required of Jewish men illustrate this principle. Orthodox men typically observe this ritual by reading the prayers in Hebrew but at the speed of light. Conservative men are less hasty in their reading, choosing English or Hebrew depending on their facility in Hebrew, but most observe this ritual only occasionally rather than on a daily basis. Reform men rarely observe it at all, and many do not even acknowledge the morning prayer as a part of their Jewish observance.

This pattern may be observed for nearly every Jewish ritual, whether it be a holiday observance, keeping the Sabbath, following kashrut (the dietary laws), or celebrating a life-cycle event. When time is expensive, we look for ways to "save" time. Now that most American Jews are college graduates and many have advanced degrees, there is much less variation in schooling within the Jewish community. This means that differences in education levels no longer explain much of the variation in the value of time and are thus not a good predictor of differences in religious behavior. Annual income levels are also less useful than they once were for predicting differences in wage rates because nonlabor sources of income vary widely from one family to the next. Yet wage rates remain the best single indicator of the value of time and hence the full price of religious observance. Differences in the full cost of an hour of Jewish observance now come mainly from differences in occupations, which in turn depend on differences in the nature of skills acquired in higher education and on the job. Whether an hour spent in Jewish observance is worth more than its full cost also depends on the skills obtained in the course of a Jewish education, which are the subject of the next chapter.

4

Jewish Education and Human Capital

MOST AMERICAN JEWS ARE *Jews-by-birth*, which usually means that their parents were Jewish.[1] In other times and places, being born a Jew was like inheriting a racial category, branding you for life whether you liked it or not. In the United States, however, "Jew" is a religious and ethnic characterization that may or may not be accepted as part of one's identity. Without some knowledge of religious Judaism, or some experience with a Jewish lifestyle, "being Jewish" has no more meaning than any other accident of birth—like being born in California, say, or having blue eyes. When Jewish parents ensure that their children get this kind of knowledge we say they are raising them to be "good Jews." *Jews-by-choice*—that is, those who convert to Judaism as adults—get some of this same knowledge by fulfilling the preconversion study requirements. Jewish identity is built through an education process that itself is part of what it means to be a Jew.

Jewish culture values learning for its own sake and speaks of the "sweetness" of pure study, but this chapter focuses on Jewish education as an investment in the next generation. It considers *what* American Jews need to learn and *how* they are taught it. Jewish education is defined in its broadest sense to include the creation of Jewish values, memories, experiences, and skills, as well as knowledge of religious matters. It takes place primarily in the home but also in the synagogue, in the classroom, in youth groups, in summer camps, and anywhere that Jews come together for social or religious purposes. Moreover, Jewish education in the United States is deeply affected by its American context and by the high secular education of American Jews. These are the subjects to which we now turn.

Education and Human Capital

In the language of Economics, education is an investment in *human capital*. Although the word *capital* can mean different things in other contexts, here it means anything human-made that makes a person more productive, makes tasks easier, or makes his or her use of time more efficient. Most people think of machines as capital, and indeed these are good examples of physical (that is, tangible) capital. Useful skills are another form of capital, for they are human-made and improve our future productivity. Unlike physical capital, however, knowledge and skills are embodied in human beings and cannot exist independently of the people who learned them. To emphasize this distinction we refer to skills as "human" capital.

The concept of human capital is much broader than just production-related skills. It also includes the skills that make us more efficient consumers (for example, sports-related skills, artistic skills, gardening skills, culinary skills, and the like). "People skills" make our interactions with others more efficient, and "social skills" increase our pleasure in their company. We invest in "parenting skills" that make childrearing activities easier, more enjoyable, and (we hope) better for our children. We have skills that are useful for our hobbies, skills that increase our enjoyment of literature and the arts, and skills that improve our relationships with other family members. We invest in these skills by reading manuals or "how-to" books, by taking lessons, by talking with others, and by practicing. Whenever we spend our money, time, and effort to learn any of these skills we are investing in our human capital.

Economists also make a distinction between skills that are *general* and those that are *specific* to a certain activity. For example, the public schools teach general subjects—English, mathematics, American history, and social studies—to children of all religions. Religious groups make supplemental arrangements for teaching skills specific to their own religion, skills related to the ceremonies, rituals, customs, language, and music that distinguish that religious culture from the others. Each group's religion-specific skills make the practice of that religion easier, more efficient and enjoyable, but they have little or no impact on other activities. *Jewish human capital* refers to specific skills that enhance participation in Judaism's religious, communal, and cultural life without necessarily affecting the other dimensions of American life.

Investment is simply the act of creating capital, using resources to make something as a tool to make something else in the future. Economists often use the term *education* broadly to include many different ways in which we learn new skills. In a previous chapter we saw that American Jews invest heavily in formal schooling, whether public or private, and acquire high levels of skill related to their future occupations. Occupation-related skills are also acquired on the job, sometimes through an internship or employer-sponsored training, sometimes through informal instruction by co-workers, but sometimes simply through experience performing the job itself. Other skills are acquired during the course of social interactions, leisure activities, or even family life. (Language, for example, is an important job-related skill. Even before acquiring basic literacy, anyone who has watched a toddler learn to speak knows that this is a time-intensive project involving great effort on the part of both child and caregiver.) If the skill is relevant for our job it usually earns a higher hourly wage rate. Nonwork skills increase our efficiency and enjoyment of the many unpaid activities that make up the rest of our lives. No matter where we learn it, any skill that makes us more productive workers or consumers raises the value of our time.

Jewish Human Capital

Few American Jews make a career of the study of Judaism and Jewish subjects, but nearly all of them invest in some Jewish human capital for themselves and for their children. Like any investment in education, an investment in Jewish education is a process that takes time and money, the two scarce resources for which a family must budget. As we saw earlier, for most American Jews the value of time is an important determinant of the full cost of Jewish education. Its full benefit is determined by the usefulness of the additional skills for Jewish life, augmented by whatever usefulness these skills may have for a person's secular activities. The economic incentive to invest in Jewish education thus depends not only on improved efficiency of Jewish time but also on the importance of Jewish-specific skills for an individual's American lifestyle.

For example, Hebrew is the language of Judaism's Great Tradition, the Jewish-specific language in which its scriptures are written, its traditional prayers are recited, and its synagogue ritual is conducted. Torah is written in an antique Hebrew, differing from the modern language much as Shakespeare's English differs from modern English. Most of the remaining works are composed in "modern" Hebrew, which itself dates back at least 2000 years. Even with the same language, usage varies over time, as the U.S. Supreme Court demonstrates every time it has to "interpret" the Constitution (written in eighteenth-century English) to resolve a current problem. Much of Judaism's scripture is also written as poetry, which is notoriously difficult to capture in translation. English translations exist for most (but not all) of this literature, but they vary considerably, and the Hebrew original remains the common point of reference. Moreover, language is an important dimension of culture, facilitating a personal identification with the Jewish people and an emotional connection with Jewish ancestors and their traditions.

Israeli Jews speak Hebrew as their native language, but American Jews learn it as a second or even third language. Learning any foreign language requires time and effort, less for a Romance language that is linguistically close to English (such as Spanish) and more for languages that are linguistically distant (for example, Korean and Chinese). Hebrew is a Semitic language that falls between these two extremes, written from right to left with its own alphabet and a distinctive grammar. For most Americans, learning Hebrew is a time-intensive process that creates few skills useful for nonreligious activities. It is therefore an expensive activity, especially for people with attractive alternative uses of time.

American Jews with a high value of time who conduct their religious ritual in English, whether at home or in the synagogue, see little benefit from investing in Hebrew language skills and tend to stop their Hebrew education at the basic level.

The relative importance of human capital that is specifically Jewish, a major determinant of the cost of being Jewish, depends on the balance between universal aspects of Judaism and its parochial aspects. Some skills that might have been Jewish specific (parochial) in other times and places are shared by the larger society in today's United States. For example, American notions of ethical behavior, of social justice, and of responsible stewardship of Earth's resources are so close to Jewish values that children need not attend Hebrew school to learn them. High-wage American Jews face strong economic incentives to emphasize these values as the essence of Judaism and to deemphasize the importance of traditions that require specifically Jewish human capital.

This principle helps explain how Judaism adapts to new socioeconomic environments, both historically and in our own time. In the nineteenth century, Reform Judaism emphasized the universal in Jewish theology, dismissing as "obsolete" any customs or laws that were deemed "parochial," replacing Hebrew with the vernacular as the synagogue language, and drastically reducing religious ritual at home and in the synagogue. This movement originated in Germany, a modernizing country where many Jews were highly educated and held high-wage occupations. Reform Judaism also had great popular appeal in the United States, where many synagogues adopted similar customs at the grassroots level. Not all innovations, however, can stand the test of time. By the mid-twentieth century Reform Judaism had reintroduced many of these parochial traditions, often modified to enhance the religious experience of congregants with few Jewish-specific skills. Meanwhile, the Conservative and Orthodox synagogue movements developed different responses to these same economic circumstances with religious adaptations that were less radical. For example, both of these movements retain Hebrew as the language required for full participation in religious ritual and encourage advanced study of religious texts, although Conservative synagogues are more likely than the Orthodox to rely on English translations and transliterations for both ritual and adult education.

Jewish Education

As religions go, we say that Judaism is human-capital intensive because education yields a relatively high benefit. Its sacred texts and their commentaries are both broad and deep, a large body of writings with layers of meaning that can be very rewarding for the sophisticated student. Serious study of these texts requires some knowledge of Hebrew, the language in which they were originally written. (Advanced students also need to learn Aramaic, a Semitic language very similar to Hebrew that was in daily use some 2,000 years ago in the Near East.) Hebrew is also the usual language of Jewish religious ritual, whether in the synagogue or at home, where each person's experience depends on familiarity with the requisite knowledge and background. In the United States, the most common form of religious education is the Hebrew school, which introduces Jewish children to the Hebrew language as well as the basics of religious practice. Most American synagogues either operate their own Hebrew school or affiliate with one that emphasizes Jewish skills corresponding to the lifestyle associated with their respective synagogue movements.

Formal education—that is, schooling—is not the only way to acquire human capital. Many Jewish-specific skills are acquired through experience with synagogue services or home-based religious rituals. Others are learned as part of everyday Jewish family life or by participating in Jewish life-cycle rituals. The annual cycle of Jewish holidays also provides a context for the formation of much Jewish human capital. Each Jew is connected to the community and to the Jewish people as a whole—past, present and future—to a degree determined largely by shared memories and experience, as well as the kind of knowledge that is acquired outside of the classroom. Whether learned at home, at school, in the synagogue, or in the Jewish community, Jewish human capital includes all of the knowledge, experience, and memories that enrich the value of time spent in Jewish observance today. The creation of this human capital in all of its forms is the essence of Jewish education. And because education is a time-intensive activity, economic incentives encourage Americans to seek Jewish practices that reduce the cost of acquiring Jewish-specific skills.

Synagogue Ritual and Jewish Human Capital

The Conservative synagogue that my family attends follows a *siddur* (prayer book) prepared by the Conservative movement and made available to everyone in attendance. Congregants can follow the service by listening, by reading along in the siddur, or some combination of the two. The synagogue also provides each congregant with a book in which he or she can follow the portion of Torah that is read aloud (in Hebrew) during the service. Both of these books use Hebrew and English on facing pages, Hebrew (read from right to left) on the right-hand page and an English translation (read from left to right) on the left. Congregants familiar with the Hebrew script can follow the service in that language, even if their comprehension skills permit no more than a vague understanding. People with partial competence in Hebrew may find the language easier to comprehend if the spoken and written words are experienced together. People with limited Hebrew skills rely on the English translation to follow the service.

Both the liturgy and the Torah readings are traditionally chanted to melodies, tunes that have accumulated over the centuries so that on any one day they can range from the very ancient to the very modern. These melodies serve three functions for a listener whose knowledge of Hebrew is imperfect. They are a memory device, especially useful for Jews who lived in times and places where books were expensive and not available for each congregant. Music also heightens the emotional experience of the service, at the same time providing connection to the traditions of Jews in other communities, both contemporary and historical. A third function that I find useful is that melodies tend to slow down the reading, making it easier for me to follow the written text and enhancing my comprehension. For many Jews, tunes used for chanting the Hebrew words are an important part of the synagogue experience, some nostalgically familiar and others new and exciting.

Literacy in the Synagogue

The widespread use of a siddur in the synagogue presumes a literate congregation. Literacy in Hebrew has been a requirement for Jewish males for at least 2,000 years. (Female literacy in Hebrew has been less widespread, probably more common in certain times and places than in others.) The siddur itself dates back at least to the Middle Ages and was among the first books produced by the early printing press. Traditionally published entirely in Hebrew, the siddur familiar to many American Jewish immigrants from Eastern Europe divided each page in half, placing a Yiddish translation below the Hebrew original. This was feasible because Yiddish uses the same alphabet as Hebrew and is also written from right to left. Once English replaced Hebrew as the vernacular of American Jewry, the English translation was moved to a separate page.

The Hebrew text is very similar for every version of the siddur, the main differences being omissions made for the sake of brevity. English equivalents vary widely, however, ranging from literal translations—which themselves can differ—to readings that capture the spirit rather than the language of a particular passage. We find the same format being used for the siddur when we visit synagogues in other countries, with Hebrew and the local language presented on facing pages. The Hebrew page is always familiar to us, but we cannot vouch for the translations because our command of other languages is rudimentary at best.

Orthodox synagogue services that I have attended follow much the same patterns. Each congregant follows the service and the Torah reading in his or her copy of the appropriate books. Some Orthodox synagogues provide books in Hebrew only, but today most follow the familiar format with English and Hebrew on facing pages. English versions used by the Orthodox sometimes differ from those in the Conservative movement, reflecting differences in style and interpretation with which translators inevitably wrestle. (This is why Jewish scholars must be so familiar with the Hebrew language that they can read the original for themselves.) The Orthodox siddur includes a few (rather long) passages that the Conservative liturgy drops or shortens as a time-saving measure. However, the total length of the synagogue service—about two and a half hours on a typical Saturday morning—is about the same because the Orthodox read their liturgy much more quickly and with less singing. Thus, an Orthodox Hebrew education is more likely to focus on the kind of fluency that enables a person to read quickly, a fluency that comes in part from frequent repetition as well as comprehension. In contrast, a Conservative Hebrew education relies more heavily on reading comprehension than on speed.

The Reform synagogues that I have attended follow the same basic liturgical structure but have a very different ambience. Although Reform congregations differ and some now use Hebrew extensively, most still rely on English and use Hebrew mainly for short prayers that represent the core of traditional liturgy. A Reform Hebrew education typically focuses on conversational Hebrew—that is, the modern idiom spoken in Israel today—and the Hebrew used in Reform synagogues reflects this emphasis. Like the Orthodox and Conservative, Reform synagogues use Hebrew for traditional songs, but they like to sing these songs with new melodies, and sometimes they break with Jewish tradition by using musical instruments on Shabbat.

Reading the Torah in Hebrew

In every synagogue, regardless of movement, a central feature of the Sabbath service is a public reading of the Torah, the first five books of the Hebrew Scriptures, sometimes called the Five Books of Moses. The Torah itself, in its original ancient Hebrew script, is written by hand on a parchment scroll that is kept in the *Ark* (a special cabinet near the pulpit), a central feature of every synagogue. The parchment scroll is wound around two rollers, "dressed" in a cover made of cloth (in the Ashkenazi tradition) or wood (in the Sephardi tradition), and adorned with a breastplate and crowns traditionally made of silver.

The Torah service begins when the leader opens the Ark, removes the dressed Torah, carries it around the room for everyone to see and (if desired) touch, and lays it on a reading table near the pulpit after removing its various coverings. The Scriptures are available in book form, and congregants will follow the reading in such a book, but the public reading is done directly from the scroll. The Torah scroll retains an ancient format, omitting all vowels and most punctuation, so reading from Torah requires more than a casual acquaintance with the ancient Hebrew language. Afterwards the Torah is held up for everyone to see before its cover and adornments are replaced. Then a passage from the later Scriptures (usually from Prophets), known as a *Haftorah*, is read. Unlike the

Torah, the Haftorah is not on a special scroll but rather in a book with vowels and punctuation, so it is less demanding of the reader's language skill. At the end of the Torah service, the leader again carries the scroll around the room before returning it to its place in the Ark.

The Torah reading is embedded in a ceremony that is part of Judaism's Great Tradition, common to all Jews regardless of ethnicity or synagogue movement. It takes place in the synagogue every Saturday morning and on the major holidays, with a shorter version during the morning service on Monday and Thursday. More than a thousand years ago, the rabbis of Babylon (the main center of Diaspora Jewish scholarship at that time) divided the Torah into fifty-four weekly portions, so that reading one portion each Shabbat would allow congregants to hear the entire work during the course of a year.[2] Each portion is further subdivided into seven parts, giving seven congregants the honor of participating in its reading. Each person called to the Torah recites a brief blessing before and after the reading of the portion. A congregant can be so honored even if his Hebrew skills are not up to the actual Torah reading, in which case he recites the blessings and a substitute does the actual reading. Other congregants participate by opening or closing the Ark, by carrying the Torah scroll around the room, by undressing or dressing the Torah scroll, or by lifting the open scroll for the congregation to see. Each of these acts honors a congregant by giving an active role in the Torah service.

Although anyone is welcome to attend a synagogue service, only Jews participate in the Torah and Haftorah readings. In many traditions, including the European Ashkenazi tradition from which most American Jews descend, only men may conduct the synagogue Torah ritual. In the twentieth-century United States, however, women played an increasingly active role in all aspects of Jewish life. In the later decades of that century women achieved full participation in the synagogue ritual, first by the Reform movement and then by the Conservative. Even among the Orthodox, where synagogue ritual remains a male-only domain, some congregations permit women to conduct their own Torah service separately from the men.

(Apart from tradition, there is a semantic ambiguity affecting our understanding of what it means for "Jews" to read from Torah in the synagogue. The Hebrew language has separate plurals for males and for females, but uses the masculine plural for a mixed group because it does not have a separate plural form for a group of both men and women. Thus the injunction limiting participation in the Torah service to Jews (masculine plural), traditionally interpreted as meaning Jewish men, might instead be interpreted as including both men and women. There is some debate as to how this term was understood in antiquity, although it is agreed that it has been interpreted as men-only in recent centuries.)

Whether the synagogue ritual is "egalitarian" (that is, includes men and women on the same footing) or male only, only adult Jews are called to the Torah. In Jewish religious tradition a child becomes an adult at the age of thirteen. (In some traditions, girls reach adulthood at the age of twelve and boys at thirteen.) The first time a person is called to the Torah, usually during a Sabbath synagogue service just after the thirteenth birthday, marks the point at which a person becomes a *Bar Mitzvah* (for a boy) or *Bat Mitzvah* (for a girl), translated literally as a Son or Daughter of the Commandment, and accepts membership in the Jewish People as an adult. It is also customary for him or her to read the day's Haftorah portion and to deliver some remarks (in English) teaching the congregation something about their content. Among American Jews this ceremony, traditionally followed by a modest festive meal for family and friends, has evolved into a major celebration that brings together relatives even from distant places and often includes a party comparable to a wedding reception.

Although the party afterwards sometimes seems like the most elaborate part of the Bar or Bat Mitzvah observance, children typically spend years preparing for their adult role in the synagogue. At a minimum they need to read Hebrew and chant the Torah and Haftorah melodies, to recite the blessings before and after the readings, and to lead the blessings associated with the festive meal. Hebrew schools typically provide at least this level of language skill, usually accompanied by some personal tutoring for the specific Torah portion and the Haftorah assigned to the designated date. As a practical matter, the Bar or Bat Mitzvah is the culmination of a basic Hebrew education and is essentially the same in every synagogue, although Orthodox women do not read from Torah and thus need not celebrate in the synagogue.

Jewish Education in the United States

When I was about nine years old, my parents enrolled me in a Conservative-movement Hebrew school. We lived in a suburb with few synagogues, where everyone who was not Catholic attended the local public school. Twice a week, at the end of the regular school day, Jewish children were carpooled to Hebrew school for another hour or two in the classroom. As children, we placed a low value on improving our religious skills and understood only dimly that religion might turn out to be important for our adult lives. At the same time, we were very aware that Hebrew school came at the cost of other after-school activities like sports, glee club, Scout meetings, or just playtime. Our parents, however, insisted that Jewish children belonged in Hebrew school, and in the end we learned to accept this as part of the cost of being Jewish.

Differences in the use of Hebrew by the various synagogue movements dictate differences in their requirements for a basic Hebrew-school education. The Orthodox is the most time intensive, requiring a high degree of Hebrew fluency and consequently longer hours of preparation for boys. Orthodox parents are thus more likely to send their children to day schools that have longer hours of Hebrew and Torah study than the after-school programs permit. The Reform is the least time intensive, not only because the services are shorter but also because many Reform synagogues use more English and rely less on Hebrew. Each movement designs its Hebrew-school curriculum to give preteens the language skills needed for its respective synagogue culture, culminating in the Bar or Bat Mitzvah ceremony when the child becomes a full participant in the religious congregation.

The Synagogue Schools

In recent decades, a growing number of Jewish children attend day schools that include an expanded Hebrew-school curriculum in the regular school day. This helps resolve a student's time-use conflicts, but it serves only a small minority of Jewish youth and is not even available in most Jewish communities. Synagogues in the United States typically operate a Hebrew school to which members send their children several times a week, usually twice on school-day afternoons and a third time on Sunday mornings. Younger children go once a week to Sunday school, where they are introduced to the stories, observances, and holiday customs that are the heritage of all American Jews. Sunday school also introduces children to the sound of Hebrew, often with simple songs plucked from the synagogue liturgy or short blessings said during the Sabbath and holiday rituals.

By the fourth grade (about age nine) children begin the three-day-a-week Hebrew school that is at the heart of the American Jewish educational system. The Hebrew-school curriculum includes Jewish history and culture, religious rituals observed in the synagogue and at home, and an introduction to the study of the Jewish scriptures. It also includes Hebrew language instruction, the subject that gives this branch of Jewish education its very name. Students continue their Hebrew-school studies at least until the Bar or Bat Mitzvah on their thirteenth birthday. Some synagogues have supplementary classes for teenagers, but these are not as common as the Hebrew schools for children, and the attendance is generally much lower.

The Bar or Bat Mitzvah ceremony is a rite of passage into adulthood for religious purposes, but in other contexts it marks the transition from childhood to adolescence. As a Jewish parent, I think of my children's adolescence as the decade between Bar Mitzvah and college graduation (approximately ages thirteen to twenty-two), a period during which they thought they could learn more from their peers than from parents or teachers. Teenagers can be blasé about the Jewish holidays, restless in the synagogue, and impatient with Hebrew school classes. They are eager to participate in the many activities available at their public high school, activities that sometimes conflict with the exigencies of Jewish observance. They are also characteristically anxious to fit in with the teen culture, a particularly trying concern for youngsters whose very Jewishness makes them "different" from most other high school students. While some teenagers continue their Jewish education in a Hebrew high school or evening classes, most of them end their formal Jewish education soon after their Bar or Bat Mitzvah.

Jewish Camping

The highlight of my own teenage years was the summers I spent at a Jewish camp. Originally intended to give disadvantaged city children the salutary benefits of a rural experience, summer camps continue to be popular with American Jews for many reasons. Campers enjoy the age-appropriate summer activities—hiking, camping, water sports, singing and dancing, arts and crafts—in a social setting dominated by peers with similar interests. Free from the supervision of parents and teachers, summer camps nevertheless provide a structured environment to reassure parents of the health and safety of their children. Jewish camps provide all of these benefits in a Jewish environment, where Judaism is something that everyone has in common and can express freely. Teenagers from small Jewish communities can extend their circle of Jewish friends, developing relationships that often continue into the following year. Many campers—especially those coming from communities with few Jews—find that living in a completely Jewish environment for a month or two provides a new perspective on Jewish life, giving the summer an important place in the education of young American Jews.

Just as there are many different Jewish lifestyles in the United States, so there are many different ways in which summer camps are Jewish. They range from the religiously observant to the determinedly secular. Each of the three major synagogue movements (and some of the minor ones) operates camps that practice the corresponding style of religious observance. Most of the Zionist youth groups also operate camps, as do youth groups organized under other auspices. Some camps observe kashrut, and some do not. (Children from a nonobservant home may find that observing kashrut is itself a new experience.) Shabbat observance ranges from the strict to the casual, but all Jewish camps observe Friday evening and Saturday as a special day when relaxing, socializing, and quiet activities replace the active weekday schedule. And, increasingly, all Jewish camps incorporate Hebrew into their everyday language, ranging from camps where common Hebrew words are thrown into the usual English conversation to camps that use total immersion to achieve fluency in conversational Hebrew.

Just as parents choose their children's school and synagogue, they have a major voice in selecting a summer camp. My own parents had been attracted in their youth to the early American Labor Zionist movement, and as a high school student I attended one of that movement's summer camps. *Zionism* is a movement supporting Jewish life in Israel, and Labor Zionism is a branch of Zionism that was especially supportive of *kibbutz* life in Israel. (A kibbutz is a community organized as a collective, like an extended family, where everyone shares in the work and income is pooled so that everyone can also share in the consumption.) To feel what it might be like to live in a kibbutz, we campers did all of the daily chores (except food preparation), used Hebrew words and phrases as much as we could, learned about Israel's history and culture, and entertained ourselves with Israeli singing and dancing. Of course we also enjoyed the swimming, hiking, crafts, and amateur theatrics characteristic of all summer camps. Yet my lasting memories—and those of the other middle-aged former campers who still come to reunions—arose out of the distinctively Jewish spirit that infused every camp activity.

The Israel Experience

In my generation, summer camp was the most important setting for learning about Jewish life in Israel. Today, however, there are many opportunities for Jewish youth to actually go there. The synagogue movements and other Jewish youth groups organize summer trips for teenagers, called "Israel Experience" tours, usually before or after the sophomore year of high school. Grouped in units of one or two busloads, teens from all over the United States typically spend a month in Israel, sometimes preceded by a one-week "heritage" visit to a Holocaust-related site in Eastern Europe. They see Israel's major tourist sites, engage in summer sports (for example, kayaking on the Jordan River, rock climbing in the Negev desert), join with Israeli teens for activities and discussions, and experience the special feeling of life in the Jewish State. These Israel Experience tours have become a popular feature of the American Jewish lifestyle. Special savings plans help young people finance their trip, motivating a variety of fund-raising activities by young teens and providing an appealing option for Bar and Bat Mitzvah gift giving. Parents help with the funding, and scholarships are also available. The community's willingness to provide support for this purpose is evidence that the Israel Experience trip is considered an important part of a teenager's Jewish education.

Young Jews have other opportunities to spend time in Israel during their college years. Birthright Israel provides a highly subsidized ten-day tour for young people who have never before been to Israel with a youth group, sort of an abbreviated Israel Experience for youths ages eighteen to twenty-six. A number of Israeli universities and *yeshivas* (schools for intensive religious studies) have special yearlong programs in English, programs that attract recent high-school graduates who want to spend a "gap year" in Israel before entering college. Many colleges enable students to spend a semester or year abroad, and young Jews sometimes choose to attend classes in one of Israel's excellent universities. American youth can also enroll in one of the many *ulpan* (modern Hebrew language) programs in Israel, either in conjunction with their regular university studies or independently as a separate activity. In addition, families (for example, parents and younger siblings, grandparents) of students in one of these longer-term programs may choose this time to visit Israel as tourists. Whatever the motivation or length of stay, people invariably find that an experience in Israel increases their Jewish human capital and strengthens their identity as American Jews.

Holidays, History, and Jewish Human Capital

Although I remember complaining as a child about the need to go to Hebrew school, I don't think I ever complained about our family's observance of the Jewish holidays. These came throughout the year at uneven intervals, approximately once a month, each one contributing painlessly to my Jewish education. Every Jewish holiday is layered with meaning, some layers aimed at children and others at adults, some layers related to religious ritual and others to ethnic tradition, some layers expressed communally in the synagogue and others at home with family and friends. Simply observing these holidays would add to one's Jewish human capital by providing experience and accumulating memories. In addition, each holiday serves as a vehicle for learning something about Judaism's religious culture.[3]

The Annual Cycle of Jewish Holidays

Table 4.1 provides a list of the most important Jewish holidays, using the Hebrew names by which they are known along with their most common English translations. Each holiday comes on the indicated date according to the Hebrew calendar and lasts the indicated number of

TABLE 4.1. *The Major Jewish Holidays.*

Date* (Hebrew calendar)	Holiday	Length	English name
Weekly holidays	Shabbat	1 day	Sabbath
Monthly holidays	Rosh Hodesh	1 or 2 days	New Moon
Fall holidays			
1–2 Tishri	Rosh Hashanah	2 days	New Year
10 Tishri	Yom Kippur	1 day	Day of Atonement
15–21 Tishri	Sukkot	7 days	Feast of Booths
22–23 Tishri	Shmini Atzeret/ Simchat Torah	2 days **	Day After Sukkot/Rejoicing in the Torah
Winter holidays			
25 Kislev–2 Tevet	Chanukah	8 days	Festival of Lights
15 Shevat	Tu B'Shevat	1 day	New Year of the Trees
14 Adar	Purim	1 day	Festival of Lots
Spring holidays			
15–22 Nisan	Pesach	8 days **	Passover
27 Nisan	Yom Hasho'ah	1 day	Holocaust Remembrance Day
5 Iyyar	Yom Ha'atzma'ut	1 day	Israel Independence Day
18 Iyyar	Lag B'Omer	1 day	33rd day of the Omer
6–7 Sivan	Shavuot	2 days **	Feast of Weeks
Summer fast day			
9 Av	Tisha B'Av	1 day	9th day of Av

* All holidays begin at the sunset before the first day and end at sunset on the last day.

** Jews in Israel and Reform Jews observe all but the last day of these holidays. Simchat Torah always coincides with the last day Shmini Atzeret is observed.

▒ Torah-based holidays on which work is forbidden. On the long holidays of Sukkot/Shmini Azeret/ Simchat Torah and Pesach, work is forbidden on the first two and last two days, but not the days in between.

days. Viewed from the perspective of the familiar Gregorian calendar that governs everyday life in America, Jewish holidays seem to come on different dates from one year to the next. This is because the Hebrew calendar is synchronized with the phases of the moon, each month beginning when the moon is "new." Jewish holidays always come in the same season, however, because every few years, on a set schedule, the Hebrew calendar adds an extra month in late winter. The days start and end at sunset. For example, in a year when the first day of Tishri falls on September 15, Rosh Hashanah would start right after sunset on September 14 and end two days later at sunset on September 16. Jews learn at a young age that our religious lives follow the Hebrew calendar, while all other activities follow the secular calendar. Because of this, every Jewish holiday poses a potential conflict with secular schedules that may raise the cost of religious observance.

The comedian Woody Allen liked to joke that when he was a young man a diversity-minded firm hired him as their "token Jew," but he lost the job because he took off too many Jewish holidays. Table 4.1 lists thirteen, not counting the New Moon at the beginning of each month or the Sabbath that comes every Friday evening and Saturday. Holidays specifically described in the Torah are marked by shading and constitute the core of religious Judaism. Except for the High Holy Days of Rosh Hashanah and Yom Kippur, which are the same everywhere, the Torah holidays are a day longer for Jews living outside the land of Israel than for Israeli Jews. Reform Judaism rejects these extra days on ideological grounds and drops them even in the Diaspora. For the sake of simplicity, I will speak of each holiday lasting the number of days indicated in Table 4.1. The reader should be aware, however, that holidays marked with asterisks (*) are observed for one fewer day by Israelis and by Reform Jews in America.

The Torah describes the weekly Sabbath as a day of rest on which we should refrain from any kind of work activity. Sabbath is also a day when Jews gather in the synagogue and listen to a portion of the Torah. All of the holidays described in the Torah (shaded in Table 4.1) follow this pattern, days on which no work is to be done and with a special synagogue service. An exception is made for the two eight-day holidays, Sukkot followed immediately by Shmini Azeret and Simhat Torah in the fall and Pesach in the spring. For these, the Sabbath-like observance is limited to the first two days and the last two (one for Israelis and Reform Jews), leaving four or five days in the middle when work is permitted even though it is still a religious holiday. Altogether, the Jewish religious calendar contains six such holidays (not including the Sabbath) for a total of twenty-one days, of which thirteen are days when an observant Jew must not work. The remaining eight religious holidays listed in Table 4.1 were added after Jews received the Torah (more than 3,000 years ago) and therefore do not require abstaining from work.

Holidays and Jewish Human Capital Formation

The use of history as a vehicle for teaching religious concepts is a fundamental characteristic of Judaism, and the annual holiday cycle is a continuous lesson in Jewish history. The Torah itself describes an annual holiday cycle on two levels, one relating to ritual observance and the other relating to the educational function of each holiday as a "reminder" of fundamental Jewish principles. Every fall, the High Holy Days remind us of the origins of Judaism, when the patriarch Abraham made a covenant with God committing us to our monotheistic religion and connecting us to the Land of Israel. Early in the spring, Passover reminds us that "we"—that is, the ancient Israelites who were our Jewish forebears, and therefore us as well—were redeemed from slavery to the Egyptian pharaoh. In late spring the holiday of Shavuot reminds us that God gave "us" the Torah at Mount Sinai. The fall holiday of Sukkot reminds us that the first forty years after redemption from slavery were spent wandering in the Sinai desert, during which time "we" became organized as a free people and developed religious institutions. The Sabbath is a weekly celebration of both Creation and the Exodus from Egypt, marked by reading the Torah with its history of early Judaism. Refraining from everyday production on the Sabbath is a reminder that even the most productive person is not all-powerful, dependent on God who created not only life but also the Jews as a People.

This use of holidays to teach history is explicit in the Torah and is a core concept of religious Judaism, whether the history is real (that is, corroborated by the archaeological record) or mythical (as some prefer to believe). In the same spirit, Chanukah and Purim joined the holiday cycle much later in classical antiquity when Hellenism presented the Jews with new questions about religious observance. The Chanukah story, about events in Israel under the rule of Seleucid Greeks, raises issues about how far to bend religious practice when an inhospitable (or even hostile) cultural environment threatens the continuity of religious Judaism. The Purim story, about events in Persia at about the same time, describes a situation where anti-Jewish hatred threatens the physical safety of Jews. Each of these holidays uses a specific historical event to illustrate communal threats to Judaism and to Jews *qua* Jews (that is, regardless of their individual characteristics). These stories help Jews of every generation recognize such threats and provide a model for facing them with integrity, courage, and self-esteem.

Later additions to the Jewish holiday cycle mark milestones in Jewish national history. Tisha B'Av is a day of mourning for the Temple in Jerusalem, the center of Jewish religious life for 1,000 years, totally destroyed by the Romans nearly 2,000 years ago. Lag B'Omer commemorates the subsequent rebellion against Rome, which ended disastrously with the utter destruction of Judea as a political entity although not Judaism as a national identity. Today the Jewish religious calendar also includes Israel Independence Day, to celebrate the restoration of a Jewish national state in 1948, and Holocaust Remembrance Day to help us recognize modern symptoms of anti-Semitism and to honor the memory of its victims. These holidays are "minor" in that they present no important new religious lessons, but together they remind us that history did not end 2,500 years ago and that each generation contributes to the story of the Jewish People.

Holidays, Ritual, and Economic Incentives

In addition to marking a particular historical event, each Jewish holiday is accompanied by religious ritual in the home as well as the synagogue. People who differ from each other by age, by personal histories, by scholarly sophistication, or simply by personality may experience the holiday differently even though they share the same ritual observance. In every case, however, the holiday is an occasion to build Jewish memories, to practice Jewish skills, and to acquire Jewish experiences. All of these are forms of human capital accumulated by Jews everywhere, not in isolation but in the company of fellow Jews. Observing these holidays year after year gives us something in common with Jews who live in other places and with Jews of the many generations that came before and those that will come after us. This shared Jewish human capital binds us to each other and defines us as part of the Jewish People. Accepting membership in the Jewish People may or may not be associated with religiosity, but for many Americans it is the most meaningful aspect of Jewish identity.

Except for the few fast days, each holiday also has its characteristic family meals and festive traditions, some of which are dictated by

Judaism's Great Tradition but many of which are specific to the Small Tradition to which a family belongs. In the United States today, holiday observances are greatly influenced by the high value American Jews place on their time. They either ignore any home-based rituals that involve extensive Hebrew prayers, or they conduct them in abbreviated form, often in English. Most Americans join a synagogue at some point in their lives, but except for the High Holy Days (Rosh Hashanah and Yom Kippur) in the fall they seldom attend synagogue services. Few American Jews observe a full day of rest on the Sabbath or holidays. Many simply ignore the longer holidays, with the partial exception of Passover in the spring and Chanukah in the winter.

Even though time is costly, we cannot shorten our holiday observances without limit unless we choose to ignore them entirely. We can, however, develop strategies that increase the value of time spent on Jewish holidays. One such strategy is to use our general human capital—of which American Jews have a lot—to good advantage in our Jewish practices. The most obvious way that we do this is by using English translations of the Hebrew ritual literature, but there are many ways that Jews throughout the ages have adapted religious practices to their social environment. In the language of economics, we say that they sought to make their Jewish skills more complementary to their general skills. (The reverse is also true: High levels of Jewish human capital constitute an incentive to invest in those general skills that are most complementary to Jewish skills. That, however, is another story that we'll save for later.)

Complementary and Anticomplementary Human Capital

As a small minority group in a larger society, Diaspora Jews are always faced with the problem of positioning themselves within two (or more) cultures. A good general education builds human capital to enhance our experience as workers, consumers, and citizens, and a good Jewish education creates human capital—skills, experience, and memories—to enhance our Jewish experience. As long as Jewish human capital and general human capital are mutual *complements*, investment in either one stimulates more investment in the other, and a strong Jewish education helps create successful participants in the larger society. When the two kinds of human capital conflict, however, we characterize them as *anticomplements* because acquiring one set of skills makes it more difficult (and therefore costly) to acquire the other. In a society where general and Jewish skills are anticomplementary, a child might learn things at school or on the street that are in direct conflict with the Jewish values learned from parents and rabbis. When this occurs, it is more efficient to emphasize one or the other type of education rather than investing heavily in both. Thus, anticomplementarity induces an outcome where Jews with a high level of secular education have little Jewish human capital and, conversely, those with lots of Jewish human capital typically have less secular education, sometimes even to the point of being economically disadvantaged.

In America today, we are fortunate that much of our Jewish human capital is highly complementary with our general human capital. The United States was founded on principles of democracy, equality of opportunity, religious freedom, and ethical values rooted in Torah (via Christianity) and thus fully compatible with the Jewish religion. Unlike other societies in the past, a high level of education is not limited to the Jewish minority but is rather spread throughout the entire American population. This means that for most practical purposes our Jewish education need not compromise our ability to function in the larger society. It also means that Jews can excel in secular pursuits without sacrificing their Jewish identity. Yet Jews remain a small religious minority, and some cultural conflicts with the larger society are inevitable, especially at holiday time.

Human Capital Anticomplementarities: Chanukah and Purim

Despite the glitter and excitement of the season, I remember December as the most difficult time to be a Jewish child. Apart from my home and my Hebrew school, Christmas saturated the entire atmosphere. At school we sang only Christmas carols, sacred music that troubled my young Jewish conscience. Every store seemed to advertise wonderful toys for Christmas presents that I as a Jew would not be eligible to receive. The beautiful colored lights and the decorated Christmas trees in our neighbors' homes and in public places were constant reminders that we Jews were outsiders at this time of year. December was a season of good cheer for Christians, few of whom were sensitive to the discomfort of a Jewish child. Even in today's multicultural America, Jewish parents still face the "December Dilemma": how to deal with the pervasiveness of Christmas while neither observing it nor demonizing it.

At the heart of the December Dilemma lies an anticomplementarity between general and Jewish human capital, the inherent tension between assimilation and tradition. American Jews in the twentieth century faced a stark choice: They could either withdraw into isolation (even if it was only psychological) for the entire month of December, or they could join everyone else by accepting Christmas as a "general" holiday. If you took the former approach you felt uncomfortable, as though you lacked generosity, cheerfulness, and good will, sort of like the literary characters Ebenezer Scrooge or the Grinch who stole Christmas. Many Jews preferred to break with tradition partially and emphasize the secular side of Christmas, characterizing the decorated tree as a purely secular seasonal decoration, a "pagan" custom that need not be associated with religious Christianity. To avoid the sacred music of Christmas carols, Jews looked for songs about winter, snowmen, reindeer, and an imagined nostalgia. In this spirit Irving Berlin, arguably the most famous Jewish composer of his day, contributed the classic "White Christmas" to the American seasonal repertoire (and another classic, "Easter Parade," to the spring holiday season). Apart from the popularity of secular "Christmas" songs, American culture has since become more religiously neutral and thus more compatible with Jewish observance. In contrast to the American customs of my youth, today's public schools and many stores have either secularized their December celebrations entirely or generalized them to include Chanukah and the midwinter holidays observed by other non-Christian religions.

In the Book of Maccabees, Scriptures describe a Jewish rebellion in late antiquity against the Seleucid Greeks, and the Talmud includes details about the commemorative holiday of Chanukah. Because it is not mentioned in the Torah itself, however, Chanukah is a "minor" religious holiday with no requirement that we refrain from work. It is especially prominent on the American Jewish calendar because it usually comes in December during the Christmas season. Sometimes translated as the "Festival of Lights," Chanukah is traditionally observed for eight days by lighting candles in the home: one on the first night, two on the second night, and so on until the climactic eighth night when eight candles are lit. It is also traditional to give children small coins, nuts, or similar treats at the brief candle-lighting ceremony. Chanukah celebrations in the United States (but rarely elsewhere) now include gift giving on a scale that gives Jewish children a counterweight to the commercial side of Christmas and the presents received by their neighbors and classmates. American Jews also like to characterize Chanukah as marking the earliest struggle for religious freedom, a theme that resonates especially well in the United States with its deep commitment to religious pluralism. Both of these Americanisms may be viewed as enhancing complementarity between practices that are Jewish-specific and those of the general society.

The Jews of medieval and early modern Europe faced a similar conflict with the larger Christian culture, not in December but rather during the late-winter weeks before the beginning of Lent. Christians celebrated this period with merry entertainments, masquerade parties, and general licentiousness in anticipation of the coming period of self-denial. Facing many of the same problems that gave American Jews their December Dilemma, European Jews developed an analogous solution. They added costume parties and comic Purim *spiels* (entertainments) to enhance the traditional reading of the Book of Esther and exchanging small gifts of food. They encouraged merriment and festive drinking; there is a saying (oft repeated, seldom carried out) that on Purim one should drink until it's hard to tell the difference between the hero and the villain of the Purim story!

In America today, Mardi Gras is one of the few vestigial reminders of this pre-Lent Christian tradition, and our Purim celebrations are much less flamboyant than they once were. Yet masquerades and comic theater remain a distinct part of our Purim heritage. American children have costume parties in Hebrew school, and people even wear fanciful costumes to the synagogue when the Book of Esther is read. Gifts of food (usually sweet treats) are also sometimes exchanged, especially the triangular pastries called *hamentashen*. Some synagogues (including ours) celebrate Purim with a comic play or a satiric review poking fun at the Jewish community and its leaders. We enjoy these customs not only for their own sake but also as links to another time and place where Jews celebrated Purim observance in a society that was different from our own.

Human Capital Complementarities: Passover

Passover commemorates the exodus of the Jewish people from ancient Egypt, the passage from slavery into freedom which is the quintessential act of redemption in Judaism. (This event is commonly referred to simply as the Exodus, with a capital *E*.) The Torah tells us that each generation should experience this redemption vicariously, and at Passover you should tell your children this story as though you yourself were an actual participant. It also tells us that during the entire eight days you should remove all leavening (that is, yeast and yeastlike products) from your diet and from your possession. Instead of bread we should eat *matza*, a yeast-free crackerlike food baked quickly from flour and water (or in some cases fruit juice), to help those of us who are otherwise comfortable to experience one aspect of the urgent flight from oppression.

These two observances, telling the story of the Exodus and eating matza on Passover, have been observed by all Jews everywhere and continue to be observed by nearly all American Jews today. On the first night (remember, on the Jewish calendar each day begins just after sundown), when the entire family gathers around the dinner table, we tell the Exodus story before the food is served as part of the ceremony called a Seder (about which more later). The entire ceremony is repeated on the second night of Passover by Orthodox and Conservative Jews, although Reform Jews and Israelis conduct a seder only on the first night. Reform Jews do not always observe the full eight days of Passover. Conservative Jews are much more likely to refrain from working on the first two days and from eating leavening for the entire week, but they seldom observe the last two days as a nonwork holiday. The Orthodox, however, will often observe all eight days, with both the first two and the last two as full religious holidays.

By now the reader should recognize the time-use patterns explaining these differences. American Jews with a very high value of time will tend to choose a Jewish lifestyle with shortened religious observances and one which deemphasizes the importance of particularistic—that is, specifically Jewish—observances. The Reform Movement is the most explicit in justifying such a lifestyle, but the members of other synagogue movements may also reduce or adapt their actual religious observance if time seems to be more valuable in some other use.

Passover in Different Cultures

The Seder itself can be viewed as a similar adaptation to changes in the cost of Passover observance. In fact, the Torah doesn't describe a Seder at all. Torah tells the Israelites wandering in the Sinai desert after their escape from Egypt to observe the first night of Passover by slaughtering a lamb, roasting it, and eating all of its meat before morning. Families too small to eat an entire lamb by themselves are instructed to join together for this purpose. This simple ritual was well suited to nomadic shepherds, whose occupational skills would have made kosher slaughtering a routine activity, but today's urban American Jews prefer to buy their meat from a butcher.

Nor would this ritual have been easy for the Jews of ancient Israel with its semi-urban economy of farmers and craftsmen. The Torah itself recognizes this and gives different instructions to be followed once the people had settled in the Promised Land and built the Temple in Jerusalem. It tells them to celebrate Passover (among other holidays) by making a pilgrimage to that Temple. Everyone should still offer a lamb for sacrifice and eat it for the Passover meal, but the Temple priests would do the actual slaughtering. As befit a nation of farmers, the holiday became the start of the spring harvest and hence a celebration of spring itself.

By the second century BCE (that is, Before the Common Era, comparable to the Christian notation BC), economic conditions had changed yet again, so much so that the pilgrimage to Jerusalem was extremely expensive and very time consuming for many Jews. For one thing, not all Jews were living in or near Israel. Jews had settled in many places, from Babylon (Mesopotamia) to Alexandria (Egypt) and even Rome, where many of them were merchants and urban tradesmen. An observant Jew of means could travel to Jerusalem by caravan or by ship, exchange his money at the Temple to buy a lamb for the sacrifice, and follow the rituals described in Torah. It would be very costly, however, to do this every year (or, rather, three times a year if the other pilgrimage holidays were observed), and many Jews would simply not bother. In response, the religious leaders of the time (usually referred to as Sages) developed an alternative set of rituals to be carried out at home. These rituals developed over several centuries and became the core of our modern Seder, codified in the *Mishna* (the earliest part of the Talmud) and required of all Jews after the Temple in Jerusalem was destroyed. The only vestige of the earlier Passover sacrifice is a roasted meat bone (referred to as a "lamb shank" even though it might belong to a chicken if that is the meat being served for dinner) symbolic of the Temple practice.

Human Capital at the Seder

The Seder itself is designed as an educational experience. The Hebrew word *seder* means "order," or in this context an "agenda." The Seder takes place at the dinner table, and indeed serving the meal is one of the agenda items listed. Its format is that of a symposium, one that was familiar to the educated Hellenistic Jews of classical antiquity and therefore highly complementary with their secular skills. Unlike the typical Greek symposium, however, the Seder requires participation by the entire family so that the leader (usually the father) can teach the children about the experience of the Jewish people. The table is set with various special foods (for example, matza, parsley, horseradish, salt water) that are child-friendly symbols of the Passover story, serving also as little snacks to occupy the young ones during the ceremony. Early in the Seder the leader takes a portion of the ceremonial matza to hide, and the children hunt for it to produce at the end of the meal. The entire ritual is interspersed with songs and digressions into side stories, many of which have been added by Jews in subsequent generations over the last two millennia.

The Seder ritual even has a "textbook," called the *Haggadah* (telling) because its centerpiece is a retelling of the Exodus story with all of its layers of meaning. (We do not actually know when the Haggadah took its present form, but the oldest one still in existence today comes from thirteenth-century Spain.) The basic text of the Haggadah is part of Judaism's Great Tradition, but the actual books vary in their format, their artwork, and in the additional songs, stories, or commentary that editors chose to add. American Jewish bookstores typically display a variety of *Haggadot* (plural of Haggadah) in the months before Passover, ranging from the very traditional to the very innovative. Some families and communities even compose their own Haggadah, adapting tradition to their own special needs and experiences. One of the earliest American versions is the *Maxwell House Haggadah*, introduced as a promotion for Maxwell House coffee and distributed free in grocery stores every year since 1934. (The original *Maxwell House Haggadah* was an inexpensive reproduction of the 1695 *Amsterdam Haggadah*, the first illustrated Haggadah produced by a printing press, and newer versions are still used by many American Jews.) The *Maxwell House Haggadah* has a special place in our American Jewish tradition although it now has to compete with the many other modern Haggadot available today.

As a Jewish child growing up in the United States, I experienced the Seder differently in different homes. My paternal grandparents were old-country Orthodox. At their table my grandfather read the entire Haggadah verbatim, in Hebrew, and very quickly. My father was the only other participant with the skill to follow along; the rest of us just sat there wondering how soon he would finish so we could eat the savory meal my grandmother had spent all day preparing. When my father conducted the Seder in our own home, however, the experience was very different. Except for the elementary knowledge of my sister and me, the gathered family—including my maternal grandparents, aunts, uncles and cousins—had little Jewish education and virtually no command of Hebrew. Everyone at the table would have a copy of the Haggadah that included an English translation, usually on the page facing the Hebrew text. Instead of the leader reading aloud to everyone in Hebrew, we took turns around the table reading the Exodus story and its commentary in English. As leader, my father made a point of including us children and explaining anything he thought we might not understand.

My father's Seder seems to have been fairly typical for Conservative Jewish families of that generation. The Seders that my children experienced were similar except for two important differences. We lived far from other relatives, so grandparents, aunts or uncles, and cousins rarely joined us. One of our two Seders would be small, intimate, and focused on teaching our own children, but for the other Seder we liked to join friends in similar circumstances to give our children a "traditional" extended-family experience. The other difference between our Seders and those of my father was that almost everyone at our table had some Jewish education, was more or less literate in Hebrew, and had some familiarity with the songs. We still read the stories in English, taking turns around the table, but we could all say the prayers and sing the songs in Hebrew. As leader, my husband would often interrupt the flow with an anecdote from his reading or a question for the children, and this might develop into a general conversation before we returned to our place in the Haggadah. These extra discussions became more interesting as the children got older, and we all valued them as an entertaining part of the learning-and-teaching experience.

The spiritual lesson of the Passover Seder is one of redemption in this life, on Earth rather than in heaven, couched in the story of how God led the Jews out of slavery and into freedom. This story has meaning for every generation, but it has a special resonance for modern American Jews who like to think of Passover as the Holiday of Freedom. My grandparents, all of whom came to the United States from Russia or Poland at the turn of the twentieth century, were part of a wave of immigrants who came in their own exodus from persecution to freedom, from poverty to opportunity, from stigmatization to full participation as citizens in a new world. They and their descendents witnessed the birth of the State of Israel in midcentury and the consequent ingathering of Jewish refugees from the horrors of Europe and from oppression in Arab lands. The last decades of the twentieth century saw the airlift to Israel of Ethiopian Jewry and the rescue of Soviet Jews, mostly to Israel but also to the United States, where they are now our neighbors. These recent escapes, still fresh in the experience of today's American Jewish families, are often the subject of digressions at the Seder table. Many American versions of the Haggadah acknowledge them explicitly with additional passages in the form of a prayer, a reading, a song, or a combination of these. This naturally leads to discussion of the evils of any kind of oppression, including discrimination experienced by other (that is, non-Jewish) people in the United States and elsewhere. No wonder, then, that so many American Jews are outspoken civil rights advocates who attribute their activism to lessons learned at the Seder table.

Complementarities in the United States

Despite the occasional conflict, American secular and Jewish educations are generally mutually complementary, so that an investment in either one increases the effectiveness of investment in the other. Hebrew-school teachers expect arriving students to be literate in English and familiar with the age-appropriate subjects taught in their secular schools. Teaching methods designed with this in mind are more efficient than, say, an old-country style of rote learning. At the same time, learning the literature and language of a second culture can improve a Hebrew-school student's ability to grasp various secular subjects. This mutual complementarity suggests that students who are high achievers in their secular school subjects can make more effective use of additional Jewish education, while a good Jewish education contributes to a higher level of secular educational attainment.

The traditional stereotype of a Torah scholar is a bearded man, usually elderly, wearing a hat and a *tallit* (prayer shawl), reading from a Torah scroll or poring over a page of Talmud. American Jewry has its share of Torah scholars, but they rarely fit this picture, and not everyone who looks like this is a Torah scholar. As with any specialist, a true scholar must acquire a high level of skill and deep knowledge of arcane technicalities specific to that profession. When Jews lived in preindustrial societies and had few opportunities for professional education, Torah scholarship provided one of the few outlets for a Jewish man to exercise his intellectual capabilities. In contrast, today's United States offers many such opportunities and Jews—men and women—are free to choose whatever specialty leads them to a fulfilling career. Religious scholarship is still the choice of some people, but most American Jews spend their time studying other advanced subjects at the expense of higher Jewish education.

Even "ordinary" Jews (that is, those who do not become Torah scholars or professional clergy) acquire a lot of Jewish human capital. Just participating in synagogue services and observing Jewish holidays involves liturgical skills and knowledge specific to the practice of Judaism. Many of us take our Jewish human capital for granted, perhaps because we spend much more time and money on our secular education or perhaps because so much of our Jewish education is so informal that it just seems "natural." Yet Jewish skills, like any other skill, improve with use and atrophy with disuse. People who do not practice some form of Judaism as adults find that their Jewish skills depreciate over time. As the language, history, and culture of Judaism become increasingly unfamiliar, they become less efficient participants in the synagogue and less efficient transmitters of Judaism to the next generation. In contrast, people who are actively Jewish—whether by making a Jewish home, by participating in religious ritual, by celebrating Jewish holidays, or by attending classes on Jewish subjects—accumulate additional Jewish skills and find their religious experience correspondingly enriched.

Mutual complementarity is characteristic of many different forms of human capital. This is why people with high levels of educational attainment not only earn higher wages but also tend to make greater investments in on-the-job training, in health, in consumer education, and in leisure-activity skills (like sports, music, or art appreciation) than do people with lower education levels. Advanced Jewish studies help develop the language, study habits, and analytical skills that are useful for learning other subjects. Because these skills are very useful for any student, we say that they are highly complementary to the general skills Jewish children learn as part of a general American education.

Because of this complementarity, an investment in Jewish human capital—whether it be Hebrew school, synagogue attendance, holiday observance, Jewish summer camping, or an Israel experience—thus raises the probability that a Jewish student will do well in his or her secular studies. This would make any investment in education more efficient, and this in turn raises the likelihood of investing in various other forms of complementary human capital. Certainly Jews are not the only Americans that invest heavily in all of these forms of human capital, and this may be one reason why Jews assimilate so easily into American society. Yet high levels of secular human capital are so characteristic of American Jewry that Jews who describe themselves as "nonreligious" may consider such an investment pattern as itself an expression of their Jewish identity.

Part III

Constraints and Incentives in American Jewish Life

5

Jewish Families in America

LIKE MOST COUPLES CONTEMPLATING MARRIAGE, my husband-to-be and I had serious discussions about children—how soon and how often we wanted to add them to our family, how many we wanted for our ideal family size, and how we could adapt our already-busy lifestyle to include parenting. As it happened, we both wanted two children for several reasons. One, of course, was the sheer pleasure of parenting and to satisfy our basic human impulse to nurture. Children can also be a vehicle for passing a legacy to future generations, giving our lives meaning beyond our actual lifespan. We both wanted our children's legacy to include the kind of secular human capital that is central to our own identity as individuals and as Americans. We also wanted to give them a firm knowledge of Judaism and Jewish values, as part of our contribution to the intergenerational continuity of the Jewish People.

Judaism recognizes the central place of marriage and family in our lives in many ways. It imbues each of the four major life-cycle events—birth, coming of age, marriage, and death—with religious ceremonies that elevate their meaning. Every religious holiday (including Shabbat) involves some ritual in the home that includes all family members, and many of these home-based celebrations involve explaining to children some aspect of their Jewish heritage. Each generation frames these explanations in the idiom of their time and place, resulting in an accumulation of stories, songs, and customs that become a legacy to their descendents. Most if not all of the religious observances and customs embedded in the Jewish calendar are clearly designed to reinforce families with children.

Torah itself emphasizes our lifelong relationship with our own parents, first in the laws of Noah which apply to all humanity and then as one of the Ten Commandments given specifically to the Jews. It speaks of the husband–wife relationship as one of "cleaving," a seamless bonding into a lifelong partnership. It tells parents to educate their children about their Jewish heritage, repeating the story of the Exodus each year, explaining the meaning of each Jewish holiday, and observing the Sabbath as a reminder of God's creation. Talmud adds to this the obligation of a father to teach his son three things: an occupation with which to earn a living, literacy with which to study Torah, and the ability to swim. (We don't know whether the sages viewed swimming as an investment in health, in survival skills, or in a skill that enhances pleasure, but they evidently considered it important.)

We sometimes complain about our children, of course, but we derive much pleasure from them, learning in the process a lot about ourselves and our place in the world around us. Yet many if not most of our parenting activities are actually investments in our children's future. Recall that economists define an investment as anything to which we devote resources for some future benefit. Our children certainly fit this definition, absorbing a large share of our resources—mainly time and money, but also our attention and energy, neither of which is unlimited in supply—over a period of years and even decades. For many of us, our children represent the largest investment we will ever make.

Less obvious, perhaps, marriage itself is an investment. We search for a marriage partner with whom we can build a future life and raise a family and on whom we can depend for security and companionship in our old age. Once we find such a partner, we invest time and energy building good relationships with our spouse's birth family, creating an extended family in which we and our children obtain comfort and support. We begin to reap the benefits of marriage and parenting almost from the beginning, but our investment doesn't stop there. Whether for maintenance or for growth, investment in family relationships is a lifelong project.

The Economics of Marriage

Marriage is a partnership between two people, a contract with important benefits for each spouse. Some marital benefits are simply efficiencies that arise from shared living conditions, but roommates and unmarried cohabitating couples can also benefit from these gains. A more important benefit of marriage is the long-term commitment to a shared companionship, giving each partner the emotional security to face life's uncertainties, both good and bad. The marital partnership also greatly raises the efficiency of investments in children, a complex, long-term enterprise that is far easier when shared with a partner. Raising Jewish children in a non-Jewish society is an even more complex undertaking. A marriage contract expresses the willingness of both spouses to work together as a team in the enterprise of building a family.

The Marriage Market

Any contract involving a large investment over a long period of time requires identifying a partner well suited for the enterprise at hand. Consider, for the moment, that you are an employer seeking to fill a position called "spouse" for an enterprise called "family." You want to find someone attractive, both physically and emotionally, whose life goals are compatible with yours and with skills that complement your own. You reject some of the applicants for your job as "unqualified." Some people are qualified but show no interest in your job, presumably because it doesn't meet their own criteria. Your objective is to find a qualified partner who wants the position you would like to fill.

In analogy to how we choose a career and search for a job, we also make a lifestyle choice and look for a spouse to share it. The analogy between job search and the search for a marriage partner is very apt. We speak of a marriage "market" where you close the deal with a marriage "contract." Searching for a spouse involves an investment of time and money, so the search itself is an investment in one's future family. You start by looking in the least expensive places—your neighborhood, your workplace or school, your synagogue or social organization—where you can meet people while engaging in other activities without spending extra time or money. If you don't find someone there, you would look elsewhere in a more purposeful—and more costly—search. You can even hire a marriage "broker" or its modern equivalent, an Internet dating service, to make your search more "efficient." As a general principle, the longer it takes you to find a good match, the more you are willing to spend on an additional search activity.

At each stage of your search, any time you meet a potential partner you have to decide how suitable he or she would be as your spouse. This is not the whole story, however, because a contract requires that both parties agree to the match. The people you are considering are also in the marriage market, searching for the best partner to achieve their own goals. If you are "attractive" (that is, your traits make you a desirable spouse) you may get more offers of marriage, but you might also be more likely to find a better partner if you keep looking. The cost per hour of search goes up the longer you are in the marriage market, including the risk that your potential partner will withdraw the earlier offer if you wait too long. The economic question is not whether the new match that you might find from continued search is better than this one, but rather whether the new match is enough better to be worth the extra cost of search. At some point the answer to this question is "no," and you are ready to enter into a contract.

Conventional wisdom insists that nobody is perfect, and few of us are married to the "ideal" spouse. Today's young Jews have a complicated set of criteria, searching in the marriage market for a good match with respect to age, schooling, career goals, lifestyle preferences, socializing styles, leisure interests, childrearing philosophy, and religious beliefs, as well as physical attributes such as good health and good looks. Other criteria can also be important, like geographic or political preferences or willingness to invest in family-related skills. In general, the more attributes a person seeks in a marriage partner, the more difficult it is to find a "perfect" match, the longer he or she will search, and the more likely the final result will involve compromise on the spouse's actual characteristics.

Human Capital and Marriage

If the purpose of marriage is to build a family, a high level of human capital makes a person more desirable as a spouse. Education not only raises a person's earning power, it also generally improves his or her efficiency in household tasks, as a parent, and as a consumer. Each type of human capital not only makes your partner more productive in his or her role as "spouse," it also makes your own human capital more efficient. For example, it is easier for you to stay healthy and raise healthy children if your spouse has healthy habits and values good medical care. Your investments in parenting or in building relationships in the extended family are more effective the more skilled your spouse is in these areas. Making a Jewish home, and raising Jewish children, is more efficient if your partner has skills related to the Jewish lifestyle that you have chosen. In each of these examples, the higher your partner's level of human capital, the more productive you can be with your own skills and the greater your joint productivity from working together.

Because education and career are important aspects of our lives, it should be no surprise that they influence our choice of spouse. When our grandparents got married, social and legal norms limited career opportunities for married women. Women thus had less incentive to invest in education leading to a profession, investing instead in skills related to homemaking and childrearing. Their training took place in the home and prepared them for marriage at a young age. Men had higher earning power than their wives and tended to be more educated, but they were older before they reached the financial independence necessary to be the sole support of a family. The most productive partnership was based on a division of labor, the husband specializing in job-related activities and the wife specializing in home- and family-based activities, and a man tended to be somewhat older than his wife. This within-family division of labor, which would become even more efficient as each spouse gained experience and became more skilled in his or her own area of responsibility, was a solid economic basis for the marital partnership.

In the United States today, the fact that Jewish women and men have nearly similar economic opportunities leads to marriages between people with similar characteristics, a process that economists call *positive assortative mating* that results in marital *homogamy*. More educated people look for a spouse who is also more educated, and people who want a Jewish lifestyle look for a partner whose goals are similar and whose Jewish skills are an appropriate match. We saw in an earlier chapter that

American Jews in high-level occupations typically marry someone who also has a high-level career. Sometimes the match is even more specific, as when both spouses are medical doctors, both lawyers, or—as in my own marriage—both are economics professors.

An investment in education not only raises your own earning power, it also improves your attractiveness in the marriage market and thus increases the contribution to family income you can expect from a potential spouse. A similar incentive applies to investments in other kinds of human capital. For example, investments in Jewish religious skills are desirable for themselves but also because they make it easier to attract a spouse with similarly high Jewish skills. Just as a two-earner household will have twice the income as a comparable one-earner household, so a family where both partners have a Jewish education will have twice the religious human capital as a family with only one such person. Differences between rich and poor households would be greater in a community of two-career couples than in a community of single-earner families, and differences in Jewish human capital would be similarly greater in a community where men and women receive the same level of religious training. Because gender-neutral education and two-career families are now the norm, the American Jewish community in the twenty-first century may well exhibit a greater degree of inequality than in the past.[1]

Religious Intermarriage

Perhaps the most widely discussed statistic in the American Jewish community is the so-called intermarriage rate, the percentage of married Jews whose spouse is not Jewish. This rate had been increasing for decades, and by the end of the twentieth century it came close to 50 percent among young American Jews. In an earlier era, when two people of different religions matched up on other characteristics and wanted to get married, one of them—most often the Jewish partner—converted to the other's religion. This kept the intermarriage rate low, for it identified the new family with one religion or the other. This is no longer the case, and it is not unusual today for a Jew and a non-Jew to marry without either changing their religious identification.

As noted earlier, the marriage market tends to pair up partners with similar skill levels. This is so for each type of human capital, including religion. A person weakly attached to Jewish religious life and with little Jewish human capital is unlikely to pair with someone who wants to make a Jewish home and has a high level of Jewish religious skills. American Jews with low levels of Jewish human capital thus tend to marry each other. The families that they form place little emphasis on Jewish observance, and their children's Jewish education is often perfunctory. When their children reach adulthood and look for a life partner, the marriage market matches them with a spouse who also has little or no Jewish human capital.

For an intermarriage to occur, several conditions must be met. First, the life goals of the Jewish partner must not place heavy emphasis on Jewish religious observance in general and home-based religious ritual in particular. Second, the life goals of the non-Jewish partner must also deemphasize home-based religious observance. This is easiest for non-Jews weakly attached to their own religion, but it can also work for those who consider religion a purely personal matter not to be shared with anyone, not even a spouse. Third, each partner must be able to overcome any prejudice against the other's religion with which he or she was raised. Fourth, the two partners must feel that they are a good match on other characteristics. Finally, young people of different religions must be able to meet each other in sufficient numbers for a marriage market to arise.

Socioeconomic trends in the United States during the second half of the twentieth century raised the probability that all of these conditions would be met, thus contributing to a dramatic increase in intermarriage among American Jews. As we shall see in the next chapter, Jewish human capital declined between the immigrant generation and their children and declined even further in their grandchildren's generation. Several non-Jewish religions experienced similar declines (although perhaps with different timing), especially among mainstream Protestant denominations and certain ethnic Catholics. A marked decline in anti-Semitism, both overt and covert, especially after WWII, has increased the acceptability of Jews by non-Jews in many areas of American life, including marriage partners for themselves and their children. Young Jews today grow up in an economic, social, and cultural environment where non-Jews receive the same education, both formal and informal, making them eligible marriage partners on every criterion except religion. And because Jews are such a tiny minority in the population—about 2 percent overall and rarely as high as 10 percent in the professional occupations where they concentrate—even a fairly small fraction of non-Jews meeting the eligibility criteria could generate a high rate of intermarriage in the Jewish community.

The convergence of all these trends increases the likelihood that an American Jew will choose a non-Jewish marriage partner. This is a voluntary decision that a young person makes in his or her own best interest, but it has implications for the Jewish community as a whole. Of particular concern is that the Jewish partner in such a marriage will be unable to transmit Judaism to the next generation, thus violating a religious injunction crucial to the continuity of the Jewish People. Some interfaith couples simply ignore religion because they don't think it matters, raising children with no religious human capital for either faith who as adults will identify themselves as agnostic, atheist, or with "no religion." Other interfaith couples create families that combine religious customs from both parents, giving their children some human capital from each religion so that when they are older they can choose the one that suits them best. Judaism is very human capital intensive, however, and such families rarely invest enough in Jewish skills for their children's Jewish religious experience to be very productive.

Marriage and Family

Marriage partners are chosen with a view toward future family lifestyles, especially with regard to childrearing goals, and parenting experiences have a big effect on the relationship between spouses. Marriage is more than a simple partnership between spouses, however, because it also unites their two families. The parents of each spouse will share grandchildren, giving them an important common interest. (The English language has no name for this relationship, but in Hebrew the parents of the bride and the groom are *m'chatanim* to each other.) Siblings of each spouse become the in-laws of the other, and their children will be cousins. An important marriage-specific investment involves building good relationships with each other's birth family, an investment that begins to yield benefits immediately in the form of belonging to an extended family. The long-term benefits include mutual aid in times of sickness or adversity, including a shared responsibility for aging parents.

A Jewish marriage thus requires each partner to make "marriage-specific" investments in his or her spouse, in their children, and in the relationship with their extended families. If the marriage ends, these skills may lose some of their usefulness. Some, however, remain important, especially those involving children. For example, even as divorce severs much of the relationship between husband and wife, it merely alters the relationship that each has with their children and with their children's grandparents, aunts, uncles, and cousins on the "other side" of the family. These altered relationships require new investments, even more so after a divorced spouse remarries. The greatest need for new investments occurs in so-called blended families, families in which each partner has children from a previous marriage as well as joint children with the current spouse. In this case the extended family includes not only the families of both parents but also the ex-spouses, their parents, and possibly even other members of their extended families.

Marriages between young people from different backgrounds in any dimension, but especially religion, can lead to very complicated relationships with their extended families. Whether a Jew-by-birth marries a Jew-by-choice (that is, a convert) or a partner who continues to profess another religion, the spouse's parents and other family members remain adherents to that other religion. The couple may choose a Jewish lifestyle and agree to raise children as Jews, but the children still have two sets of grandparents with two different religions. Each wants to include their grandchildren in holiday celebrations and share with them their own family's religious traditions. At worst, grandparents vying for the children's loyalty to their own religion can be very disturbing, but even at best the very fact of two religions has the potential to undermine the importance of Jewish identity.

The Economics of Parenting

Statistics show that American Jews are having so few children that the Jewish population is shrinking. The "replacement" fertility rate—that is, the rate at which the next generation will be the same size as the current one—is an average of 2.1 children per adult woman. American Jewish fertility is below the replacement rate not so much because families are small but rather because childlessness is on the rise. More Jewish women than ever before are not getting married at all, and more married couples than ever before are remaining childless. Jews are also marrying at an older age when women are less fertile. (Jewish couples in this situation may turn to adoption to form a family, but adopted children are not included in fertility measures.) Many couples, however, simply choose not to complicate their busy lives with the additional demands of parenting, allocating their scarce resources elsewhere instead of raising a family with children. The community gives childless adults other outlets for their nurturing impulses, for example as aunts and uncles, as teachers, or as caring professionals. Yet the combination of low fertility, high intermarriage, and low immigration of Jews from other countries means that the total number of Jews in the United States is shrinking.

Although Jewish immigrants at the turn of the twentieth century came from old-country families with many children, they and their children adopted the small-family ideal almost immediately on their arrival in the United States. As Figure 5.1 indicates, Jewish women who

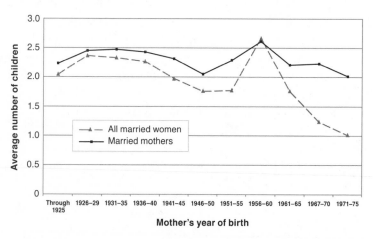

FIGURE 5.1. *Average number of children by mother's year of birth, for married women with children and for all married women.*
SOURCE: Computed from NJPS 2000/01. See Schwartz et al. (2004).

were ever married with children and who were over the age of seventy-five in the year 2000, all of whom were born before 1925, averaged 2.3 children each. The average number of children for younger women in this category varies from year to year but remained near 2.2 throughout the twentieth century. (Even Jewish women of childbearing age during the "baby boom" after WWII brought the average up to only 2.8.) Today's Jewish mothers average a bit more than the replacement rate with 2.2 children each, thus following their own mothers and grandmothers when they and their husbands choose to have small families. Two children per family is still the most common, although many families have three children or just one child. Families with four or more children are considered large, especially outside of the small (but growing) ultra-Orthodox communities.

The Cost of Raising Jewish Children

If we were to ask people how they decided to limit their family to two children (or whatever number they chose), a common response would be that they could not afford to have any more. This suggests that children are a "normal" economic good, defined as something we would want more of if only we had more resources. Yet the notion that we are resource constrained is something of a paradox, for our immigrant grandparents (or great-grandparents as the case may be) had many more siblings even though their old-country families were extremely poor. If we, with our much higher incomes, feel that we can't afford more children, Jewish children must be more expensive in America than they were in the old country. The resolution of this paradox therefore lies with the high cost of raising Jewish children in the United States today.

Quite apart from the money that we spend on them, children absorb a great deal of the time, attention, and energy of their parents. Family life is a complex of relationships and activities that are desirable, enjoyable (mostly), and important. As the saying goes, our children are our jewels. We want to spend time with them and interact with them, not only to raise them properly (by which we mean invest in their socialization) but also to enjoy their company. The cost of that time is very high for a parent in a high-wage occupation and even higher for two-career couples where both spouses earn high wages. Adding an additional child to the family may increase the money costs proportionately (assuming that we spend the same amount of dollars on each child), but the time costs increase even more as within-family relationships become more complex. Because the norm in America's Jewish community is the two-career couple where both spouses are in high-wage occupations, time is so costly that they can't "afford" to have many children.

High educational attainment in secular subjects, especially fields leading to careers in high-level occupations, is such an important part of our own American Jewish culture that most of us want to bequeath it (or its equivalent) to the next generation. We saw in an earlier chapter how investments in higher education have persisted for several generations to the point where they are now a stable feature of American Jewry. Jewish parents are willing to sacrifice other consumption items to help support children—both male and female—through graduate or professional school. Sometimes this requires paying tuition, living expenses, or both. Even those children who finance their own education, however, typically rely on parents in emergencies or for loans to cover unusually large expenses such as a hospital bill, a wedding, or a down payment on a home.

American Jewish parents also place a high priority on medical care for their children, taking them for regular checkups with a doctor and quickly turning to specialists when faced with a difficulty. We want to benefit from the latest advances in medical technology whenever we think it will improve the health of our children. Medical costs per child are higher than our own parents had to pay, but our dollars usually buy treatments more effective than the ones available in our childhood. If American Jews spend more than ever on health care, it is largely because they believe that medical technology makes it a better investment than ever.

Jewish education is also an investment in children's human capital, but its importance varies considerably from one Jewish lifestyle to another. As we saw in an earlier chapter, non-Orthodox day-school parents probably invest the most money per child in Jewish human capital. Parents who observe the Sabbath and home-based holiday rituals probably invest the most total time but not necessarily the most time per child. Parents who choose a secular Jewish lifestyle, or limit their children's Jewish education to a synagogue-based Hebrew school, probably make the smallest investments in their children's Jewish human capital. Whatever the choice, however, the cost of Jewish education—including parents' time as well as money—must be added to the cost of secular education when we estimate the net benefits from investments in our children.

Quantity–Quality Trade-Offs

With this in mind, young Jewish couples can choose among various parenting lifestyles. For a given resource budget, they can have many children with low expenditures per child, few children with high expenditures per child, or something in between. The technical jargon of economics calls this spectrum of choices a trade-off between *child quantity* and *child quality*, an unfortunate label that seems to imply that parents can get "better" children only by spending more money on them. I find it more helpful to think of the economic good as "parenting" rather than children. We can satisfy our desire for increased parenting by having more children, but we also can satisfy it by parenting our existing children more intensively. We parent more intensively by spending more resources—time, attention, energy, and money—on each child, and we buy things for our children that make us feel like "better" parents. This is what the jargon tries to express by saying that we increase the "quality" of our children. Quality, of course, is in the eyes of the beholder, and different parents choose to buy their children different things. Sometimes we indulge our children (and ourselves) with higher-quality—or more expensive—clothes, meals, vacations, or sporting events. American Jewish parents generally place a high priority on investments in their children's human capital, like education and medical care. This parenting choice, made by individual families in the past, is an important determinant of the high education, occupation, and income levels observed in today's Jewish community.

The economic incentives underlying the balance between the number of children and expenditures per child, like any economic trade-off, depend on relative prices. Larger families usually cost more money in total, but if there are *economies of scale* the money spent per child will be lower than in smaller families. The same principle applies to other resources, like the time and energy required for parenting, resources in especially short supply for two-career couples. American Jewish couples in high-wage occupations face economic incentives to reduce the time-intensity of parenting activities, typically by having smaller families so they can spend more time with each child and still spend less time over-all. High-earning couples also find it relatively inexpensive to increase the intensity of their parenting by substituting market-based services (for example, child care or Hebrew lessons) for their own time in many activities. This permits the fewer hours spent with their children to be "quality time" that builds relationships and satisfies the desire for parent-ing per se.

The parenting lifestyles chosen by individuals and couples have implications not only for Jewish religious observance within the fam-ily but also for the Jewish community in which they live. For example, families with many children observe the Sabbath and Jewish holidays with a festive gathering that includes aunts, uncles, and cousins. Any couple who moved far away from the extended family would find it dif-ficult to attend these events, a high cost that tends to reduce geographic mobility in such a community. Holiday observances are less festive in small families, many of whom come from extended families that are geographically scattered. One way of dealing with this is to celebrate the holiday meal in a group, so some synagogues and other Jewish organi-zations host communal Shabbat dinners and Passover Seders for their members and guests. Another custom is for several small families to join each other for a festive gathering. This approach creates the flavor of an extended family celebration as well as the custom of inviting "strangers" (that is, people without their own families) to the table. Families without either of these options, whether by choice or by circumstance, find home religious observances less satisfying and therefore have a lower incentive to perform them.

Legacy, Human Capital, and Social Change

If bequeathing a legacy to the next generation is important for all Jewish parents, the way in which this is done can depend on the number of children in each family. In some cultures, for example, the oldest son is groomed to follow his father's occupation or inherit the family business, and the oldest daughter is primary caretaker for her parents in their old age. Among Jews, fathers traditionally performed religious rituals in the synagogue and at home and passed these skills on to their sons, while mothers were responsible for observances related to food and homemaking and passed these skills on to their daughters. The American Jewish community has moved away from this pattern of specialization by gender, in part because parents who want to pass their legacy to the next generation have fewer children to receive it.

Despite high birth rates in the ultra-Orthodox communities, the fertility data clearly imply that most American Jews have small families. As Figure 5.1 suggests, the two-child average persisted in the American Jewish community for almost the entire twentieth century so that today's young adults are the third or fourth generation of parents who themselves grew up with few siblings. Traditions differentiating children by gender or birth order that seem "natural" in a community with large families tend to break down in small families with few children. Today the "natural" order of things is a small family in which neither birth order nor gender confers preferential treatment.

Parents' own skills and interests affect the home environment and become an important part of the legacy to their children. For example, the children of highly educated parents have an advantage at school, in part because they are exposed to learning in the home, in part because their parents interact with them to reinforce school lessons, and in part because the home environment encourages completion of homework assignments and school projects. Similarly, parents with high levels of Jewish human capital create a home in which children absorb Jewish knowledge, experience, and values, a legacy that makes their Jewish education more productive and their religious observance more valuable. These types of home-produced human capital contribute to much of the intergenerational stability we see in American society.

Unlike an inheritance of, say, financial resources, inheriting human capital requires a child to be cooperative as well as receptive to the legacy. As any parent can tell you, it is fruitless to insist that your child go to medical school if he or she wants to be a concert violinist, and vice versa. Similarly, if the father is a doctor, the larger his family the more likely he is to have at least one child willing and able to follow in his foot-steps. The fewer children he has, the less likely this will happen. Suppose he has two children, a son and a daughter, and only the daughter shows interest and aptitude for the medical profession. Then the daughter is his only opportunity to pass this legacy to the next generation. This is always the case for parents with no sons, a group that includes much of the Jewish community because it accounts for one-fourth of all two-child families and fully half of the one-child families. A similar logic applies to Jewish religious skills, a form of human capital that used to be gender based but that is now virtually the same for boys and girls.

The transition from large to small families was already changing the American Jewish community early in the twentieth century. The sons of Jewish immigrants quickly acquired high levels of secular ed-ucation and moved into high-level occupations. Jewish daughters also attended college in families that could afford it, but because market op-portunities were low for women they were more likely than their broth-ers to fill unpaid (or low-paid) positions in a family business or in Jewish communal organizations. By the post-WWII generation, however, most Jewish parents could afford college for all of their children, and the labor market for women was widening. From the 1970s onward most Jewish families expected both sons and daughters to achieve a high level of edu-cation in preparation for a correspondingly high-level career.

The same phenomenon also transformed gender roles within the Jewish community. During its early phases, when labor market activities were much more attractive for men than for women, women filled many roles in Jewish social services and communal organizations previously dominated by men. As the Hebrew-school curriculum adapted to the needs of children with strong secular schooling but little knowledge of Judaism, boys and girls attended class together and received the same religious training. (Some very Orthodox communities continued to edu-cate boys and girls separately, but these were the exception rather than the rule.) Women even became teachers in Hebrew schools and Sunday schools, a job that was once an entirely male preserve. As women entered more and more high-level careers, the notion that they by nature were less able than their brothers to grasp sophisticated texts, or to achieve spiritual heights, became more and more dissonant with their secular achievements. By the beginning of the twenty-first century most non-Orthodox American synagogues are fully egalitarian (that is, gender neutral) in their ritual practices, and female clergy are now commonplace in non-Orthodox synagogue movements.

The legacy motive in small families also has other implications for the American Jewish community. Behaviors that were once considered extremely antisocial, even a threat to the coherence of the Jewish community itself, could be punished by expulsion or even excommunication. Parents of a homosexual son, for example, or a daughter who married a non-Jew (often requiring conversion to another religion), might disown the child, sometimes even to the point of observing rituals associated with death and mourning. Such extreme measures are always painful, possibly more so for the parent than for the child because a parent experiences this as failure to pass his or her legacy to the next generation. The cost to the parent of losing a child is greatest if there are no other children to inherit this legacy, so disowning a child is more costly for parents with small families than large ones. Communities with many small families have a greater incentive to "accept" such children even though they may disapprove of their behavior. When it comes to the religious life of American Jewry, any stigma attached to participation by women, divorcees, homosexuals, and even intermarried Jews is rapidly becoming a thing of the past. This is reinforced by changing attitudes in the larger society, which itself is characterized by an increase in the proportion of families with few children.

Age, Marriage, and the Jewish Community

One of our sons met the love of his life at a Jewish summer camp while they were still young teenagers. The two "children" attended different high schools and then different colleges, but they remained close friends throughout those years. (There was an interlude during college when they each dabbled in the marriage market—the inevitable subtext of college social life—but soon concluded that they already had a good match and further search would not be worthwhile.) They became a couple while earning graduate degrees and establishing their careers, so by the time they actually got married they had been together for more than eight years. It would be two more years before they had a child, at which point they became parents and my husband and I became grandparents.

Age at Marriage

Much has been written about the fact that today's young American Jews marry much later than their parents did and they are older when they start to have children. They remain students well into their twenties and are closer to thirty by the time they are established in a career. These older students typically focus narrowly on the heavy investment required by their profession, postponing whatever additional investments they might need to make in other areas. They may not even have a clear vision of their life goals until their professional training ends and their career begins. For whatever reason, however, marriages made too early in the educational process—that is, when the couple is "too young"—are less stable and more likely to end in divorce.

Even though adult singles' economic incentives argue for postponing marriage, their physical, social, and emotional maturity are not so readily delayed. Many American Jewish singles solve this imbalance by cohabitation, an informal marriagelike living arrangement for partners not yet ready for a lifelong commitment. Cohabitation is now so common among older students and young professionals that it receives wide acceptance within the American Jewish community. Once they are ready to start a family, however, the couple are expected to commit to a marriage (that may or may not be with their cohabiting partner) before having children of their own.

The only thing unusual about our son's experience was that he and his wife were high-school sweethearts and got married in their mid-twenties. Most of their classmates were older when they found a good match but otherwise followed a similar pattern by first establishing a career and then marrying in their late twenties or early thirties, often after pairing up in a stable cohabitation arrangement. In effect, the decade-long interval between high-school graduation and a Jewish wedding has become a new life-cycle stage that demographers call "young adult singles." Adult singles were rare in the Jewish community when marriages typically took place right after graduation, but they are an important share of the American Jewish population now that so many Jewish men and women pursue advanced studies and professional careers.

Adult Singles and Empty Nesters

American synagogues are still adjusting to this new demographic fact of communal life. Traditional Jewish observance and religious custom assigns a role for everyone to participate, whether they are children, parents, or grandparents. Young adult singles fall into none of these categories. Jewish children formally undertake adult religious responsibilities with a Bar or Bat Mitzvah ceremony on their thirteenth birthday, but it will be another five or ten years before they leave their parents' home and nearly two decades before they themselves become parents. During adolescence they may join youth groups, attend Jewish summer camps, spend time in Israel, or even continue their Jewish education. Some synagogues have special services in which teenagers assume adult roles, and college students may have the same opportunity in services organized by Hillel (a parareligious organization supporting Jewish life on campus). Adult singles in their twenties, however, often feel out of place within the typical family-oriented structure of Jewish religious life.

One consequence of this situation is that many adult Jewish singles neglect religious participation in favor of activities that at the moment seem more rewarding. Yet increasingly these young adults are forming new congregations with innovative religious lifestyles. Their idiosyncratic religious styles range from the very traditional (almost) to the very secular (almost). They may or may not hire a rabbi and cantor, but even when they do their services tend to be very participatory. Few of these congregations formally affiliate with one of the major synagogue movements, perhaps styling themselves as "nondenominational" or even "postdenominational." Once their children reach Hebrew-school age, however, they typically lose members to a more conventional synagogue for the sake of its Jewish education. This allows the young synagogues to remain youthful and brings young parents with new religious experiences to invigorate the older synagogues.

The emergence of young adult singles as an important demographic group within the Jewish community has as its mirror image the group that we now call *empty nesters*. My husband and I probably became empty nesters as soon as our younger son left home for college, but we certainly belonged to this group once he graduated. Empty nesters are married—and formerly married—adults whose grown children do not yet have children of their own. Within Judaism's religious context, empty nesters are no longer parents raising a family, but they are not yet grandparents. They are joined in the community by never-married older singles, by childless married couples, and by grandparents whose children live far away.

Holiday observances can be particularly difficult for this group because so many Jewish holidays are family centered and involve children. Because Jewish parenting no longer dominates their religious lifestyle decisions, empty nesters may reduce their Jewish observance or—like adult singles—seek a new congregation better suited to their own religious needs. Many, however, miss the Jewish family celebrations that they enjoyed when their children were growing up. It is not uncommon for empty nesters to fill this void at home by turning to the synagogue, whether with increased religious participation, with a study group, or with adult education classes. At a stage in their life cycle where they can afford more time and money for Jewish causes, empty nesters are an important source of lay leadership for today's synagogues and communal organizations.

The New Jewish Demography

Demographers traditionally describe the age distribution of a community as a *population pyramid*, with the largest group at the bottom being children, the smallest group at the top being the elderly, and the middle-sized group in between being prime-age adults. The American Jewish community is more aptly characterized as a *population cylinder* with five levels instead of just three. As long as the average married couple has only two children, children as a group do not outnumber their parents. If we think of adult singlehood as bracketed by the Bar or Bat Mitzvah and the wedding, there are essentially the same number of adult singles as there are children and about the same number of empty nesters. At the top of the cylinder are the grandparents, "senior citizens" who are more numerous than ever before because they are much healthier and likely to live longer than their own grandparents did.

The geographical distribution of the American Jewish community has also changed since the days of a population pyramid when the different generations of the same family were likely to live near each other and know each other well. The typical transition from childhood into single adulthood now means leaving home, first to go to college and a place of advanced education and then to follow the best opportunities for establishing a career. Because siblings often live in different cities by the time they marry and become parents, many Jewish children grow up far from their aunts, uncles, and cousins as well as their grandparents. Senior citizens who followed careers and raised families in Northern cities might move to a friendlier climate in the Sun Belt (mostly states in the American Southwest, including Southern California, and Florida). Many retired people, whether grandparents or empty nesters, become "snow birds," living most of the year near their children and grandchildren but spending winter months in Sun Belt communities with others in their age group.

This new demographic reality of American Jewry has implications for parareligious and Jewish communal organizations, as well as for its religious institutions. Young adult singles earn more than ever, but they are investing heavily in career-related human capital and only weakly motivated for supporting traditional Jewish institutions. Parents in two-career families are typically time constrained, interested in communal life primarily as it contributes to the Jewish upbringing of their children. The main burden of supporting the Jewish community thus rests on empty nesters and senior citizens. This works well in a stable community, where parents and grandparents can identify the needs of young families by recalling their own youth and where their leadership affects the lives of their own children and grandchildren. In today's community, however, lay leaders and their adult children often live in different cities, and

American Jewry is still a community in transition. Among other things, this means that the decisions of lay leaders affect other people's children rather than their own. In this situation, a community's elders sometimes find it a real challenge to anticipate the Jewish needs of the next generation and to shape institutions that can meet them.

6

American Jewish Immigrants

MOST AMERICAN JEWS TODAY HAVE AMERICAN-BORN parents and even grandparents. Yet the immigrant experience is an important part of American Jewish identity and culture. For a century and a half—from 1840 to 1990—the story of American Jewry was a story of immigrants, their children, and their grandchildren. We love to hear about Jews who grew up in poverty, flourished in the American land of opportunity, and became wildly successful in their chosen field—in the arts, in science, in business, and even in crime. We also know that many of our Jewish communal institutions began by serving the needs of immigrants. Whether we speak of German Jews in the middle of the nineteenth century or Russian Jews early in the twentieth, the economic adjustment of immigrants dominated the lives of Jewish families for so long that it had a major impact on the community as a whole. To understand today's Jewish community, we cannot ignore its immigrant roots and the economic forces that transformed it in America.

The Human Capital of Jewish Immigrants

Photographs of immigrants landing at Ellis Island (in New York harbor) show them carrying bundles with all of their worldly possessions. Although the bundles look large and unwieldy, they could not possibly have contained anything comparable to the wealth of the average American citizen of that day. Most immigrants would spend their first years after arrival in poverty. In addition to their meager tangible assets, however, every immigrant arrived with a stock of human capital. Even those with little or no schooling brought skills, experiences, and talent to their new country. The first arrivals may have been venturing into the unknown, but those arriving later had the benefit of letters with information about conditions in America. For example, many Russian Jews who had learned that garment-industry skills would be useful in America learned tailoring in anticipation of their move. Some men even carried ashore a sewing machine among their personal possessions.

Transferable and Country-Specific Human Capital

Some of the human capital with which an immigrant arrives will be useful in the new country, but some will not. We say that their human capital is either *transferable* between countries or *specific* to a particular country. An immigrant's initial disadvantage relative to natives arises because only some of his or her human capital is transferable. The immigrant can overcome this disadvantage by investing in *U.S.-specific* forms of human capital, a process that we describe as adjusting to the new country. Even though an immigrant may be fluent in his or her native language, for example, only English is fully transferable to the United States. Workers whose English is weak are limited to low-wage jobs in America, so learning English is an important investment in U.S.-specific human capital. Other forms of U.S.-specific human capital improve production skills, workplace relationships, knowledge about how and where to find better jobs, and an understanding of American technology.

New immigrants are disadvantaged not only in the workplace but also in their role as consumers. An important part of an immigrant's adjustment process is acquiring new, U.S.-specific knowledge about such basics as neighborhoods and housing, food and food preparation, child care and schooling, transportation and entertainment. It takes time and effort to learn where to shop for the best goods at the lowest prices, to know which neighborhoods offer the best urban environment for the cheapest rents. Whether acquired through study, conversation, or simply by experience, new knowledge also opens doors to other investments. Once an immigrant learns English, for example, he or she can participate in a variety of nonwork experiences beyond the immigrant enclave—politics, journalism, theaters and concerts, public libraries, museums—each of which would benefit from additional U.S.-specific human capital. Little wonder, then, that a new immigrant is sometimes overwhelmed by how much there is to learn in the new country.

An immigrant's adjustment process is made easier the more his or her human capital is transferable. New-country-specific investments are also more efficient if they complement skills that the immigrants bring with them, even if these skills are not themselves directly transferable. This is why immigrants often seek work in occupations similar to the ones they held before leaving home. People choosing to immigrate to a new country also tend to be adventuresome, adaptable, open to new possibilities, and willing to take risks. These characteristics may not be very useful in a rigid or stagnant economy, nor are they always transferable to a wage-earning factory job. Yet they are highly complementary to the entrepreneurial skills required to start a business, and the United States has always been a place where entrepreneurship is admired and can flourish. Immigrants with these characteristics find them to be highly transferable to American economic and social life. Because immigrants as a group are more entrepreneurial than the average worker, they are also more likely to become self-employed as long as there are no significant barriers to starting a business.

Although old-country-specific human capital, by definition, is not transferable to the new country, it is never "lost" because the skills, experiences, and memories that make up a person's human capital are inseparable from the person in whom they are embodied. Old-country-specific human capital becomes part of an immigrant's "ethnic" identity even if it has no other function in the American economy. Every immigrant faces a choice between preserving traditions associated with the old country and assimilating into the new country by investing in U.S.-specific human capital. Working in an ethnic immigrant occupation, or living in an ethnic enclave, can make the choice seem less difficult, but the basic nature of the trade-off is always present.

Jewish Immigrant Occupations

The earliest Jewish immigrants in what is now the United States were Sephardi Jews who arrived in New Amsterdam (New York) from Brazil in 1654. They were followed by others, refugees or their descendents from Spain and Portugal (including their Latin American colonies) or from the Portuguese Jewish community in Amsterdam. Few in number, Sephardi Jews would soon become a community of merchants and financiers trading on connections with European Jews in those occupations. By the time the United States gained its independence at the end of the eighteenth century, these Jews were well integrated into the economy and financially well off. Sephardi Jewish immigrants and their descendents established synagogues, schools, and communal institutions in the major port cities of colonial America. The trickle of Ashkenazi Jewish immigrants arriving from Europe during the early decades of American independence found small but well-established Jewish communities in these cities.

During the 1840s and 1850s a large wave of German-speaking immigrants arrived in the United States. (We usually refer to them as German immigrants, although it would still be several decades before their places of origin were united into the country that we now know as Germany.) Among the German immigrants were some Jews, a small fraction of the total but nevertheless in far greater numbers than the existing Jewish community in America. Quite a few of the German Jewish men became itinerant peddlers, an occupation characteristically Jewish in Germany, selling dry goods to small rural towns and isolated frontier farmsteads. A typical peddler in America might begin on foot, carrying his goods in a large pack, and progress to a horse-drawn wagon that served as a mobile shop. When he had accumulated enough assets, he would choose a likely spot on his itinerary and open a general store, perhaps expanding it into a small retail emporium as a town grew up around him. Jewish shopkeepers innovated in other ways as well, eventually transforming the retail industry by building "department" stores, many of which are still known by the names of their German Jewish immigrant founders.

If the arrival of German Jews in 1840–1860 constituted a wave of immigration, the Russian Jews arriving fifty years later were a veritable tsunami. In 1890, when German immigrant families still accounted for most American Jews, more than three-quarters of all Jewish men worked in clerical and sales occupations. By 1900, only one decade later, so many new immigrants had arrived that those clerical and sales occupations made up less than 10 percent of the Jewish male workforce. During this same decade the proportion of Jewish men in blue-collar occupations, most of whom were new immigrants from Russia or Eastern Europe, rose from 16 percent in 1890 to fully 80 percent in 1900. The Russian immigrants so dominated the Jewish community numerically that as recently as 1990 their descendents accounted for over 90 percent of all American Jews.

Russian Jewish Immigrants

English proficiency is only one example of a U.S.-specific skill that Russian Jewish immigrants lacked on their arrival. The tsarist country from which they came was poor and stagnant, the most technologically backward economy in Europe, and the Jews came from the Pale of Settlement, one of its poorest regions. In contrast, the United States already had a bustling industrial economy and was modernizing at a breathtaking rate. Immigrants entering at Ellis Island found themselves in New York, the country's leading city in size, in economic development, in modern urban amenities, and in the performing arts. Only a fraction of the human capital that they brought with them was transferable to the U.S. labor market. Before landing a good job or starting a small business they needed U.S.-specific occupational skills and an understanding of how American labor markets worked. They also needed to learn American ways of relating to supervisors and co-workers, salespeople and customers, before they could take full advantage of American economic opportunities. There was plenty of work, but many of the workplace skills useful in Russia had little or no value in New York.

By the turn of the twentieth century the German Jews were already assimilated into the American economy and social fabric, identifying themselves as American Jews rather than immigrants. In contrast, Russian Jewish immigrants were still in the early years of the economic adjustment process, living mostly in poor immigrant neighborhoods but investing heavily in U.S.-specific human capital. Russian Jewish men worked as craftsmen and low-skilled laborers in various manufacturing activities, especially in the garment industry, which was dominated by small firms. Many of them soon became entrepreneurs, setting up their own small factories that employed even newer immigrants. Russian Jews as a group were also very imaginative in the way they embraced the economic promise of America. Some found their economic niche in entertainment—including sports, music, theater, and the new motion-picture industry—while others worked with new technologies as innovators, inventors, or researchers. By the early 1920s, when the United States closed its doors to unlimited immigration from Europe, the typical Russian Jewish immigrant of the late nineteenth century had already joined the American middle class.

Other Twentieth-Century Jewish Immigrants

Subsequent waves of Jewish immigration to the United States were much smaller in size. Refugees from the Nazi Holocaust in Europe—both before and after World War II—immigrated in midcentury; Jews from Israel and the Middle East came in its later decades; and a significant wave of Jews from the former Soviet Union arrived in the last decades of the twentieth century. Each of these groups followed the typical pattern of economic assimilation already described, choosing an occupational niche in the U.S. economy that complemented the skills with which they arrived and learning the U.S.-specific skills needed to "become American." Although none of these groups of postwar immigrants was so large as to change the basic structure of the Jewish community, each contributed its own culture to the fabric of American Jewry.

The experience of Russian Jewish immigrants so dominates the story of American Jewry in the twentieth century that most of this chapter focuses on them as the source of our Jewish traditions. Yet every wave of Jewish immigrants faced similar problems of economic, social, and religious adjustment. They all invested heavily—and for the most part wisely—in U.S.-specific human capital. They showed creativity in their choice of economic niches, studied new subjects, and worked intensely to realize the opportunity that America promised. For the most part their American-born children achieved the middle-class prosperity to which the immigrants had aspired. By the third generation, each wave of Jewish immigrants was fully integrated into the American labor force and was disproportionately concentrated in high-level occupations.

Immigrant Enclave Communities

When many immigrants with poorly transferable human capital all come from the same area, the initial adjustment is made easier by forming an immigrant *enclave* community. An enclave community effectively allows old-country human capital, which would otherwise have little if any value, to be at least partially transferable to the new country. In the Jewish neighborhoods of New York's Lower East Side, for example, or Chicago's Maxwell Street, one could buy kosher foods and speak Yiddish in neighborhood shops, making home life more familiar. American Jewish immigrants celebrated Jewish holidays and established small Jewish synagogues, often formed by people who grew up near each other and were familiar with the same local customs. They even formed *landsmenshaften*, informal mutual aid societies made up of people from the same town or region in the old country.

Russian Jewish immigrants arriving in America during the forty years from 1881 to 1920 came from a place where "Jew" was a trait determined at birth and from which there was no escape, a place that confined them to live in crowded and impoverished Jewish enclaves and that severely limited their economic and political freedom. They used their new freedom in America to generate a flowering of Yiddish culture, making the immigrant neighborhoods an exciting place to live. Yiddish books and newspapers proliferated and found wide readership within the community. The Yiddish theater was very popular, and *klezmer* bands played "Yiddish" tunes at weddings and parties. Restaurants and coffee shops (often called "candy stores") that served kosher food encouraged socializing and community spirit. These are all examples of Jewish *ethnic goods*, goods and services specific to a particular ethnicity because they have few other customers and thus depend on the ethnic community.

For all its appeal, the Jewish neighborhood was still a poverty-ridden enclave in the midst of a land of opportunity. The immigrants understood well that "becoming American" was their best hope for improving their economic circumstances. The Yiddish press published how-to books and advice columns that were widely read and discussed, making many kinds of U.S.-specific human capital accessible to those not yet fluent in English. Night classes for learning English were very popular, as were Americanization classes offered by the Settlement House in immigrant neighborhoods. Many non-Jewish immigrants in this period came for temporary jobs to escape from poverty in their homeland, viewing their enclave neighborhoods as a means of preserving their homeland culture even if it meant resisting assimilation into the American mainstream. In contrast, Jews had little desire to return to Russia and were enthusiastic about "becoming American" even—or perhaps especially—if it meant rejecting Russian tradition. They found a balance between the twin goals of assimilation and cultural preservation that greatly favored the former and led to rapid economic success.

The Economics of Jewish Immigrant Adjustment

Each wave of Jewish immigrants followed a path to economic as-similation typical of most immigrants to America. When they first arrive they are "greenhorns," unfamiliar with the environment and at a distinct economic disadvantage. Once they orient themselves to the new country they invest in both human and nonhuman capital, demonstrating in-dustriousness and imaginativeness that pays off with upward economic mobility and gives rise to the stereotype of diligent immigrants willing to work hard and for long hours. As their economic situation contin-ues to improve the immigrants may eventually earn as much as their U.S.-born peers, people whose entrepreneurial drive and good decision-making abilities typically yield incomes above the average. Thus immi-grants who arrived as young adults in poor enclaves might raise their children in middle-class urban neighborhoods and spend their senior years with grandchildren in suburbia. Their economic assimilation at this point is such that popular language no longer calls them "immi-grants" but rather hyphenated Americans: Italian immigrants become Italian-Americans, Polish immigrants become Polish-Americans, and Jewish immigrants become American Jews.

Economic Assimilation

The Russian Jews followed the path common to nearly all immigrants as they adjusted to the American economy. For the first few years, everything was new, and they had to work hard just to find their way around. Then they found a place for themselves and began to advance up the economic ladder. For some it was a job with a firm promising advancement for those who work hard; for others it was a small business with promise of future prosperity. Younger Jewish immigrants became doctors, accountants, or teachers, professions that required additional schooling in the new country. Whatever the choice, they typically spent the next decades investing heavily in both human and nonhuman capital, earning a reputation as dedicated workers as they strove for success in their new world.

We can see the results of this effort in Figure 6.1.[1] Whereas in 1900 some 80 percent of all Jewish men—nearly all of whom were recent immigrants—worked as laborers or craftsmen, by 1920 this fraction

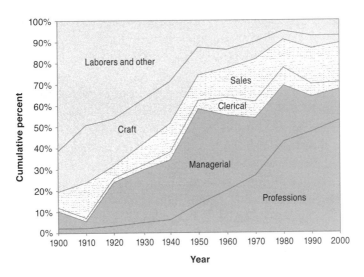

FIGURE 6.1. *Changing occupations of American Jewish men, 1900–2000.*
SOURCES: Computed from B. Chiswick (1999), pp. 68–98, Table 2; and B. Chiswick (2007), pp. 80–111, Table E-1.

had fallen to 68 percent. The managerial occupations (not including the owners of small "mom-and-pop" establishments) accounted for only 8 percent of Jewish men in 1900 but more than 20 percent by 1920. Some immigrant men worked for firms that promoted them into managerial positions, but often they started small businesses that grew into larger companies. By 1920 many of them also had American sons old enough to work, some of whom had arrived with their parents as young children but most of whom were born in the United States. Fewer men in this second generation worked in blue-collar occupations. Many of them would enter the professions, while others would become owners or managers of successful medium-sized businesses.

By midcentury some 45 percent of the Jewish men worked in managerial occupations and, as we saw in Figure 2.2, another 7 percent had professional occupations in medicine, law, and college and university teaching. More than half of the American Jewish men were financially secure enough for the next generation to pursue higher education. Subsequent decades thus saw more and more Jewish men entering the labor force in professional occupations. The professions accounted for 43 percent of the Jewish male labor force by 1980 and fully 53 percent by 2000. By that time two-thirds of the men in the American Jewish community worked in high-level occupations, either as professionals or in management.

Jewish women followed a similar path to economic assimilation. In the earliest years they worked in low-wage jobs, often as "sweatshop" labor in the home or in the garment factories. The typical Jewish immigrant woman worked both before and after marriage but withdrew from the labor force once she started having children. Because she would then become a full-time mother and homemaker, her human capital investments focused on new-country skills relevant for that kind of work. Jewish immigrant women flocked to settlement houses to learn not only English and civics but also American ways of housekeeping, cooking, health care, and parenting. They read self-help books written in Yiddish just for this market. The wives of self-employed entrepreneurs would often work full-time or part-time in their husband's business, perhaps beside him in a "mom-and-pop" shop or perhaps in a supporting role as secretary or bookkeeper. Jewish immigrants had ambitions for their daughters as well as their sons, keeping them in school as long as they could. Second-generation Jewish women were very likely to earn a high-school diploma, and they were more likely than other American women to go to college.

During this phase of adjustment the immigrants could see the re-sults of their investment as their wages rose or their business prospered. They also saw their families grow, raising their children as "real" Ameri-cans. Immigrant Jewish parents took full advantage of the American public school system, prepared to make sacrifices to keep their children in school as long as possible. They moved out of the immigrant slums as soon as possible so that their children could grow up in a less crowded neighborhood with more comfortable homes, better schools, healthier air, and fewer threats from underworld seductions. By the time the chil-dren had finished high school, the most successful immigrant parents could afford to send at least some of them to college or professional school, especially to the "free" public colleges in cities like New York. This was their American Dream.

Figure 6.2 illustrates these trends for both Jews and non-Jews in the United States. We do not have statistics on the educational attainment of Jews for each decade, but we know the education level in 2000 of people of different ages, and we can use this to reconstruct the time pattern of educational attainment. About 20 percent of the Jewish men and 10 per-cent of the Jewish women born before 1925 not only finished college but continued on to earn some sort of advanced degree. (These are people who would have graduated from college before or during World War II, whose schooling may have been interrupted by a period of work or mili-tary service.) Because Jews make up such a small proportion of the total population, the U.S. Census figures can serve as a comparable estimate for non-Jews. These data suggest that non-Jews born before 1925 were only half as likely as Jews to earn an advanced degree, and this discrep-ancy seems to have increased with each generation. Educational attain-ment increased with each younger age group through those born during the post-WWII baby boom, but the increase is much more dramatic for Jews than for non-Jews, and women lag only a couple of decades behind their brothers.[2] Among people born in the late 1960s, about 40 percent of the Jews—41 percent of the men and 37 percent of the women—had

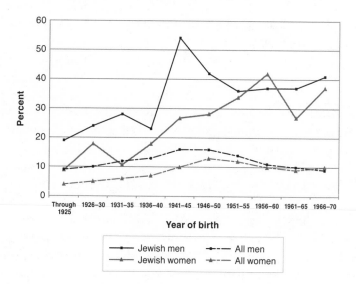

FIGURE 6.2. *Advanced degrees earned by age and sex, Jews and non-Jews, 2000.*

SOURCES: Computed from NJPS 2000/01 for Jews, U.S. Census of Population, 2000 for all persons. See Schwartz et al. (2004) and U.S. Bureau of the Census.

earned advanced degrees by the year 2000, as compared to only 10 percent of the non-Jewish men and women.

The high levels of educational attainment among children and grandchildren of immigrants contributed to the dramatic economic success of American Jews. Jews and non-Jews alike enjoyed the benefits of new technology and economic development of the U.S. economy throughout the twentieth century. As Figure 6.2 shows, however, Jews were investing in higher education much more than non-Jews, permitting them to move into high-level occupations in much more dramatic numbers. This had two direct consequences. It raised the hourly wage rate of Jews, increasing the cost of time and making time-intensive activities more expensive. It also gave them higher incomes, making all consumer goods and services more affordable. This combination of incentives and opportunities induced an affluent consumption pattern in which money could be used to "buy" time, for example by hiring a housekeeper, to free up time for family activities.

By the third generation—the grandchildren of immigrants—nearly half of all Jewish men would work in professional occupations. By the 1970s fully two-thirds of all American Jewish men would be in the high-level occupations, a fraction that would remain fairly stable for decades thereafter. As the decades passed, however, the immigrant generation retired or died, and more and more third-generation men entered the labor force. The statistics reflect this as an occupational shift as managers are replaced by professionals.[3] In 1970 about half of the Jewish men in high-level occupations were still in managerial occupations, but by 2000 this fraction had dropped to one-fourth. By the end of the twentieth century, some two-thirds of all American Jewish men worked in high-level occupations that placed them comfortably in the upper middle class.

Judaism as an Immigrant Religion

Legend has it that a great pile of tefillin lies undersea at the entrance to New York harbor. (Reminder: Tefillin are the two small leather boxes with leather straps that a Jewish man wears, one bound to his forehead and the other to his arm, during the weekday morning prayers.) Whether or not there is such a pile, the symbolism is clear. Jews arriving in America during the 1880–1920 era came mostly from tsarist Russia and Eastern Europe, where the legal and social penalties imposed on Jews were especially severe and Jewish religious authority seemed especially restrictive. People who chafe under such strictures are the ones most likely to risk moving to a new country, and for them America meant freedom from all authority in Russia, whether secular or religious. In the excitement of his first sight of the Statue of Liberty, we can easily imagine a young man throwing his tefillin overboard in his enthusiastic hope for a new beginning.

Even for immigrants who looked forward to practicing Judaism free from persecution, religious observance was rarely the highest priority. They wanted to find work, to find housing, and to learn English so that they could participate fully in the economic promise of America. They reveled in the freedom to participate actively, if not always as equals, in the political and social life of their new country. They were delighted by the many cultural activities available in American cities of that time and the new technologies that were transforming household consumption. To achieve these goals the new immigrants invested heavily and enthusiastically in U.S.-specific skills, a process described as "Americanization" or, equivalently, "assimilation."

Jewish religious behavior in the new country followed a pattern typical of many immigrant groups. As best they could in their new environment, they continued to keep familiar home-based religious practices, such as kashrut, Shabbat observance, and the most "important" holiday celebrations. They also established small "storefront" synagogues (*steibls*), typically on the ground floor of a home or tenement. The Jewish equivalent of an "immigrant church," a storefront synagogue replicated familiar religious rituals of the old country and provided a safe haven from the strangeness in language and culture that might otherwise overwhelm the newcomer. Its appeal was practical as much as it was spiritual, providing a place where an immigrant could meet other Yiddish speakers with similar backgrounds, perhaps even from the same old-country town or region. Old-timers (that is, people who had already been in the United States for a few years) could help new arrivals find housing or jobs or at least give them advice from their own experience. Immigrant synagogues facilitated investment in U.S.-specific human capital, at the same time giving value to old-country human capital that was otherwise nontransferable to the United States.

There were many lapses, of course, not only by those who rejected religion as old-country "superstition" but also by well-intentioned Jews distracted by the many other activities competing for attention. Sabbath observance conflicted with the six-day workweek of that era and was especially costly for owners of a small business. Even though Jewish immigrants could easily find a familiar congregation close to home, the *steibls* were plagued by poor attendance almost from the beginning. To make a *minyan* (the ten-man quorum) for the synagogue service these congregations might even need to approach a Jewish passer-by on the street.

In hindsight, the economic incentives were clearly stacked against the *stiebls*. An old-country religious lifestyle may have been suitable where earnings were meager and economic opportunity nonexistent, but turn-of-the-century America was not such a place. The initial wage rate of new immigrants exceeded their old-country wage even though it was low by American standards. The value of their time was higher than that, however, if they were investing in human capital that would raise their future wages even higher. The immigrants clearly understood this, whether purposefully enrolled in a class or acquiring country-specific human capital in the course of daily life. What with an immigrant's long work hours and heavy human capital investments, any time-intensive religious observance would have been much more costly in America than it had been Russia. Aside from the High Holy Days (Rosh Hashanah and Yom Kippur) in the fall, synagogue attendance was far lower than the number of people professing Judaism as their religion.

Family life and religious observance are both very time intensive, so combining them is efficient for people with a high or rising value of time. Sabbath and most holiday observance could take place at home, becoming family occasions that also had religious content. Yet ritual has little value in itself other than for the spirituality that it stimulates. A time-intensive ritual may be much less effective for this purpose when it is truncated, or even when it is conducted in a hurry. Reducing the time spent on religious observance thus led many Jews to deemphasize the importance of ritual itself, whether at home or in the synagogue. Some observances persisted out of habit, but others were simply ignored. Holiday observances might remain important despite their loss of spiritual content if they provided an opportunity for family gatherings. American Jews also relaxed their observance of kashrut, whether because they viewed it as an old-country "superstition" or because of the constraints that it posed on meals eaten with non-Jewish friends and colleagues in lunchrooms or restaurants.

American Synagogue Movements

Earlier waves of Jewish immigrants had faced similar adjustment problems when they first arrived in the United States. By the time Russian immigrants began arriving in large numbers in the 1880s, however, the Jews who had preceded them were well integrated into the American mainstream. The German Jews already lived in middle-class neighborhoods with good housing, good schools, and convenient access to stores and workplaces. They had synagogue buildings with comfortable seating—typically with men and women seated together—and they could afford to hire a rabbi and cantor to lead the religious service. German-American synagogues had adopted many "reforms" of Jewish religious practice, modifications influenced by the new Reform Judaism gaining popularity in Germany. Even though German-Jewish theologians justified these reforms in various ways, the high value of congregants' time was at least as important in explaining their widespread appeal to ordinary American Jews.

The changes introduced by Reform congregations met the needs of a community dominated by immigrants adjusting to their new economic environment. If Jews were "too busy" for regular synagogue attendance, then perhaps the ritual could be modified so as to be "meaningful" for congregants who attended only rarely. Two obvious time-saving modifications were to make the service shorter and to conduct at least part of it in English. Another was to have the rabbi give a sermon (in English, of course), in effect "translating" that week's Torah portion into an idiom understood by congregants unfamiliar with the religious literature. Although the Sabbath begins at sundown on Friday, the synagogue service could be rescheduled for later in the evening (especially in the winter with its early sunset) to avoid conflicts with the secular workweek. Some synagogues even scheduled the Sabbath service on Sunday because American jobs and small businesses—especially in retail trade—often required a six-day (Monday through Saturday) workweek.

Many Jewish religious leaders bemoaned the low synagogue attendance and the seduction of American secular ways. Others, however, sought creative adaptations to Judaism's new economic realities. Rabbi Isaac Mayer Wise (1819–1900) sought to reinforce the popular grassroots reforms by uniting American synagogues into a single umbrella organization to serve their common interests. (An "umbrella" organization is one whose members are synagogues rather than individuals.) Rabbi Wise was instrumental in establishing the Union of American Hebrew Congregations (UAHC) in 1873, the basic organization of the Reform synagogue movement in America, which remains active to this day as the renamed Union of Reform Judaism. In 1875 the UAHC established the Hebrew Union College, in Cincinnati, to train rabbis and cantors in the "American custom." Although the Reform movement had its roots in Germany and was established in America primarily by middle-class German Jews, it was a "natural" response to rising wage rates, and hence the rising value of congregants' time, and would develop throughout the twentieth century in distinctively American ways.

By the time the Yiddish-speaking immigrants began arriving in large numbers, most established American synagogues were "reformed," and many were already affiliated with the UAHC. During its first decades in America the Reform movement was very radical and met with strong resistance among the new Russian immigrants with different synagogue traditions. A few decided that Reform Judaism was simply the "American" way of being Jewish and adopted it right away. For most, however, it didn't seem "Jewish enough." In part, of course, this was because the Reform ritual was so different from the Jewish observance with which they were familiar. In part, however, the strangeness of Reform synagogues reflected cultural differences between the Jews from Germany and those from Eastern Europe and Russia. Recognizing the usefulness in America of an umbrella organization, and to counterbalance UAHC, in 1898 the non-Reform synagogues formed the Union of Orthodox Jewish Congregations of America (known today as OU, sometimes referred to as "Modern Orthodoxy" to distinguish it from the various "ultra-Orthodox" communities).

As the Russian immigrants continued to assimilate economically, they faced the same rise in wage and income levels that had influenced their German-Jewish predecessors. Inevitably, some congregations responded to these incentives with modifications of religious practice that "saved" time, even when this meant paying a higher money price to maintain the synagogue community. In 1913, some of the more "liberal" congregations broke away from the Orthodox Union to form United Synagogue of America (USA), the umbrella organization of the Conservative movement that was recently renamed the United Synagogue of Conservative Judaism (USCJ).

The Jewish community's religious leadership during this formative period included some of the greatest thinkers of the time, people who understood the realities of grassroots changes in religious practice and sought creative innovations in ritual to strengthen its Jewish content. Mordecai Kaplan (1881–1983), for example, saw Judaism as a religion embedded in an entire civilization and looked to ancient Jewish sources for "new" traditions that would resonate in the American milieu. Among other things, he encouraged the transformation of the Bar Mitzvah ceremony from a small family affair to the major celebration that it is today, and Kaplan's daughter is said to be the first Bat Mitzvah in the United States.[4] Solomon Schechter (1847–1915) became head of the Jewish Theological Seminary in New York in 1902, where he encouraged the use of modern scholarship for the study of Jewish texts. This seminary would eventually be supported by the United Synagogue of America (USA) and train clergy for Conservative congregations throughout the United States. These are but two examples of Jewish leaders who glimpsed the emergence of a new Small Tradition, were excited by its possibilities, and contributed constructively to the development of contemporary American Judaism.

Americanization and Immigrant Synagogues

Like the "immigrant churches" of other American religious groups, *steibls* played an important social role by supporting members in the twin tasks of assimilation into their new country and preservation of their religious heritage. As Jews found their niche in the American economy and moved into the middle class, however, they abandoned them in favor of new middle-class "American" synagogues, mostly affiliated with the Conservative or Reform movements. Within a few decades, these synagogue movements came to define the mainstream religious practice of American Judaism.

Some immigrant synagogues moved to the new, middle-class neighborhoods along with their members. Even as wage rates rose and time became more costly, they continued to conduct traditional ritual in the face of steadily declining attendance at religious services. They also continued to support the Americanization needs of congregants, providing a Yiddish-speaking social environment even as the immigrants became more and more comfortable with English in their everyday activities. These synagogues had less appeal to the second generation, however, and even less to the third, the American-born children and grandchildren whose native language was English and who felt little or no nostalgia for an "old country" that they never knew.

Many of today's urban congregations were originally established by immigrants or their children trying to "Americanize" their religious practice. There are still a few Sephardi congregations remaining from earlier periods, but most of today's older synagogues were founded by German Jews or by immigrants from Russia and Eastern Europe. The Conservative synagogue to which our family now belongs began as a German Ashkenazi congregation in the mid-nineteenth century, shifted to a Russian Ashkenazi culture in the early twentieth century, became affiliated with the Conservative synagogue movement in the mid-twentieth century, and now maintains multiple religious lifestyles within that movement as it adapts to the needs of a new generation.

Adult children of the earlier immigrants sometimes remained in the Orthodox synagogues of their youth, typically until either they or their parents moved away or their parents died. At that point they might join a Conservative or Reform synagogue, or perhaps join one of the less well-organized communities of "secular" Jews, "cultural" Jews, "humanistic" Jews, or "Jewish atheists." The immigrant synagogues as such rarely survive much beyond the immigrant generation. More recent arrivals—especially those from the Middle East and from the former Soviet Union—formed new immigrant synagogues in their respective traditions. Because these later immigrant groups were small relative to the existing Jewish population, however, they often assimilated into already-established Jewish communities. Yet each group left its mark on American synagogue practices even as their members' economic and religious adjustment followed patterns similar to those of the earlier arrivals.

Immigrant Adjustment and American Judaism

The small amount of data that we have suggests that the children of turn-of-the-twentieth-century Jewish immigrants from Russia and Eastern Europe received considerably less Jewish education than the typical Jewish youth of today. The immigrants arrived with their own religious human capital, acquired informally in a closed community with little competition from outside opportunities. Perhaps they thought that their children would follow the same pattern, acquiring religious human capital informally by living in a Jewish family in an enclave with other Jews.

Coming from a culture in which Jewishness was an ascribed trait and thus inescapable, they may have assumed that the children of Jewish parents would automatically remain Jewish by default. (Even people whose parents had converted to Christianity and who were raised as Christians were still considered "Jews" in Europe and Russia.) Yet the Jewish neighborhoods were wide open to non-Jewish influences, and Jewish immigrants spent less and less time on religious observance as their time became more and more costly in America. Reliance on informal learning taught the children of immigrants much more about ethnic Jewishness—cuisine, humor, mannerisms, and a smattering of Yiddish vocabulary—than it did about the ritual, theology, and culture of religious Judaism.

The religious education that did exist in the immigrant neighborhoods was very different from the Hebrew schools of today. Children were expected to work hard in their public-school studies; they were encouraged to engage in leisure activities; many also held after-school jobs. This left little time and energy for religious training. Parents' goals for religious education were minimal, so almost any Jewish man with old-country synagogue experience could get a job as a Hebrew teacher if the pay was low enough. As a consequence, Hebrew teachers were often new immigrants who had yet to acquire enough U.S.-specific skills for a better-paying job. Their students—mostly boys—learned rudimentary religious skills for a simple Bar Mitzvah ceremony, often by rote, but without further reinforcement these skills were quickly forgotten. In any event, the synagogue skills learned in immigrant communities would have limited use in the middle-class Reform and Conservative synagogues to which the American-born second generation was headed.

Even though the turn-of-the-twentieth-century Russian immigrants often sacrificed their own religious observance in their eagerness to Americanize, that generation would become the repository of Jewish knowledge for their future family and community. Their children attained high levels of secular education; worked in professional, technical and management occupations; and moved to comfortable middle-class suburbs with good schools. Yet these achievements usually came at the expense of investments in Jewish human capital. Few children of immigrants learned much Hebrew or synagogue liturgy, not even the traditional prayers for home-based religious ceremonies. Bar Mitzvah candidates studied their Haftorah portion and the relatively simple blessings recited in the synagogue before and after reading from Torah, but few of them mastered the fluency needed to understand what they were reading. (The Bat Mitzvah for girls was extremely rare until late in the twentieth century.) As adults, these second-generation immigrants faced a high value of time and low religious skills, a combination that increased the cost and decreased the benefit of time-intensive religious observance.

By the middle of the twentieth century, Orthodox Judaism was increasingly associated with elderly immigrants, a small and shrinking proportion of the Jewish population that was widely expected to disappear from the American scene. Even among the non-Orthodox, it would be immigrant grandmothers who would prepare Shabbat and holiday dinners and immigrant grandfathers who would conduct whatever rituals were observed at home. This arrangement may have been an efficient division of labor for second-generation adults with low levels of Jewish human capital, but it also spared them from any incentive to acquire adult religious skills. The second generation had incomes high enough to support expensive American synagogues, complete with new buildings and a professional rabbinate, but they rarely attended religious services more than a few times each year. They enrolled their children in after-school Hebrew programs, but few of them had the inclination or the skills to reinforce those lessons at home. The children and grandchildren of immigrants thus came to associate religious Judaism with the elderly and the old country, neither of which was especially attractive to a fully Americanized younger generation. They thought of themselves as Jews who were "not religious," and even the few observances that they kept—like the Bar/Bat Mitzvah and the Passover Seder—typically gave more emphasis to the family celebration than to its spiritual foundations.

By the later decades of the twentieth century, American Jewry as a community was characterized by extremely high secular human capital and extremely low religious human capital. That meant that time spent in secular activities was very productive while time spent on religious observance yielded low benefits. A person in this situation is not using resources—in this case time—to best advantage if they participate in both kinds of activity, an unstable position that induces one of two alternative responses. Some Jews simply distanced themselves from religious Judaism by spending less time in the low-benefit activity (religion) and more time in high-benefit activities (work and leisure). Others decided to raise the value of religious activities by investing in Jewish human capital, for example by learning Hebrew, reading Jewish books, visiting Israel, studying Torah, participating in the synagogue service, taking classes in college or in the community, or raising the intensity of Jewish observance by joining an ultra-Orthodox religious group.

These two alternative responses to the imbalance between secular and Jewish human capital explain the paradox of "apathy and renewal," a renaissance in modern American Judaism even as most American Jews drift further away from the religious community.[5] The roots of this phenomenon, with all of its implications for today's American Jewish community, are an unintended consequence of the path to economic assimilation chosen by our immigrant forbears. Ironically, the very same resource-allocation decisions that made Jewish immigrants so successful in America, and in which we take such pride as a community, have also led many of today's American Jews to drift away from Judaism as a religion.

Economics and the Jewish Community

In our collective memory, the Yiddish-speaking immigrant neighborhood was a vibrant, exciting place to live. Despite their economic hardships, the Jewish immigrants were optimistic, creative, and energized by the prospects of American opportunity. We have much evidence for this. The Yiddish press was prolific, publishing newspapers, magazines, and books, fiction and nonfiction, for a public that read widely and frequently. The Yiddish theater flourished, producing everything from Shakespeare (well-translated into Yiddish) to vaudeville entertainments for appreciative audiences. Their creativity extended to the workplace, innovating new management techniques, especially in the garment industry, or organizing labor to improve working conditions. Jewish immigrants and their children seemed especially interested in frontiers of economic progress, like the new movie industry and modern medical research. All this activity was decidedly secular, having little or nothing to do with Judaism per se, but it came to be associated with American Jewish life during the first half of the twentieth century.

The immigrant Jewish community also included a wide variety of educational, charitable, and related service organizations. In countries where civil and religious authority overlap, the religious leadership typically takes care of charities, hospitals, schools, and other communal services, activities associated with religious obligations but not by nature religious in character. In the United States, where civil and religious authorities are separate, churches and synagogues are *congregational* in structure. This means that congregations are founded, funded and operated by their own members, typically laymen who then hire clergy to serve the congregation that they manage.[6] Nonreligious functions associated with a religious community, like a Jewish hospital, orphanage, or lobby group, are performed by parareligious organizations that stand apart from the synagogues themselves. Jewish parareligious organizations—that is, Jewish organizations involved in nonreligious activities and not associated with any synagogue movement—are an integral part of the American Jewish communal structure.

There may have been a small synagogue on every corner in the Jewish immigrant neighborhoods, but religion often took second place to its secular life, not only for cultural activities but also for parareligious opportunities to serve or be served. A Yiddish-speaking immigrant could feel completely immersed in Jewish life without ever stepping into a synagogue. Upwardly mobile second-generation Jewish immigrants treasured the vibrant culture of the immigrant neighborhoods and accepted responsibility for maintaining its Jewish communal organizations. They felt little of this nostalgia for its religious life, which they completely "Americanized" as they moved into the middle class. Their legacy to later generations emphasized Jewish traditions of social justice and community service rather than the ancient traditions of religious ritual. Today's American Jews—most of them grandchildren and great-grandchildren of immigrants—are rediscovering these traditions, not only among the ultra-Orthodox but within each of the American synagogue movements.

Parareligious Organizations for Jewish Immigrants

Care of the needy—widows, orphans, the destitute, the aged, and the infirm—is an obligation shared by all Jews, and every Jewish community has some arrangements for providing these services. Other services, like providing kosher meat, operating a *mikva* (ritual bath), or maintaining a burial ground, are often provided by private entrepreneurs, but if not the community steps in to ensure these needs are met for everyone who desires them. Each wave of Jewish immigrants to the United States established parareligious organizations to serve these basic functions almost as soon as they formed a community. Even secular organizations and charities, like hospitals and schools, might serve the religious community by making kosher meals available to their workers, clients, patients, and students.

The huge influx of immigrants from tsarist Russia and Eastern Europe also generated a wide variety of Jewish organizations whose main purpose was to facilitate investments in American human capital. A Jewish Community Center (JCC) typically included a gymnasium and swimming pool to improve the physical fitness of urban youth. As early as 1885, Yiddish-speaking immigrants founded the Hebrew Immigrant Aid Society (HIAS) to help new arrivals, an organization that served as a model for other groups and continues to this day to help Jewish and non-Jewish immigrants adjust to their new economic environment. The National Farm School was established in 1896 to teach urban Jews a new "American" way to earn a living. (Although some of its graduates did indeed become farmers, many of them went into research and made important contributions to modern agricultural technology.) An astonishing number of Jewish fraternities and sororities—Greek-letter social and professional organizations, especially in medicine, dentistry, and law—helped an upwardly mobile immigrant population adjust to its new socioeconomic environment.

Parareligious organizations also formed in response to anti-Semitism, never as oppressive in the United States as in Europe or Russia but a presence nonetheless in the lives of American Jews, especially prior to WWII. Jews mostly avoided hostile neighborhoods and occupations where they would be subject to discrimination, made easier by America's openness in a period of rapid economic change. The Young Men's Hebrew Association (YMHA) could provide Jewish boys with the same services as the local YMCA. If it was hard for Jews to gain admission to the best medical schools and practice medicine in the best hospitals, it was possible to establish Jewish medical schools and hospitals that did not discriminate on the basis of religion or race. Turn-of-the-century Russian-Jewish immigrants were especially concerned about tuberculosis, and by 1909 there were more than five Jewish establishments—including the National Jewish Hospital at Denver—specializing in its treatment.

Jewish immigrants worked diligently to establish themselves as "real" Americans. B'nai Brith (a men's fraternal organization founded in 1843 by German Jewish immigrants) organized the Americanism Commission in 1921 to help Jews prepare for citizenship, the Vocational Service Bureau in 1938 to help in the "occupational adjustment of Jewish youth," and the Hillel Foundation in 1924 to serve Jewish students on college campuses. At the same time, Jews took to heart the basic American principles of religious freedom and political equality. The B'nai Brith Anti-Defamation League (now an independent organization known as ADL) was established in 1913. The ADL has a twofold approach to confront anti-Semitic discrimination, first with education and persuasion and then, failing that, with legal action.

The new immigrants were also concerned with Jews in other countries, especially the lands from which they came (where they still had relatives) and the nascent Jewish community in Palestine. As early as 1906 they founded the American Jewish Committee "to prevent the infraction of the civil and religious rights of Jews in any part of the world." The Zionist Organization of America was founded in 1897 to stimulate political support for a Jewish state, followed in 1910 by the Jewish National Fund (JNF) to buy land for Jews to live in British Palestine, in 1912 by Hadassah to provide Palestine with modern medical and public health facilities, and in 1914 by the Joint Distribution Committee to settle Jewish refugees there. Organizations aimed at helping Jews in other countries proliferated during the interwar decades, in part because of increasing distress of European Jewry and in part because of improvements in the economic circumstances of American Jews.

With the proliferation of Jewish organizations serving so many different needs, joint fund-raising efforts became very practical. Indeed, many cities developed community-wide fund raising into a parareligious organization in its own right, the local Jewish Federation. By 1932 these had formed an umbrella organization, the Council of Jewish Federations and Welfare Funds (CJF), the forerunner of today's Jewish Federations of North America (JFNA), to coordinate their activities at the national level. United Palestine Appeal, a similar umbrella organization to raise funds for various causes in Jewish Palestine, would later become the United Jewish Appeal (UJA) after Israel became an independent country. By supporting a wide variety of Jewish communal institutions, these fund-raising organizations provided another secular outlet for Jewish expression and strengthened the community's sense of common purpose. They also kept their administrative costs low and were very effective in raising money from a Jewish community that was only modestly affluent at the time.

Economic Assimilation and Communal Organizations

While time-intensive Jewish religious traditions had trouble competing with secular activities (that is, Americanization), many immigrants expressed their Judaism primarily by supporting Jewish cultural and parareligious organizations. The immigrant community's inattention to religion was partly the result of self-selection: People strongly attached to traditional religion in the old country were leery of the presumed "decadence" in America, while those who chafed at religious strictures sought the freedom that America promised. The presence of a thriving parareligious and secular culture probably undermined religious observance in the Jewish enclaves. Immigrants whose friends, neighbors, and co-workers were mostly other Jews could express their Jewish identity not only by religious observance per se but also by participating in these other Jewish activities. In contrast to religious observance, which diverted time and money from other goals, Jewish parareligious organizations facilitated assimilation into the American economic, social, and political culture even for those living in a Jewish enclave.

The number and variety of cultural and parareligious organizations in the immigrant Jewish community was truly impressive. Rapid upward mobility of American Jews, however, led to changes in the community itself and therefore in its support for these organizations. Those concerned primarily with Americanization simply became obsolete. Others lost their constituencies as non-Jewish institutions became more hospitable to Jews and as governments began providing more social services. Many Jewish organizations began to serve non-Jewish constituencies, in part because of shrinking Jewish neediness and in part because of new antidiscrimination laws. All of them faced rising costs as they competed for staff whose other earning opportunities were increasingly in high-wage occupations.

Changes in the Value of Time

The full cost of running any organization includes the value of time, even for volunteer workers, as well as the wages of employees. As immigrant men responded to economic incentives in the United States, their time became increasingly expensive. Jewish women, however, faced lower wages and fewer labor market opportunities, especially because they typically withdrew from the labor force when they became mothers. The immigrant community responded by substituting female for male labor in most of its parareligious functions. As their children grew older and their husband's income rose, Jewish women joined fund-raising organizations, worked for charities as volunteers, and found jobs in Jewish communal service. Jewish women also became teachers in Jewish schools, another traditionally male role.

Substituting for men in communal service organizations and synagogue offices gave married Jewish women important career opportunities. They may have earned little or no money for their families, but the work experience increased their American human capital. It also established a family pattern in which women with school-age children could work outside the home, mostly in white-collar occupations, perhaps part-time but often full-time when their children were older. Immigrant Jewish women in communal service roles became models for their second-generation daughters, who sought careers in the labor force, and for their sons whose future wives would have similar ambitions.

In later decades American Jewish women would have higher levels of education and better job opportunities, making their time more valuable and hence volunteerism more costly. Many Jewish organizations—including synagogues—responded to this shortage by hiring non-Jewish employees. They could do this most readily for jobs requiring secular rather than religious skills, and in charitable organizations whose clientele was increasingly composed of non-Jews. Yet each shift in the workforce composition—first from Jewish men to Jewish women and then from Jews to non-Jews—affected the way American Jews understood the very Jewishness of their communal institutions.

Changes in Communal Support

The many communal organizations—religious, parareligious, and cultural—in the immigrant Jewish neighborhoods were supported by donations of both time (volunteerism) and money. Some of this support came from high-income German and Sephardic Jews through the organizations that they had founded earlier, but much of it came from the low-income Yiddish-speaking immigrants as part of their Americanization effort. As their economic situation improved, however, the immigrants developed new patterns of giving. They retained a strong commitment to Jewish communal service, reinforced by gratitude for the help they had received from parareligious organizations during their own adjustment process. In their support for religious and parareligious organizations, however, they gave far more generously of their money than their time, a reflection of the rising full cost of volunteering as education and wage rates rose over time. They were strongly committed to religious freedom, supporting (again, with money more than time) the new "American" synagogues even as the old-country immigrant congregations withered from neglect. Their giving also extended beyond the Jewish community as non-Jewish educational, medical, and cultural institutions increasingly changed policy and opened their doors to Jewish clients and (especially) patrons.

Many communal organizations that served Jewish immigrants in the past still operate today. Some of these have lost their Jewish focus, shifting their attention to needy non-Jews if not declining in importance entirely. The most successful, however, were able to adapt their mission to the needs of a nonimmigrant Jewish community. Schools, nursing homes, and Jewish Community Centers moved to the suburbs and now provide the modern facilities demanded by upper-middle-class families. An identity-building Israel Experience, often subsidized by the community, has become a new rite-of-passage for Jewish youth with spillover effects for their parents and for Jewish tourism in general. Whether they originated with the immigrants or were formed in later years, however, today's American Jewish communal institutions are an important part of our immigrant heritage.

These changes in Jewish support for communal institutions were more than just responses to changing economic circumstances because they altered the very identity of American Jewry. The decline of Jewish-specific parareligious and cultural organizations as a dominant aspect of the American Jewish experience contributed to a blurring of boundaries between Jews and non-Jews and a loss of the community's sense of its own distinctiveness. There was a time when American parareligious organizations and synagogue movements distinguished American Jewry from other Jewish communities around the world. This distinctiveness remains even today, but is declining as economic development in Israel and elsewhere gives rise to a convergence of economic conditions among Jews in every country.

The Immigrant Legacy of American Judaism

Jews were only one of the many immigrant groups assimilating into a larger American society in the late nineteenth century and throughout the twentieth century. American society itself was constantly changing during this period as more and more people attained higher education and as economic development transformed the economy. The Americanization of Jewish immigrants also occurred within the context of larger events affecting the entire community. In the first half of the twentieth century the United States instituted severe immigration restrictions, experienced the Great Depression, and fought in two world wars. The loss of so much of European Jewry in the Holocaust had a large emotional impact on American Jewry, increasing their sense of urgency for preserving the Jewish heritage and especially for acquiring Jewish knowledge.

The subsequent establishment of the State of Israel in 1948 also helped shift the American Jewish self-image from old-country victims to new-country success stories.

American Jewish institutions tried from the beginning to counteract—at least partially—the decline in Jewish human capital intrinsic to the immigrant adjustment process. Communal institutions supported immigrants socially and politically as well as economically, strengthening bonds of Jewish identity that might otherwise have disappeared with the loss of religious tradition. The American synagogue movements developed ways to practice Judaism without large investments in traditional religious human capital, and in the process they developed new forms of Jewish human capital consistent with the educational background of American Jews. Perhaps most dramatically, the emergence of a vibrant Jewish community in Israel moved the Hebrew language out of the exclusive province of religion and religious scholars to become—along with English—the common language of the Jewish people.

The Ashkenazi Judaism of Russian immigrants remains an important part of the American Jewish heritage. It is not, however, American Judaism. Like most American Jews of my generation, I have outlived my immigrant grandparents and my second-generation parents. We are now the third-generation parents of our fourth-generation American children and the grandparents of their fifth-generation children. Despite the more recent arrivals of smaller waves of Jewish immigrants, the overwhelming majority of American Jewish families have no members with direct experience of Ashkenazi Europe. While we learn about our immigrant forebears and their religious customs as part of our heritage, our own religious customs are distinctively American.

In the United States, the twentieth century was a period of transition between the traditional Ashkenazi Judaism of nineteenth-century Europe and American Judaism as it emerges in the twenty-first century. The way in which this transition played itself out was influenced by the economic circumstances in which the immigrants and their descendents found themselves. Dramatic and persistent increases in the value of time—approximated by the difference between hourly earnings in the old country and the new, augmented by increases in American economic development and Jewish educational attainment—induced them to replace time-intensive religious customs with other, less time-intensive expressions even if these might be more expensive in money outlays. Rising income levels meant that people could afford to spend more resources—both time and money—on Jewish activities and institutions. The economic incentives for change are now greatly reduced. High levels of education, wages, and incomes have persisted for at least two generations and show no signs of dramatic change in the near future. In contrast to the twentieth-century experience of our immigrant forebears, twenty-first-century changes in American Judaism will probably be dominated by different sets of economic conditions. The final chapter in this book will take a look at the impact that today's economy may have on the Jewish community during the next few decades.

Before leaving this chapter, we should note that Judaism and Jewish observance were changing throughout the twentieth century even outside of the United States. Judaism is still very "traditional" only in countries where well-educated, high-income Jews live in a small enclave community among their less-educated compatriots. Less wealthy Jewish communities, however, were affected by the economic transformations occurring everywhere during the twentieth century. Modernization and economic development raised real wages and incomes in many countries, increasing the value of time and discouraging time-intensive religious customs. As a result, Conservative and Reform Judaism (and their indigenous counterparts) gained ground among European Jews during the early decades of the century, cut short only by the destruction of much of European Jewry in the Holocaust. Today, Israel's economic development is having a similar impact on the religious practices of Israeli Jews. Conservative and Reform synagogues in Israel (and their indigenous Israeli counterparts) are beginning to influence Jewish religious behavior in that country. Although often referred to as "Americanization," the immigrant experience described in this chapter suggests that rising Israeli wage rates and incomes are the driving force underlying these changes in Israeli Judaism.

Part IV

Exchange and Change in American Judaism

7

Israel and American Judaism

WHENEVER I TRAVEL TO ISRAEL, I always enjoy visiting my Israeli cousins. Our grandparents were two of eight brothers in the part of tsarist Russia that would later become Poland. Four of these brothers (including my grandfather) migrated to the United States late in the nineteenth century and joined the upwardly mobile American Jewish community. The remaining brothers never left Poland, but two of their teenage children moved to British Mandate Palestine in the 1930s to join its immigrant Jewish community. Cousins on all three continents stayed in touch the old-fashioned way, writing snail-mail letters in any of the three languages (Yiddish, Hebrew, and English) that someone in the family could either read or have translated. Although none of our European cousins survived the Nazi Holocaust, the American and Israeli branches of the family remained intact and continue communicating with each other to this day, whether by telephone, by e-mail, or by personal visits.

The first time I met my Israeli cousins—second cousins, actually, but cousins nevertheless—was sixty years ago when we were still children. It was only a few years after Israel's War of Independence, and the country was still absorbing a huge inflow of Jewish refugees, first from war-torn Europe and then from the hostile Arab countries of North Africa and the Middle East. Israel's economy was that of an LDC (less-developed country), and living standards were correspondingly low. Our cousins lived in a *moshav* (cooperative settlement) where they raised grapes for the nearby winery. Six people (two parents and four children) lived in a two-room house that had recently been expanded by adding a bedroom for an elderly American aunt who had decided to join them. Although their semi-rural environment had many attractions, I remember being surprised by the crowded conditions, the poor heating (there was none), and a bathroom that seemed primitive to my American eyes.

What I did not fully grasp at the time was that my father's Israeli cousin and her husband were immigrants, just as my grandparents had been immigrants to the United States some fifty years earlier. The young couple spent their first years in British Mandate Palestine (as it was then called) investing in Israel-specific human capital, mainly the Hebrew language and farming skills. They also invested in Israel-specific Jewish human capital, emphasizing national rather than ritual aspects of Jewish culture, with on-site experiences that gave fresh meanings to the Jewish Scriptures. Our first visit to them came during the upward-mobility phase of their adjustment period, while they were still working long hours to build an economic base in their new home. Twenty years later my Israeli second cousins would have university degrees, work in professional occupations, and have middle-class families of their own. Despite the marked differences between Israel and the United States, and between their childhood and mine, my cousins' children and our children grew up in similar economic circumstances and now enjoy a similar standard of living.

Zionism and Immigrant Adjustment in Israel

Immigrants to Palestine in the early decades of the twentieth century faced very different economic conditions than did immigrants to the United States. Before World War I, the land of Israel was a stagnant backwater of the Ottoman Empire; between WWI and 1948 it belonged to the League of Nations Mandate of Palestine, administered by Great Britain. Its labor force had little education; its urban centers were mainly collections of small shops; and most of its population farmed the land with antiquated technologies. Its economic infrastructure was poorly developed, the pace of modernization was—at best—slow, and the British Mandate government's ambitions for economic development in this region were low.

Country-Specific Human Capital

During the early decades of the twentieth century Israel's economic environment was so different from that of Europe and Russia that most of its Jewish immigrants had little transferable human capital other than their entrepreneurial skill. They began by working as unskilled laborers while investing in unfamiliar skills that would be useful in their new country. The economy that they faced, however, was not an economy into which they wished to integrate. Its agriculture was poor and antiquated. Manufacturing establishments were small shops using old technologies. Its cities were ancient, with few modern conveniences and even fewer cultural attractions. Its Arab population resisted living and working side by side with Europeans in general, but especially with Zionist Jews. Everything that worked in the United States to encourage immigrant assimilation seemed to be the opposite in prestate Israel.

Secular Jewish Human Capital

Faced with this situation, the immigrants used their Zionist ideology to create a new economic enclave within the larger environment. If they viewed themselves as returning to the land itself, they invested in land and made it suitable for modern agriculture. If they viewed themselves as laborers, they would build factories to manufacture modern machinery and consumer goods. If they admired the principles of socialism, they would live on collective farms and form institutions for collective ownership of factories and infrastructure. If they craved the benefits of Western culture, they would establish schools and hospitals, theaters and publishing houses, everything to stimulate healthy minds in healthy bodies. If they wanted to establish a new Jewish culture in the Promised Land, they would revive Hebrew as their national language and use their knowledge of Scriptures to identify places and rituals connecting them to their ancient roots. If they wanted freedom from the violence experienced in the old country, with a degree of security greater than that provided by the Ottoman and later the British Mandate governments, they would organize militias to defend themselves from physical attack.

Most of these institutions began early in the twentieth century, but they matured during the interwar period (that is, between WWI and WWII) when Israel was part of British Palestine. A new, larger wave of immigrants also arrived during this period, in part because the United States had virtually closed its doors to new arrivals from Central and Eastern Europe and in part because conditions of life were rapidly deteriorating for European Jewry. When my father's cousins arrived during this period, the fledgling Jewish economy was still in its formative years but was nevertheless one into which they could assimilate. The country-specific skills in which they invested were the skills of this new Zionist economy. The same human capital investments that would lead to their own upward economic mobility would also create the economic, social, and political institutions of what would later (in 1948) become the State of Israel.

Coping with Mass Immigration

Israel's immigrants would follow the usual path to economic assimilation, beginning by learning Hebrew and acquiring other basic country-specific skills, followed by a period of hard work and upward mobility. The pattern in Israel was complicated, however, by the arrival of immigrants in huge waves. In 1951, for example, more than half of Israel's Jewish population had been in the country five years or less, most of them in the very first phases of immigrant adjustment. (By way of comparison, even during peak years recent immigrants to America never exceeded 14 percent of the U.S. population.) About half of the new immigrants were refugees from war-torn Europe, mostly Ashkenazi Jews who had survived the Nazi Holocaust one way or another. The other half were refugees from Arab lands in the Middle East and North Africa, most of whom were Sephardi (whose religious culture originated with Spanish exiles in 1492) or *Mizrachi* (in the tradition of Babylonian Jewry). Few of these immigrants arrived with any means of support, with transferable human capital (that is, skills for the Israeli economy), or with fluency in modern Hebrew. All of them had immediate needs for food and housing, items already in such short supply that they were severely rationed.

Large numbers of immigrants from the same background typically form enclaves in the new country in which they can use some of their old-country-specific human capital. However, an enclave shelters newcomers from exposure to new-country-specific skills, slowing down their absorption into the larger economy and sometimes avoiding it altogether. To prevent this, Israelis developed some new institutions to facilitate rapid assimilation of new immigrants from different backgrounds. *Ma'abarot* (temporary absorption centers, mostly tent cities) sprang up all over the landscape to house the new arrivals. Intensive Hebrew classes used the newly developed *ulpan* method, intensive language instruction designed to familiarize immigrants with the idioms and customs of daily life in Israel. Doctors and nurses staffed clinics in the *ma'abarot*. Women were taught modern Western ideas about health, nutrition, food preparation, and child care. Men without marketable modern skills received training, often for jobs in a construction industry struggling to relieve the severe housing shortage. In only a few years the new immigrants acquired enough Israel-specific human capital to move out of the *ma'abarot* and begin building their own economic success stories.

There has never been a year since then when Israel did not receive immigrants from a variety of backgrounds. There have also been periods of mass immigrations from particular communities, although none was as large relative to the Israeli population—or so swamped the domestic economy—as those first post-Independence waves. During the 1970s and 1980s North American immigrants arrived in substantial numbers. A few years later Israel received a wave of Jewish refugees from Ethiopia and a much larger wave from the former Soviet Union. By then the absorption centers were apartment houses rather than tent cities, the *ulpan* method seemed less revolutionary, and the professional staff was more experienced at adapting to the needs of each group of immigrants. To this day, Israel's institutions continue working with new immigrants to facilitate investments in Israel-specific human capital.

International Institutions for Investments in Israel

American Jewish communal institutions helped in the effort to settle refugees in the new Jewish State of Israel. (They also helped immigrants adjust to life in the United States, but by 1924 the United States had begun four closed-door decades of severely limited immigration.) The Joint Distribution Committee (JDC, known also as "The Joint") was especially active, its primary mission being to rescue Jewish communities in distress. The primary mission of Hadassah, an extremely popular and influential organization of American Jewish women, was to provide public health and medical services to Israelis in general, and Hadassah doctors and nurses were especially active in the *ma'abarot*. Each of America's Zionist organizations contributed in its own way, and many synagogues worked to send food, clothing, and money to the refugees in Israel.

Financial contributions from Diaspora Jewry, especially from the United States, combined with the labor of Israel's citizens to produce a remarkably successful effort to absorb new immigrants into the new country. These efforts were largely coordinated by the Jewish Agency for Israel (formerly the Jewish Agency for Palestine), a sort of clearing house for the joint activities of World Jewry. American Jews would be represented by their relevant parareligious communal organizations. Israeli Jews would be represented by their relevant collective institutions, which after independence would become either part of the Israeli government or semi-independent parastate organizations. Financial support for the Jewish Agency would thus come partly from voluntary contributions by American Jews (raised by the United Jewish Appeal) and partly from tax-supported revenues supplied by the government of Israel.

Judaism in Israel and the United States

In the United States, most religious institutions are congregational. This means that synagogues, like most churches and other places of worship, are founded, financed, and managed by their congregants. Synagogues are run by officers and a board of directors, typically laypeople elected by the congregation's members. The synagogue board and its officers hire—and fire—clergy (typically a rabbi and a cantor) to lead congregational prayers and provide pastoral services as needed, an executive director to manage the day-to-day operations of the synagogue, and an educational director to run the synagogue's Hebrew school. The synagogue's budget, including salaries for the clergy and other employees, is financed entirely by its members, who pay annual dues supplemented by voluntary contributions solicited by various fund-raising activities during the course of the year. Many synagogues establish a cemetery, or consecrate a section of a larger cemetery, which they finance by selling burial plots to their members. Synagogues typically join an umbrella organization, like the Union of Reform Judaism (URJ, previously UAHC), United Synagogue of Conservative Judaism (USCJ, formerly USA), or the Orthodox Union (OU). These organizations provide useful services and a national religious leadership, but membership in them is completely voluntary and synagogue governance remains entirely with the congregation.

Israel also has some synagogues that are similarly congregational, but most are organized very differently. Israel's government has a Ministry of Religious Services that grants monopoly "licenses" to representatives of several religious groups, including the Muslim, Christian, Druze, and Bahai, as well as the Jewish community. Jewish religious affairs are the responsibility of a central Board of Rabbis, composed exclusively of Ashkenazi (Orthodox) and Sephardi (also Orthodox) representatives who elect a chief rabbi from among their members. This central board is aided by local religious councils funded jointly by municipalities and the Ministry of Religious Services, but the central board must approve the appointment of municipal rabbis as well as any synagogues, schools, charities, and clinics to which the Ministry gives financial support. Local religious councils thus face clear economic incentives to follow the religious directives of the central rabbinate and the administrative guidelines set by the Ministry.

The considerable power exercised by the central Board of Rabbis derives from the fact that the government of Israel recognizes them—and only them—as the highest religious authorities for Israel's Jews. This effectively grants the Orthodox establishment a monopoly over religious matters in the Jewish community, including family law in a country where civil authority does not cover this area. Local religious councils have the legal power to register Jewish marriages in Israel, but the chief rabbi and the central board decide which rabbis may perform those marriages. The Board of Rabbis also manages a central Rabbinical Court, with exclusive power for Jewish conversions, and a dozen other Rabbinical Courts with absolute authority over Jewish divorces. Local councils manage the ritual baths (*mikva*) within their municipal boundaries, but the central religious authority oversees a network of kosher supervisors, determines who may be buried in a Jewish cemetery, and responds to queries on religious matters from Jews around the world.

Monopoly versus Competition in the Religious Marketplace

In earlier chapters we saw how economic circumstances create incentives that affect the religious behaviors of individuals and the shape of communal institutions. Throughout the twentieth century, as American Jewish immigrants found their economic niches and as the U.S. experienced rapid economic development, wage rates rose dramatically, time-intensive activities became more costly, and American Jewry developed less time-intensive patterns of religious observance. For some people this led to secularization of Jewish life, but for most it meant joining a Reform or Conservative synagogue congregation and supporting Jewish parareligious communal organizations.

Israeli Jews were also immigrants with rising wage rates, and Israel also experienced rapid economic development, so we can imagine that time-intensive religious traditions were becoming increasingly costly for them as well. Yet because synagogues in Israel were established—and clergy hired—by the central Rabbinate instead of their congregants, Israeli Jews did not have the flexibility of their American cousins when it came to changing synagogue practices or establishing new congregations. After the destruction of European Jewry, the Israeli Rabbinate focused on preserving older religious traditions and showed less interest in adapting to modern times. Like many monopolists, they also took a "take-it-or-leave-it" attitude that discouraged independent innovation in religious matters. As wage rates rose and time-intensive traditions became more costly, Israel's highly educated high-wage Jews increasingly neglected the synagogues except for special occasions.

Although synagogue attendance may be low among educated Israeli Jews, Jewish expression typically emerges in the form of Zionism and nation building. Israelis have also developed forms of Jewish human capital highly complementary to their secular knowledge of history, geography, literature, and the arts. Israelis speak modern Hebrew as their mother tongue, so learning to read from Torah and the other religious classics is far less difficult—and less time intensive—than for their American cousins. Israelis live and work in the very places described in Scriptures, so biblical stories resonate as the history of their native land. Archaeology has brought modern scholarship to bear on this history, connecting past and present in a spiritually meaningful way. Because this innovative approach to religious expression typically occurs outside the synagogue and beyond the scope of the official Rabbinate, Israelis often describe it as "secular" Judaism despite its intrinsic religious content.

Many of the differences between Jewish religious observance in Israel and the United States derive from differences between the two countries in their respective "Church–State" relationships. In the United States, where government takes a laissez-faire approach to religion, Judaism is defined by its adherents, synagogues display a great deal of diversity, and the extremes—that is, the ultra-Orthodox and the ultra-secular—are relatively small. In Israel, where government confers monopoly power to a religious establishment, Judaism is defined by the official Rabbinate, few synagogues accommodate the religious interests of the majority, and a much larger proportion of the population is either extremely traditional or extremely nonobservant.

Jewish communal institutions and parareligious organizations, so vital a part of American Jewish life, are virtually absent in Israel, where most of their functions are performed by the Rabbinate or by the government itself. The official Rabbinate also functions as a lobby group on behalf of its own version of religious Judaism. Unlike the United States, where government is constrained from supporting any religious establishment, Israel's government determines not only the amount of resources allocated to the Rabbinate but also the degree to which it will use the power of the State to enforce a religious monopoly. This provides a substantial economic incentive for the religious establishment to influence government policy. It does so not only by advocacy for particular causes but also by supporting "religious" political parties that field candidates for parliament as well as for cabinet ministries. In close parliamentary elections (of which there have been many), Israel's religious parties often have determined which major party could form a government, thus exerting a strong political influence disproportionate to their representation in the electorate.

International Migration and Exchange of Human Capital

We noted in an earlier chapter that some human capital is country specific and some is transferable across national boundaries. The same is true of religious human capital. Some new forms of religious human capital developed in Israel during the twentieth century are specific to that country, and some are transferable to Jewish communities elsewhere in the world. American Jews import the transferable religious human capital by integrating Israeli language (modern Hebrew, including slang), music, art, and culture into their own culture, whether in the home, the synagogue, the Hebrew school, the youth movements, or the Jewish summer camps. They also import Israel-specific human capital with what has become known as an Israel Experience, visiting that country as tourists, students, or even temporary residents. Israeli Jews have also been influenced by American Judaism, whether through a process of "Americanization" in Israel or by experiences acquired while visiting the United States.

This implicit trade with Israel in religious human capital is now a staple of American Jewish life. Consider, for example, how the Hebrew language is taught in American Hebrew schools. In my youth the typical Hebrew teacher spoke with a heavy Ashkenazi accent and was literate mainly in the language of prayer and Torah. By the time my children went to Hebrew school, the teachers spoke with the Sephardi accent used in Israel and taught vocabulary drawn from secular as well as religious subjects. Today's Hebrew schools use textbooks, music, art, and activities heavily influenced by Israeli culture. The teachers are either native

Hebrew speakers or Americans who have learned the language either in Israel or from Israeli teachers in America. Jewish camps integrate spoken Hebrew into their daily experience, and many youth groups sponsor trips to Israel for teenagers and young adults. In recent decades an "Israel Experience"—lasting anywhere from a ten-day tour to a full school year—has become part of a typical American youth's Jewish education.

An important reason why this interchange has been so lively—and so mutually beneficial—is that changes in economic incentives have been very similar in the two countries. During the course of the twentieth century, Israeli and American Jews both experienced rising levels of education, wage rates, and incomes. These changes transformed the incentives of American Jews early in the century and Israeli Jews some fifty years later, but by now the similarities are striking. Important differences remain in their secular environments, especially with regard to the fraction of Jews in the general population and with regard to security issues in the two countries, and these differences affect the way economic circumstances influence religious institutions. Israel's Orthodox monopoly on formal Jewish institutions also limits religious innovations to an "informal" sector, in contrast to the wide variety of American Jewish religious institutions. Yet both American and Israeli Jews have found time-saving forms of religious expression, and both have adapted Jewish education to take advantage of complementarities between religious and secular human capital.

Israel's Impact on American Judaism

As we have seen, Jewish immigrants found their place in the American economy early in the twentieth century and succeeded in moving up the socioeconomic ladder within a few decades. Jewish immigrants to Israel followed a similar economic path some fifty years later. Each community experienced similar changes in their economic environment that affected religious practices, but at different times and different rates. The relationship between the two communities changed as well, responding to new economic circumstances in each country relative to the other. The effect of Israel on Judaism in America is different for my children's generation than it has been for people my age, and its effect on my generation is in turn very different than it was for my parents.

Understanding the influence of changing economic circumstances can help us understand generational differences in how we perceive Israel's importance for American Judaism.

Israel's Early Years

When my parents were young, the Jewish community in Israel (then governed by the British) was innovating new ways of expressing Jewish peoplehood, building a modern economy, and providing a homeland for Jews experiencing religious persecution in their native lands. Although some American Jews were inspired to participate in this process by moving to Israel, most were still focused on becoming Americans. Israel was a land of hardship, both economic and political, while the United States promised freedom for American Jews to prosper and for Judaism to flourish. Most American Zionists in the interwar period contributed to the creation of a Jewish homeland with financial assistance and political support, viewing it as a solution to the increasingly urgent needs of European Jewry in an era of largely closed-door immigration throughout the Western world.

By the time I was young the situation was quite different from that of my parents' youth. The State of Israel was an independent country struggling with militant enemies on its borders and hordes of Jewish refugees at home. Meanwhile we Americans were already comfortably middle class, although there were still undercurrents of anti-Semitism in housing covenants, in the admission and hiring policies of some colleges and universities, in some parts of the business world, and in McCarthy-era politics. American Jews were skittish about charges of dual loyalty (that is, to Israel and to the United States) and thus careful to avoid involvement in Israel's politics, including its wars with the Arabs. Yet we could support Israel in its domestic activities on behalf of world Jewry. We gave money for refugee resettlement and absorption, we bought Israel's government bonds so that economic development could proceed despite its wars, and we contributed our nickels and dimes to plant trees and forests that would transform Israel's ecology in a matter of decades.

My father's job gave our family an early "Israel Experience" when we lived for a year in Israel about five years after the country became independent. Israel seemed very underdeveloped to my childish American eyes, although I later realized that its living conditions were almost as good as those in post-WWII Europe. Security was also a problem, especially near the border (which ran through the middle of Jerusalem, where we lived). There seemed to be cross-border incursions daily—sometimes raiders crossing the Egyptian border to pilfer irrigation pipes from Israeli fields, sometimes Arab rifles sniping at children who strayed near the border—occasionally punctuated by out-and-out military battles. At that time there were few American Jews living in Israel and even fewer American tourists, so we were something of a novelty. Israelis were eager to show us the nation they were building and the many ways in which Jewish expression flourished in the old-new country. When we returned to the United States, our Jewish neighbors were just as eager to learn how things were going in Israel and hear about our firsthand experiences. Although American Jews continued to support Zionist causes, and tourism to Israel would increase as foreign travel became more common, throughout my youth those of us who had actually visited Israel remained a tiny minority within the Jewish community.

The Six-Day War

In June 1967, Israel's Six-Day War marked a dramatic change in its relationship with its Arab neighbors, in its diplomatic relationship with other countries, and in its relationship with American Jewry. Many older American Jews still remember the emotional roller-coaster experienced during the entire spring of 1967. Israel's security situation had always been difficult, but that year it had become much worse. The Soviet Union had supplied a modern arsenal to Israel's Arab enemies, whose armies far outnumbered Israel's. Arab rhetoric became more and more belligerent, promising Israel's Jews—all those refugees who thought they had found safe haven—nothing short of a bloodbath. Just two short decades after the Holocaust, Jews again faced the prospect of genocide.

We also faced the threat that Israel might cease its existence as a Jewish State. Even many American Jews who had not considered themselves Zionist found this possibility appalling, an indication of how fully Israel had become part of the very identity of modern Jewry. When war actually broke out in June, American Jews expressed their solidarity with Israel, and their concern for its safety, with an outpouring of generosity that defied all expectations. Our relief over Israel's decisive military victory was expressed by mass euphoria. From that time onward, we recognized explicitly that Zionism (in the sense of support for Israel's existence as an independent country and homeland for the Jewish People) had become the norm for the American Jewish community and its institutions.

The Six-Day War changed Israel's borders, making security easier to enforce and thus Israel as a country much safer to live in and to visit. (There would be different security problems in later decades, but they would not change the fundamental issues we are discussing here.) These border changes also opened for the first time since 1947 all parts of the country barred to Jews while under Jordanian rule, dramatically reducing travel times and stimulating domestic travel. Jews could again enter the ancient city of Jerusalem, live in its Jewish Quarter, visit the Temple Mount, and pray at its Western Wall. These two changes—increased security and easy access to holy sites—made life in Israel more comfortable and made it possible to develop an even more thriving tourist industry. They also stimulated a dramatic increase in Diaspora Jewish travel to Israel, whether permanent migration, a yearlong educational experience, or short-term tourism. As already noted, this has been a major factor in the evolution of today's American Judaism.

The Six-Day War clearly marked the emergence of Israel as a technologically advanced modern economy. Of course this did not happen overnight but had been developing over the previous decades without being noticed. We American Jews had bought Israel Bonds for economic development, but we didn't pay much attention to how effectively Israel used our loans. We also helped support Israeli universities and technical schools, the graduates of which were now providing technical skills to the Israeli economy. We knew that security problems required nearly every Israeli Jew to serve in the army or in the reserves, but we didn't fully realize that this implied a military with the same sophisticated human capital as the civilian labor force. The exhilaration felt by American Jews after the Six-Day War came not only from emotional relief because of the military success per se, but also from the awesome sense that our contributions had helped make this happen.

By 1967 American Jews had already achieved substantial economic success and made important contributions to the arts, to science, and to business. Yet Israel's vulnerability during its first two decades reinforced old stereotypes of Jews as victims, weaklings, and underdogs. Even its military success in the War of Independence (1948) and in the Sinai Campaign (1956) were seen as "miracles," flukes that did not change the basic nature of things. The Six-Day War put that myth to rest. Israel had become an economically developed country; its people were technologically and culturally sophisticated; and its military defenses operated with finesse. American Jews realized that Israelis were no longer poor relations desperately in need of charitable largesse. They had become a proud Jewish nation, and in so doing they enhanced our own pride as members of the Jewish People.

Israel's Place in Today's American Judaism

Israeli culture is now thoroughly woven into Jewish education and religious life in the United States. Marriages between Israelis and Americans have greatly increased the family ties between the two communities. The Reform, Conservative, and Reconstructionist synagogue movements celebrate Israel's Independence Day on the religious calendar and incorporate a prayer for the State of Israel in the synagogue liturgy immediately following the prayer for our own country. An Israel Experience trip is rapidly becoming a rite of passage that complements an American Jewish religious education. Many young Americans today see Israeli Jewish lifestyles as legitimate alternatives to the varieties available in the United States.

One day our older son came home from college and announced that he wanted to move to Israel with some of his friends. This came as a surprise to us, but perhaps it shouldn't have. Growing up decades after the Six-Day War, Jews of his generation have little of the emotional baggage or even fears still evident among their elders. They can follow their chosen career path as easily in Israel as in the United States, so that is usually not a major factor in their migration decisions. Our son and his friends wanted to live in a place where Jewish observance is well integrated into society's mainstream, a place where they could live the

Zionist dream updated for today's economic environment. Accustomed to a variety of Jewish lifestyles in pluralistic America, they saw Israel's religious lifestyles not as an alternative but rather as an expansion of their Jewish options. Like many Americans today, Jews raised in a religious lifestyle chosen by their parents may change as adults to another one more in keeping with their own preferences (and, of course, costs).

Our son is now an American-Israeli, part of an Israeli ethnic group made up of American (mostly Jewish) immigrants. Some American-Israelis immigrated as young singles, while others moved as a family unit. Some immigrated as children with their parents, others because they married an Israeli citizen, and still others after retirement from an American career. Although no longer part of the American Jewish community, most American-Israelis continue to have strong ties with parents, children, siblings, cousins, friends, and colleagues in the United States.

Israeli-Americans form a similar ethnic group composed of Israeli immigrants to the United States. Israeli-Americans are often very secular or very observant, but both of these extremes have American counterparts to which the immigrants can assimilate. Similarities between our two countries in economic life—especially technology and education—stimulate an active two-way movement of students, teachers, scientists, artists, and businesspeople, as well as tourists eager to experience life in each other's country. The cousins whom I met as a child still live in Israel, but all have spent time in the United States either professionally or as tourists, and they have many American friends and (of course) relatives. Americans now have many opportunities to meet individual Israelis, thus enhancing the personal connections between American Jews and Israel.

Israeli Religious Politics and American Judaism

American synagogue movements have also strengthened their connections with Israel. Many American-Israelis are Orthodox, comfortable with the Judaism protected by the official Rabbinate. Others prefer non-Orthodox lifestyles and establish Reform, Conservative, and Reconstructionist congregations, most of which are egalitarian (that is, they welcome both women and men in ritual roles). The Israeli Rabbinate resists all of these non-Orthodox innovations as illegitimate forms of Judaism, refusing to legitimize their clergy or support their synagogues. In response, non-Orthodox American synagogue movements have subsidized Israeli congregations, providing them with clergy and establishing rabbinic seminaries in Israel. These so-called American congregations also attract Israelis of many backgrounds, especially high-wage people trying to reconcile religious observance with competing uses of time. The non-Orthodox movements in Israel are still small, but they are growing and are challenging the Rabbinate for official recognition and support. They are also pressuring for women's rights to conduct full religious rituals in public, most notably at the Western Wall in Jerusalem.

Many Israelis, frustrated by the chief rabbis' monopoly control over family matters (especially marriage, divorce, and burial), feel the problem would be solved by introducing a civil law alternative for all its citizens. Some want to break the religious monopoly of the Orthodox establishment by officially recognizing the non-Orthodox movements, whether within the current Rabbinate or by adding a separate Rabbinate for each new synagogue movement. At some point, however, proliferation of religious establishments would become cumbersome, if not inefficient, so some people argue that the Israeli government should follow the American precedent and divest itself of all control of religion and religious matters.

As American Jews acquire more experience with Israel—whether firsthand, by personal connections, or through the activities of religious and parareligious communal organizations—they become more involved in what is essentially a domestic Israeli political controversy over the church–state relationship. Yet American Jews have a strong stake in the outcome, for it actually comes down to the very nature of Judaism in a Jewish state. If Israel is to be a homeland for all Jews everywhere, American Jews want respect for our modern Jewish religious heritage. American Judaism has been deeply affected by the very fact of Israel as an independent Jewish State and by the Jewish religious cultures that have evolved there as Israel has advanced to its current economic status as a high-technology country. Israel's influence on American Judaism in the coming decades will depend in part on how it resolves these religious issues.

Israel's Security and American Judaism

Israel's security, and its integrity as a Jewish country, pose other dilemmas that its citizens must decide at the ballot box. Yet American Jews have a large stake in these outcomes as well. We want Israel to continue to be there for us, contributing richness to the Jewish culture of the American society to which we belong. Because we are Americans, and because we are Jews, we feel free—even obligated—to express our political opinions passionately. If we think Israel's political decisions will undermine its strength as a Jewish state, we say so. We do not face the physical threats that Israelis must live with, nor do we have their military experience, which is why the decisions must ultimately be theirs. Yet we do have the perspective of distance, providing insights that might not be apparent close by. American Jews can be passionate supporters of Israel's continued security even if they sometimes seem to be arguing against some policies of the Israeli government.

Many of us also see the hostility of Israel's enemies as modern forms of anti-Semitism, focusing on Israel as the national embodiment of Jews and Judaism. Arab neighbors may have a real dispute with Israel over territorial boundaries, but the intensity of hatred directed toward Jews is fed by explicitly anti-Semitic propaganda developed in tsarist Russia and Nazi Germany. Anti-Semitism is also reappearing in Europe in new forms, sometimes by attempts to outlaw Jewish religious practices like *brit milah* (infant male circumcision) and kashrut (especially the ritual slaughter requirements for meat), sometimes by anti-Jewish vandalism or outright violence, and sometimes by supporting the delegitimization of the Jewish State of Israel. As one commentator recently observed, "Death to the Jews" is not a legitimate political slogan in any democratic society.

War, terrorism, and intractable territorial disputes are an integral part of Israeli life. Despite the way these factors dominate the international news, however, they are more like a subtext in Israel's story today. Israeli Jews—and many American Jews—are acutely aware of these dangers and work hard to deal with them effectively. Yet perhaps the greatest achievement of all is that this existential threat does not dominate daily life in Israel. The major themes of Israeli life are family, community, education, technology, consumption, culture, and religion. Israel's achievements in these areas are impressive and well documented. These are also the main source of interactions between Israeli and American Jews.

Living a full, "normal" Jewish life even in the face of mortal danger is a fundamental Jewish value and an important survival trait for the Jewish People. Living for two millennia as a small minority in various parts of the world, often subject to discrimination if not outright persecution, Jews developed a culture that emphasizes living a full life despite these external threats. Jewish holiday observances often involve stories of such threats with lessons how to face them with integrity. This approach is so fundamental that Jews sometimes take it for granted, finding it difficult to understand why people from other cultures might choose other coping mechanisms. Judaism views external threats like anti-Semitism or hostility toward Israel as situations that must be faced and dealt with, but without distracting from the main purposes of a "normal" life.

Israel's success in this regard is an important contribution to the new Small Tradition of today's Judaism.

8

Whither American Judaism?

THIS BOOK EXPLORES HOW ECONOMIC INCENTIVES influence the religious activities of American Jews and hence the practice of Judaism in the United States. It does not look at the many personal preferences, family connections, and theological issues that we know are important factors affecting religious behaviors. Nor does it claim that economics determines the behavior of any one individual at a given time. Economic incentives provide a context within which individuals make decisions that, when aggregated, affect the group as a whole. The approach used in this book is not specific to Judaism and indeed can be applied to other faith groups in the United States and elsewhere. Yet looking at how economic conditions affected American Jews in the twentieth century has yielded important insights into the religious life of today's American Judaism. By the same token, current trends in economic conditions suggest how American Judaism may change in future decades.

Economic Choices and American Judaism

Part I sketched a brief portrait of American Judaism and Jewry at the turn of the twenty-first century. Chapter One presented the notion that we make our religious choices within an economic context, and it outlined the nature of American Judaism that would be the subject of

TABLE 8.1. *Economic principles used in this book.*

- *Prices and Incomes.* People usually buy more of a good if its price is lower and less if its price is higher. Whatever the price, people with high incomes can afford to buy more than people with low incomes, and they usually do.
- *Full prices.* The full price of a good is its money price plus the value of time spent buying and consuming it. The value of an hour of the consumer's time is approximated by the wage he or she would lose (or gain) by working an hour less (or more). This means that high-wage consumers pay a higher full price than low-wage consumers for the same good.
- *Self-produced goods.* People spend time and money on goods that can't be purchased in the marketplace. Examples of these self-produced goods include religion, family, and social life. Self-produced goods tend to be time intensive in that the value of time is a large proportion of their full price.
- *Human capital.* A person's human capital includes the acquired memories, skills, and knowledge that are part of his or her identity as a person. The more human capital a person has, the more of a self-produced good he or she can make with a limited amount of time and money.
- *Investment.* Human capital is formed by an investment process requiring time and money that might otherwise be spent on consumption. Human capital investments are made in school, in the family, in the neighborhood, in the community, and anywhere else that a person can learn something new about ideas, people, places, or things.
- *Complementarity and anticomplementarity.* Different kinds of human capital are relevant for different activities. Some kinds are mutually complementary, so that more of one increases the effectiveness of the other. Other kinds of human capital conflict with each other, so that more of one undermines the effectiveness of the other.

---

this book. Chapter Two portrayed the economic context of American Jews with data on their education, occupations, and incomes. Part II developed the basic economic concepts lying at the heart of this book, summarized here in Table 8.1. These concepts are few in number and generally applicable to every religious group, but, as we have seen, their implications for American Judaism are far reaching. Chapter Three looked at budgeting choices for both time and money, showing how the full price of religious observance is affected by the value of time as well as by money prices and incomes. Chapter Four presented the case that investments in religious human capital play a central role in Jewish religious culture and that the educational choices made by American Jews affect, and are affected by, their religious lifestyles in fundamental ways.

Part III used the economic concepts developed in Part II to focus on choices made by Jewish individuals and families. Chapter Five looked at the interrelated decisions affecting marriage, fertility, and child-rearing, long-term investment decisions made by private individuals but with profound implications for the Jewish community as a whole. Chapter Six looked at the economic adjustment of Jewish immigrants early in the twentieth century, showing how grassroots investment decisions made by an entire cohort shaped the religious practices and institutions of American Jews for several generations. In each of these chapters, the economic incentives faced by American Jews as individuals provided a context within which to view important developments in American Judaism.

Part IV steps back to consider economic forces affecting the community as a whole. In Chapter Seven, we compared and contrasted modern Judaism as it is practiced in Israel and the United States. The same economic principles influence the religious choices made by Israeli and American Jews, but differences in economic environments and legal institutions lead to different religious outcomes in the two countries. These differences form the basis of trade, a mutually beneficial exchange of ideas, skills, religious practices, and institutions between the world's two largest Jewish communities. In addition, the contrast between Judaism as an official state religion in Israel and Judaism in religiously pluralistic United States is analogous with the contrast between monopoly and competition in the business world. This analogy with competitive markets provides insights into the nature of Jewish communal institutions that affect the very identity of American Jewry, especially the diverse synagogue movements with their umbrella organizations and an impressive array of grassroots parareligious organizations.

Now, in Chapter Eight, we want to compare Jewish communities across time rather than across space. We understand something about the economic environment of American Jews at the turn of the twenty-first century and about the economic incentives that shaped the way they practice Judaism. By projecting how these incentives may change during the next few decades, we can focus our expectations for developments in the future of American Judaism. It is to this topic that we now turn.

The Changing American Economy

In some ways the twentieth-century American economy was unique. The United States led the world in technological innovation, causing historians to label it the "American Century." Wages for all workers rose to unprecedented levels, with an especially high premium for people in high-level occupations that required a college, university, or professional-school degree for entry. This was the source of the high rate of return on investment in secular schooling that so influenced American Jewry. By the end of the century, however, a new technology was emerging with implications that are still not fully clear. Electronics is at its heart; computerization and information technology are revolutionizing the world of work in ways that make some forms of education obsolete and others more valuable. Decoding the human genome and DNA analysis has implications for the medical profession, for health care in general, and for everyone's longevity. Economic incentives in this new technological era may differ from those in the past in ways that are still not fully evident.

The Economic Heritage of American Jewry

Although today's American Jews still work for a living, and most have careers in high-level white-collar occupations, many of them also have additional nonwage income to provide a financial cushion against hardship. Some common nonwage sources of income include interest and dividends from stocks, bonds, and savings accounts; intergenerational transfers and inheritances; scholarships, private pensions, and government-sponsored entitlements like Medicare and Social Security benefits. This means that many young Jews can afford to choose a low-wage career without necessarily resigning themselves to a life of poverty.

A generation ago Jewish women with low-paying careers in social work, elementary education, Jewish communal services, or parareligious organizations typically had a high-wage husband who supported the family in an upper-middle-class lifestyle. Today women in these occupations often marry men with a similar career and live in families with correspondingly lower total earnings. A century ago Jews with no resources other than their own human capital chose careers in sports, entertainment, and the arts—careers with a low probability of financial security—as a high-risk route to upward mobility. Today's Jews enter these fields because their resources give them the freedom to pursue the career of their choice. These careers can attract idealistic young people even with relatively low wages, in part because their parents can help them financially. Similarly, young couples who choose some of the ultra-Orthodox lifestyles, especially those who substitute intensive Torah studies for a high-level secular education, can afford to live beyond their means because of nonlabor income from parents, charities, and government-sponsored social programs.

Jews still place a high value on secular education, especially when compared to the average American of today. Virtually every Jewish youth has a high-school diploma and nearly all—male and female—graduate from college as well. Postcollege graduate studies, however, are not automatic. The doctorate and professional degrees are required for careers in university teaching, scientific research, and certain professions like medicine and law, but a master's-level degree (or its equivalent) can be sufficient for people with careers in business, computer science, social work, education, and public administration. In the mid-twentieth century, Jewish men tended to enter careers that required professional or doctoral-level degrees and women in careers that required a master's-level degree. By the beginning of the twenty-first century, as their occupational patterns converged, an increasing proportion of Jewish women are earning a doctorate or professional degree, even as an increasing proportion of Jewish men leave school with a master's-level degree.

Today's American Jewish community is also older than that of our grandparents because families now tend to have fewer children and because the elderly are generally healthier and live longer. Because the value of time varies over a person's life cycle in a typical pattern, this has implications for full prices and hence for Jewish observance in the future. The very young may have low wages, but the value of their time is higher than their actual wage because they are investing in education or on-the-job training, acquiring human capital that will raise their wage in the future. The more they learn, the more skilled they become, and the higher the wage they can eventually earn. Up to a point, therefore, wages rise as a person grows older. Investments in human capital usually taper off as adults enter their prime earning years, say ages forty to sixty-five, when wages are at their highest and are a good approximation of the value of time.

For senior citizens (which today usually means people over the age of sixty-five), retirement from the labor force means a large drop in the value of time. This is not because they lose their human capital but rather because their income comes mostly from nonwage sources—pensions, interest and dividends, government entitlements, or support from grown children. Unlike young people, whose low wages come from low productivity and do not fully measure the high value of time, retirees with low wages still have the human capital that makes them potentially very productive even though the cost of their time is much lower than before.

A New "Modern" Technology

Technological innovations during the last decades of the twentieth century included the introduction of robots in factories and hospitals; the use of high-speed computers by managers, doctors, police officers, and students; "smart" phones and wireless access to the Internet; and medical therapies derived from miniaturization, from new pharmaceuticals and surgeries, and from new knowledge about the human genome. These and other developments were more than mere improvements in how we did things; they changed the things we could actually do and thus affected the very nature of everyday life and economic activity. By the beginning of the twenty-first century every week seemed to bring a new technological innovation that raised productivity and promised economic growth for decades to come.

My own grandparents must have experienced something like this at the turn of the twentieth century, with the introduction of electricity, telephones, automobiles, and what was then modern medicine. The "new" economy of their lifetimes was a scientific revolution that privileged professional skills of all kinds and replaced unskilled labor with high-skilled production workers. Although the final results are not yet in, twenty-first-century technology has already begun to revolutionize business. Workers in the STEM occupations—science, technology, engineering, and mathematics—still find good jobs, but workers educated with other skills often have more difficulty.

Electronic communication and information technology allow relatively few managers to perform functions that were once the province of middle-level supervisory personnel, reducing costs in large-scale enterprises and the so-called big-box stores that are displacing small entrepreneurs. (The businesses that they are replacing are small only in the relative sense, themselves having long ago replaced the truly small "mom-and-pop" establishments of an earlier era.) On factory floors, robots do tasks once performed by semi-skilled and even skilled manual workers and technicians. Computers give nurses, paramedics, and patients rapid access to the same diagnostic and treatment information once limited to physicians who had graduated from an accredited medical school. In fact, it is difficult to think of any part of our lives—whether related to production or consumption—that is not being transformed by the new information technology available with computers and the Internet.

The rapid spread of new technologies is clear evidence of their benefits. As with anything else, however, there are also costs. For every start-up firm that grows into a spectacular success, many more fail within the first few years. The management revolution appears to have hit hardest on people in middle-level positions, people responsible for the workaday operations of a modern business enterprise. As computers and robots become smaller, faster, more interconnected, smarter, and cheaper, companies in nearly all industries can function with fewer middle-level managers and supervisors. An MBA (master's in business administration), once the ticket to a good job with high earnings, is no longer a guarantee against unemployment.

Another major implication of the new technology is "globalization," by which we mean that Americans are competing far more closely than before with people in other countries. The Internet knows no borders, bringing together people with common interests regardless of where they live. It has revolutionized the way we buy things, and it has stimulated international communications and commerce. People in different countries are aware of each other in new ways, for better or for worse. We carry cell phones that are "smart" enough to access the Internet and use satellites instead of wires to put us in touch with each other. Although foreign trade and international competition have always been important, their share of the nation's production and consumption expenditure has increased. Not long ago the economic incentives facing Americans were dominated by domestic conditions within the United States, but we now speak of a "global" economy in which we must compete for goods and services produced by people beyond our borders. We live in a period of transition, when old economic relationships—and their consequent political alliances—crumble, new ones emerge, and few are as secure as we might wish.

Bubbles, Booms, and Busts

The buoyant American economy at the beginning of the twenty-first century soon gave way to the worst economic crisis in the lifetime of most of today's American Jews. In hindsight, there were plenty of early warning signs in the preceding decades, but they hardly seemed relevant to most people. The stock market was booming, and with it the nonlabor incomes and pension funds that gave middle-class workers that extra security cushion. Starting salaries for young professionals were high and rising, and homeowners saw the value of their property increase from month to month. Many empty nesters sold their house for a handsome profit, moving into smaller quarters and investing the difference in a booming stock market.

As one of my professional mentors was fond of saying, "If something can't last forever, it won't." (This is the economist's version of my parents' favorite, "If something is too good to be true, it probably isn't.") The housing bubble burst, real estate prices crashed, and homes soon were selling at a fraction of the price they had been worth the year before. Problems in the financial industry came to light that caused the mortgage market to dry up and the stock market to fall dramatically. Pension funds that relied on the stock market suddenly seemed much less secure. The financial crisis made it difficult for businesses to obtain capital, and many firms tried to forestall bankruptcy by firing workers. Employment fell, unemployment rose, and the country entered the worst recession it had experienced in many decades.

To some extent this recession was a normal characteristic of the business cycle, something that a healthy market economy copes with routinely. A number of special factors, however, made it worse and made recovery more difficult. The boom in housing prices had been fueled by easy mortgages to borrowers who, when the recession came, could no longer meet payments. Home foreclosures became routine, appearing not only in low-income neighborhoods but also in wealthier areas where buyers had been too optimistic about continued prosperity and rising house prices. The financial industry crisis derived in part from poor forecasting, in part from unsound mortgage financing, and in part from outright fraud. Some failing banks were rescued by mergers, and others weathered the crisis with government loans, but repercussions throughout the economy were harder to resolve. Some businesses failed from the shortage of capital, and others reduced production and laid off workers. As tax revenues declined along with incomes, it became apparent that many governments—local, state, and federal—had budgeted as though prosperity would never end and were now threatened with bankruptcy. Government employees might be harder to fire than workers in the private sector, but public services were reduced and new hiring frozen in response to the substantial decline in revenues.

There are no separate statistics for Jews during this period, but we can assume that they generally participated in the national prosperity and were affected similarly by the subsequent recession.[1] Jewish communal services saw a decline in charitable donations even as their hardship cases increased. Some of the needy were newly minted professionals whose high-earning positions in management or finance simply disappeared during the crisis, and others owned successful businesses whose customers had to postpone their purchases. Some were older workers who lost jobs and saw their retirement savings or pensions dissipate during the financial crisis, and others were people who lost their homes to foreclosure because their lower earnings made it difficult to meet mortgage payments. The Jewish community as a whole was better off than most middle-class Americans, however, because blue-collar workers generally suffered greater losses than professionals. Jews were also in a better position to weather the recession and participate in the recovery when it came because of their high levels of human capital.

The Economic Future of American Jews

As I write these pages, it is still unclear how long the Great Recession will last and how deeply it will dive before a true long-term economic recovery sets in. Because a recession can't last forever, though, it probably won't. Technological change is another story, however, and it is surely here to stay. To see how economic conditions will affect American Judaism in the decades to come, we must look beyond the current crisis and try to imagine the new economic world that is emerging. It will be a global economy where automation, electronics, cell phones, and the Internet are routine, and where medical technology based on gene therapy and miniaturization will increase both the length and the quality of our lives. Although we can't foresee future innovations in any detail, we can look at how economic incentives will influence some of their broad features.

The Shrinking American Jewish Population

During the last four decades of the twentieth century, young Jews began marrying non-Jews at a breathtakingly high rate. Some controversy remains over the actual statistic (depending largely on who is considered a Jew for this purpose), but it seems clear that more than 40 percent of young Jewish adults now form interfaith families. (Recall that intermarriages include only couples where the non-Jewish spouse does not convert to Judaism; a Jew-by-birth is in-married if his or her spouse is either another Jew-by-birth or a Jew-by-choice who converted to Judaism from another religious background.)

Although recent statistics suggest that the intermarriage rate for young Jews is no longer rising, marriages between Jews and non-Jews will remain common in the near term. As more and more Americans acquire education and career ambitions similar to those in the Jewish community, more and more non-Jews are entering the marriage market with characteristics attractive to Jewish partners. Non-Jews in America are also more accepting of Jews than they once were, not only in the labor and housing markets but also in social settings and in the marriage market. This means that the pool of potential spouses matched on characteristics other than religion will increasingly have many more non-Jews than Jews because fewer than 2 percent of all Americans are Jews. The similarity between Jews and non-Jews makes interfaith marriages not only more likely but also more stable, characterized by lower divorce rates than in previous generations.

In an earlier era, many "secular" or "not religious" Jews remained close to the Jewish community by participating in its ethnic activities and parareligious organizations. These are no longer a powerful source of Jewish identity, however, because non-Jewish organizations are much less likely to deny access to Jews and because so many Jewish organizations now serve non-Jewish clients. The blurring of boundaries between Jews and non-Jews in secular life weakens the nonreligious community's connection to Judaism. Like the children of intermarried parents, children raised in secular Jewish homes are less likely to be involved in Jewish religious and cultural life and hence much more likely as adults to choose a non-Jewish spouse. Recent increases in secularism as a Jewish lifestyle, like the high rates of intermarriage and low Jewish fertility rates, mean that the American Jewish population will be smaller in the future than it is today, both in absolute size and—especially—as a fraction of the American population.

As more and more Americans invest in secular human capital that approaches the Jewish norm, and as ethnic barriers blur and even disappear, religion per se is becoming the main characteristic that differentiates Jews from non-Jews. At the same time, and perhaps even as a consequence, most American synagogue movements are raising their expectations for Jewish education, emphasizing especially those forms of religious human capital that complement a high level of secular skills. This emphasis appeals not only to well-educated Jews-by-birth, but also to the growing number of Jews-by-choice and intermarried couples choosing to raise their children as Jews. In contrast, families unwilling to invest heavily in Jewish human capital are facing incentives to reduce their commitment to the religious community. Even as the Jewish community of the future shrinks to a fraction of its present size, the remainder—still mostly non-Orthodox—will have a higher commitment to religious Judaism.[2]

The Aging of American Jewry

The population pyramid is a thing of the past, and the population cylinder will almost certainly grow taller in the future than it is today. Technological breakthroughs in DNA analysis, gene therapy, organ transplants, laser and microsurgery, and pharmaceuticals—among other things—promise to provide cures for many disabling or potentially fatal conditions. They should help us manage some chronic conditions currently associated with the elderly, perhaps even slow down the aging process itself. Emphasizing healthier lifestyles can also reduce the incidence of illness and premature death. Today, people who began working when they were twenty-five or thirty years old are typically eligible for a full pension well before they reach the age of sixty-five. Someone who retires at that age can still expect to live for decades, a period that will grow longer and healthier with new advances in medical technology. Even if the retirement age rises by a few years, American Jews in the not-too-distant future can expect to be pensioners for nearly a quarter or even a third of their entire life. Families, synagogues, and parareligious organizations will have strong incentives not only to serve the needs of an aging population but also to harness the energies, use the skills, and engage the interest of its retired or semiretired senior citizens.

To highlight the implications of this phenomenon, consider an American Jewish community in the not-too-distant future that continues its current average of two children per couple, with little immigration from abroad and a high rate of in-marriage for couples committed to a Jewish family lifestyle. Suppose also that children from families weakly attached to Judaism, whether intermarried or in-married, continue to assimilate at a high rate and effectively cease to identify as Jews. Then, even though the future American Jewish population will be smaller than today, its age distribution will remain fairly stable from one generation to the next.

To make the calculation simple, suppose our life expectancy rises to about 100 years, an assumption not wildly implausible in the context of new developments in medical technology. Approximately 20 percent of American Jews will then be children and adolescents (that is, from birth to age twenty), and another 20 percent will be their parents. About half of the remaining Jewish population will be adult singles and their empty-nester parents (about 15 percent each), and the other half (30 percent) will be grandparents. In this scenario the average age at marriage is about thirty-five, and people don't become grandparents until they are about seventy. Nearly all of the grandparents and many of the empty nesters—about one-third of the Jewish population—will be retired from the workforce, living on income from past savings, investments, and public or private pensions.

Not everyone will live to be 100, although the number of people who do is on the rise. Not every retiree will be healthy, although the age at which infirmity becomes more common is also rising. Not every senior will be fully retired and have an income sufficient to remain out of poverty, but the Jewish community can deal with most hardship cases with the help of extended family members, parareligious organizations, and government benefits. Even so, the general picture just sketched is not unreasonable, and some of its features are already evident. The aging of American Jewry may carry with it new problems to solve, but it also presents the Jewish community with new opportunities for institutional growth.

The Education and Earnings of American Jews

For the first half of the twentieth century, American Jewry was overwhelmingly made up of immigrants from tsarist Russia and Eastern Europe who arrived en masse between 1880 and 1924 and who settled mostly in America's large and rapidly growing cities. Although these people were independent, innovative actors, most of them lived in similar economic environments and made their decisions in that context. As a consequence, we could speak of economic incentives that affected the whole community and shaped its institutions.

American Jews at the beginning of the twenty-first century are more diverse, so we cannot assume that economic incentives are the same for everyone. Young adults with access to financial support from high-income parents and grandparents, either directly or as an inheritance, are less constrained in their economic choices than people who must rely on their own earnings for income. They can afford more education even if it does not lead to a high-paying career; they can afford to enter the occupation of their choice even if it pays a lower wage; and they can afford to have larger families without sacrificing their children's opportunities to acquire human capital. The full cost of time-intensive activities still influences their decisions, but the availability of nonwage income expands their opportunities beyond the simple story of wage effects on economic behavior.

Higher education in the twenty-first century is more expensive, and its returns more uncertain, than in the twentieth century. The high-wage careers are now in the STEM occupations and in professions like medicine, law, and corporate management, all of which require postcollege advanced degrees for entry. Because the cost of education is high, however, fewer people will invest in the skills required to earn these degrees. Instead, more people who want careers in these fields will become paraprofessionals, perhaps earning the less-expensive master's-level degree instead of a doctorate or professional degree and accepting lower—but not necessarily low—earnings in jobs enhanced by the new technologies. The American Jewish community of the future will exhibit more variation in educational attainment, and more income inequality, than it did in the past generation.

These trends in education and income may also affect Jewish marriage and fertility patterns in the twenty-first century. Gender egalitarianism is here to stay, not only in universities and the professions but also in the home. Some married couples may be fortunate and find two high-paying careers in the same city, but for those who can't the spouse with the higher income is as likely to be the wife as the husband. Electronic communication brings flexibility in the location and timing of many work-related tasks, allowing a parent with young children to work at home with a much smaller sacrifice in earnings and career opportunities. Couples with two demanding careers and high-paying jobs will still tend to have small families, but those in lower-wage paraprofessional occupations and those whose jobs can be performed at home will face a lower full cost of parenting and thus are likely to have more children. Although we cannot be specific about the future fertility rate among American Jews, we can expect to see a larger proportion of the community in families with three or more children and a probable increase in childlessness. Even if two children per family remains the average for American Jews, it may not remain the norm with the increased disparity in family size.

Perhaps the greatest difference in the economic situation of Jews today and yesterday relates to differences in the education levels of Jews and their non-Jewish neighbors. For many decades, Jews were much better educated than most Americans and more economically successful than most other immigrant communities. Today, the descendants of these other immigrants are just as assimilated as the Jews, and higher education has reached a much larger fraction of the non-Jewish population. As new ethnic groups assimilate and gain access to higher education,

Americans of all backgrounds face similar economic conditions, and American Jews have become much less distinctive than they once were. Jews will be differentiated from non-Jews primarily by their religion and religion-based behaviors rather than by behaviors associated with their education and economic incentives. This means that the pool of potential marriage partners will have many more non-Jews than before, and the incentive for Jews to marry within the community will be strong only for those with a strong preference for a Jewish religious lifestyle. This is likely to become a permanent fact of Jewish life in the United States.

The Future of Judaism in America

If we learned nothing else during the recent economic crisis and recession, surely it should be that the future is hard to predict. I have tried to limit myself here to a few broad economic trends that began late in the twentieth century, have persisted for several decades, and now appear to be here for the long run—or at least for the next few decades. Every Jewish organization, whether synagogue based or parareligious, needs to review its fundamental purpose and how best to achieve it in the new century. Some Jewish communal institutions will have outlived their purpose and wither away. Others will thrive by adapting to the "new normal," serving the needs of small, two-career families and single-parent families, in addition to their traditional support for people experiencing hardship.

Predicting the future of religious Judaism in the United States is even more difficult. What might be useful, however, is to look at some recent developments in American Judaism from an economic perspective. These innovations in Jewish religious observance and institutions are analogous to "start-up" firms, many of which prove transitory although others persist and grow to become new "traditions." We can already see the outlines of American Judaism's response to recent changes, but at this point we can only speculate on its success. An economic perspective on this process provides insights into which innovations are most efficient, least costly, and therefore more likely to thrive in the decades to come.

Religious Roles over the Life Cycle

In the future American Jewish community, if not already, the main economic incentive for Jews to marry other Jews turns on their commitment to a Jewish religious lifestyle and the value they place on the continuity of the Jewish People. (*Continuity* is the current buzzword for passing the Jewish heritage from one generation to the next.) In other words, the only families that will remain Jewish in the future are the ones that really want to be Jewish. These will be people whose Jewish human capital consists of not only knowledge but also experiences that give them pride in their Jewish heritage and memories that make them comfortable with it. The community has already begun to focus on this, not only by revising the Hebrew-school curriculum but also by recognizing that Jewish camping, youth groups, and Israel experiences need to be an integral part of Jewish education. Today's clergy look for ways to increase the appeal of synagogue ritual for a younger generation with more Jewish schooling than their parents but also more options in the secular world. Observance of kashrut, Shabbat, holidays, and other home-based rituals is increasing among non-Orthodox families, often with reduced time-intensity and other adaptations consistent with their involvement in secular activities.

Although changes like these are well under way in the more active Jewish communities, they have yet to solidify into a clear long-run pattern. Some organizations resist this "renaissance," perhaps because they believe it to be misguided, perhaps simply from inertia or apathy. A more important problem, however, is that when the demographic pattern is "cylindrical," normal life-cycle variations in wage rates provide a strong economic incentive for Judaism to become a religion dominated by the elderly. This is because the full price of time-intensive activities is lower for retirees and other senior citizens than for younger adults, especially for two-career Jewish couples with young (that is, precollege-age) children. This suggests that a larger, healthier cohort of elders will be both willing and able to volunteer for active roles in ritual, education, or community service, not only in the synagogues and Jewish communal organizations but also within the multigenerational family. At the same time, their accumulated experience and skills may mean that these elders can perform these roles more efficiently than younger members of the community. For both of these reasons, economic circumstances favor the older generation in leadership positions within the community.

If retirees make up a large proportion of the community and are generous with their time, they can easily relieve the younger generation of time-intensive religious responsibilities. We saw a similar tendency in an earlier chapter, where immigrant grandparents performed religious roles in the family and relieved their adult children not only of responsibilities but also of the experience that generates adult Jewish human capital. The unintended consequence of this pattern was that second-generation American Jewish parents found it easy to opt out of adult Jewish roles and effectively ignore the all-important home-based Jewish education of their children. Although this arrangement was convenient for both generations, it contributed to the high intermarriage rates of the third generation and should not be repeated. This life-cycle problem is much less likely to arise when young people outnumber the elderly, in eras characterized by a population pyramid, but this will not be the case for American Jewry in the future.

Understanding the incentives that led to this situation helps us learn from our collective mistakes and avoid similar problems in the future. Raising children in a Jewish home and giving them a Jewish education is important, but we saw that it is not enough to ensure Jewish continuity unless they assume adult Jewish roles once they leave home. The challenge today is to find a place in the religious community especially for adult singles and young professionals, many of whom have Jewish skills but few opportunities to use them and grow religiously and intellectually. To survive in America, Judaism will require an intergenerational partnership that gives adult singles, young professionals, and two-career couples religious roles sufficiently satisfying to be worth the high cost of their time.

Synagogue Diversity and the Ultra-Orthodox

In the twentieth century, the overwhelming majority of American synagogues affiliated with one of the three major synagogue movements—Reform, Conservative, or Orthodox. By the end of the century, however, each of these movements was splintering. The Reconstructionist movement split off from the Conservatives in 1955 with only four synagogues and has been growing steadily ever since, although it is still a small fraction of the Jewish population. The Reform movement lost some of its potential members to groups like Jewish Renewal, Humanistic Judaism, New Age Judaism, and various new congregations styled as "postdenominational." Later cohorts of immigrants established independent synagogues, many of them similar to the Orthodox but unaffiliated with a synagogue movement. In 2000, only 62 percent of America's Jews belonged to synagogues affiliated with the Reform, Conservative, or Orthodox umbrella organizations.

A number of tiny ultra-Orthodox groups, some of them with sect-like characteristics, have grown larger and more visible in recent decades, attracting new members not only from marginally affiliated youth but also from a wide spectrum of Jewish observance. With a fertility rate higher than the rest of the American Jewish population, these small ultra-Orthodox groups are a growing fraction of the American Jewish population. Because they typically emphasize religious studies over a secular education, their members rarely have the high earnings associated with professional occupations. With wage rates lower than that of the rest of American Jewry, the ultra-Orthodox have much less incentive to avoid time-intensive activities in religious observance, in community service, and in family life. With larger families and lower incomes, ultra-Orthodox communities are characterized by a population pyramid that threatens more poverty with each passing generation.

The proportion of ultra-Orthodox among American Jews is increasing because of their high birth rates, but it is not clear how far this growth will continue or how long these communities can remain insulated from the rest of American Jewry. As long as they depend for earnings on low-wage occupations, they will need outside sources of income to remain out of poverty. Gifts from other (non–ultra-Orthodox) family members are unlikely to persist for more than one or two generations, government programs are unlikely to provide more than short-term relief, and charitable donations from other American Jews are unlikely to grow as fast as the ultra-Orthodox population.

New electronic communication technologies can provide jobs, for both men and women, that dovetail with an ultra-Orthodox lifestyle and its time-intensive schedule of religious observance. The Internet, however, is also a source of information about other lifestyles, with the potential to entice ultra-Orthodox youth away from their community. America is still a land of opportunity, where a secular education holds the promise of both intellectual and economic rewards. Like the youth of immigrant communities a century earlier, today's ultra-Orthodox youth face economic incentives to adapt their Jewish practices by finding a religious niche elsewhere in the American Jewish community. Only time will tell what this ultimately means, but the larger American economic environment and past experience suggest that the ultra-Orthodox will continue to be a small minority within the Jewish community.

Religious "Product Differentiation"

In the first half of the twentieth century, the full cost of Jewish observance was a useful indicator of the religious lifestyle choices of American Jews, ranging from the most time-intensive ultra-Orthodox to the least time-intensive secular Judaism. By the end of the century, however, two factors undermined this simple relationship. Jewish family incomes were high enough for people to choose time-intensive activities even though they might be expensive. And secular educational attainment was so high for so many members of the community that it no longer varied enough to predict differences in religious choices.

People with high wages and also high incomes are willing to spend their time and money on Jewish observance, but only if it effectively satisfies their personal religious impulses. This "new" combination of economic incentives has stimulated changes within existing congregations, as well as the proliferation of new congregations unaffiliated with the major synagogue movements. Although not every change in religious practices or in new synagogues is likely to survive the test of time, the variety of small synagogues with different religious customs and lifestyles will probably characterize Jewish communal life for decades to come.

New synagogue congregations, like new churches and new start-up firms, tend to be small but enthusiastic. Indeed, this is an important part of their appeal to their founders. Like the immigrant synagogues of the last century, most new congregations do not survive in the long run as their membership ages, lifestyles change, and enthusiasm wanes.

Some, however, will grow to become part of the future of Judaism in America. The dilemma, of course, is how to keep the enthusiasm fresh and the fellowship of a small group from being overwhelmed by the growth in synagogue membership. Eventually the new synagogue becomes an older one, its original members age or move away, and the problem becomes how to attract young families who might otherwise join even newer congregations.

Much as large automobile companies make different cars for consumers with different preferences, or large clothing manufacturers have different lines for different fashion tastes, large synagogues are finding ways to provide different religious settings for members with a variety of different needs. I have seen one of America's larger Conservative synagogues adapt to this problem by partially subdividing itself into smaller subcongregations with different religious lifestyles (but still within Conservative Judaism). On a typical Saturday morning, for example, congregants can choose among half a dozen Shabbat services. The rabbi and cantor conduct one service in the building's large sanctuary. Elsewhere in the building a more traditionally minded group (tending toward the Orthodox ritual but with women as full participants) is led by lay congregants with wide participation and only occasional leadership by clergy. Still another lay-led service is conducted by a liberal study group that recently celebrated its fortieth year of collective worship. There are also several services for children and adolescents, separated into appropriate age groups, and a group called "Young Professionals" for adult singles. Each congregant selects whichever prayer service appeals most on that particular Shabbat morning, allowing people to experience variety in their religious observance, and everyone gathers together afterwards for a light lunch and social hour.

Other large synagogues may subdivide their congregants into *chavurot* (plural of *chavura*), small affinity groups of a dozen or so families with common interests. Parents of preschoolers, for example, have schedules and social patterns that modify in similar ways as their children grow. Another *chavura* might be a group of three-generation families who belong to the same synagogue, or a group of two-career couples in the medical profession and their families. We once belonged to a *chavura* that began as a book club; our friends joined one that studied Torah together; another group emphasized community service projects; and yet another was organized simply to give young parents an opportunity to socialize together without their children. Each *chavura* is limited in size to encourage bonding within the group, with the added benefit that the large synagogue is no longer a congregation of strangers. The *chavura* movement originated in the 1970s as an alternative to synagogue membership, but we now see it as a successful innovation in Jewish religious culture within the larger synagogues.

Monolithic synagogue movements and large buildings seemed desirable in the middle of the twentieth century, when so many American Jews were at most one or two generations removed from a common immigrant background and there was less variety in their economic circumstances (broadly speaking, of course). American Jews in the twenty-first century enjoy more variety in their occupations and other secular activities, and they can support a consumption pattern that caters to their varied interests. Today's economic and religious environments also make smaller congregations more efficient than large ones and encourage variety in Jewish religious expression. We can expect American Judaism to continue adapting, not only by forming new congregations but also by incorporating a variety of Jewish experiences into the culture of large synagogues.

The American Small Tradition

For most people, the economic success of Jews in the United States during the twentieth century refers to the transformation of an impoverished immigrant community of laborers, craftspeople, and petty merchants into a well-educated middle-class American community of businesspeople and professionals in the sciences and the arts. Yet economics is not just about our lives as producers and earners; it is also about our lives as consumers, including our family life, religious life, and community life. The economic success of American Jews as individuals transformed the Jewish community, its parareligious organizations, its religious life, and its relationship with Jewish communities elsewhere in the world. What emerges is a new Small Tradition in Judaism, one that is forward looking and vibrant as it adapts Jewish observance to the freedom and abundance of secular opportunities in the United States of today and tomorrow.

This optimistic picture of American Judaism is not shared by everyone. Many people see our synagogue movements as hopeless compromises with secularism, lacking religious authenticity and encouraging the loss of Jewish identity as we drift toward religious assimilation and widespread intermarriage. Yet Judaism has a long history of crises and of adaptations to new environments, from pagan Greco-Roman civilization to medieval Christian Europe to the Muslim Ottoman Empire, to name a few examples. Each Small Tradition faced the same basic problem of how to preserve Judaism's Great Tradition for future generations, and each was surely shaped by the kind of economic incentives discussed in this book. Whether proposed by religious leaders or—perhaps more likely—arising from grassroots spontaneity, each Small Tradition must have coalesced by trial and error from earlier changes in religious observance. Many religious innovations did not stand the test of time and were lost, perhaps because they failed to preserve the Great Tradition, perhaps because they lacked popular appeal, or perhaps because they were just too costly. Cumbersome and anarchic though this process may seem, it has enabled Judaism to adapt successfully over a wide range of time, space, and cultural settings without losing the Great Tradition at its heart.

Looking at Judaism in its economic context highlights the creativity with which American Jews are forging a new Small Tradition and gives cause to be optimistic about its future. We are now more than a century away from the Small Tradition of Ashkenazi Jewry in the Russian Pale of Settlement, a tradition that is part of our Jewish heritage but not how we actually live our lives today. American Judaism is still a work in progress, however, and only time will tell whether some of our more controversial innovations will ultimately succeed. Meanwhile, to paraphrase Mark Twain, we can have confidence that the reports of Judaism's demise in the United States are "greatly exaggerated."

Reference Matter

Key Acronyms

AJIS   (American Jewish Identity Survey). Survey of American Jews conducted in 2000 with data on selected characteristics of American Jews.

ARIS   (American Religious Identity Survey). Survey conducted in 2000 with data on religious self-identification.

CJF   (Council of Jewish Federations). Umbrella organization of local Jewish Federations, each of which is an umbrella organization for local parareligious organizations. Predecessor organization of UJC and JFNA.

HIAS   (Hebrew Immigrant Aid Society). Organization founded by Russian Jewish immigrants in 1885 to help new immigrants when they first arrive in the United States.

JCC   (Jewish Community Center). Nonreligious community centers, typically with gymnasium and swimming pool, for social, cultural, and athletic activities.

JFNA   (Jewish Federations of North America). Umbrella organization of local Jewish Federations. Successor organization of UJC and CJF.

JRF   (Jewish Reconstructionist Federation). The American umbrella organization of Reconstructionist synagogues; predecessor organization of RRC.

NJPS   (National Jewish Population Survey). Surveys of American Jews conducted in 1990 and in 2000–2001with data on selected characteristics.

NSRE   (National Survey of Religion and Ethnicity). Survey conducted in 2000 with data on religious self-identification.

NSRI   (National Survey of Religious Identity). Survey conducted in 1990 with data on religious self-identification.

OU   (Orthodox Union). The American umbrella organization of Orthodox synagogues.

RRC   (Reconstructionist Rabbinical College). Seminary for Reconstructionist Clergy and successor organization of JRF.

STEM   (Science, Technology, Engineering, and Mathematics). A group of occupations in high demand with twenty-first-century technology, requiring high education levels and characterized by high wage rates.

UAHC   (Union of American Hebrew Congregations). The American umbrella organization of Reform synagogues; predecessor of URJ.

UJC   (United Jewish Communities). Umbrella organization of local Jewish Federations. Successor organization of CJF and predecessor of JFNA.

URJ   (Union of Reform Judaism). Successor organization of UAHC.

USA   (United Synagogue of America). The American umbrella organization of Conservative synagogues; predecessor of USCJ.

USCJ   (United Synagogue of Conservative Judaism). Successor organization of USA.

YMHA   (Young Men's Hebrew Association). Jewish parareligious organization modeled after the Christian YMCA.

Glossary of English Terms

Anticomplements, Anticomplementarity. Two mutually conflicting inputs in a production process, so that using more of either one reduces the productivity (efficiency) of the other.

Ark. The cabinet on the front wall of a synagogue in which Torah scrolls are kept. (Synagogue prayers are traditionally said facing Jerusalem, so in the United States the Ark is usually on the room's eastern wall.)

Assortative mating. Pairing into marital couples based on the characteristics of each individual partner. Assortative mating is positive if spouses have similar characteristics and negative if they have opposite characteristics.

Cantor. *(lit., singer).* Person who leads the musical portions of a synagogue service. Synagogues typically hire a cantor as part of their clergy.

Capital. Anything human-made that is desired not for its own sake but because it makes other activities easier, more efficient, or more enjoyable.

Child quality, child quantity. Child quantity is the number of children in a nuclear family. Child quality is the parents' perceived benefit derived from each child. Child quality is conventionally measured as the amount of money and time spent on each child, on the assumption that parents spend resources only if they expect them to improve the child's quality.

Complements, complementarity. Two mutually reinforcing inputs in a production process, so that using more of either one raises the productivity (efficiency) of the other.

Congregationalism. An organizational structure in which individual religious congregations (for example, synagogues and churches) are formed, managed and financed by their members.

Conservative Judaism. The **synagogue movement** formed in 1913 whose American **umbrella organization** is now the **United Synagogue of Conservative Judaism (USCJ)**.

Diaspora. (*lit.,* scattering) That part of a community residing outside of its home-land. In Judaism, the Diaspora is (1) any place where Jews live that is not in the Land of Israel; (2) all Jewish communities in (1); or (3) all Jews living in (1) or (2).

Economies of scale.   Efficiencies that are realized when production is increased; for example, economies of scale occur if doubling the inputs in a production process yields more than twice as much output.

Education.   Investment in **human capital**.

Enclave.   A community or neighborhood whose culture differs from that of the larger society in which it is located.

Ethnic goods.   Goods or services that have value for members of one ethnic group but little or no value for members of other ethnic groups; for example, an ethnic church, marriage market, or newspaper.

Exodus.   (1) The biblical event in which the Jewish People escaped from slavery in ancient Egypt. (2) The biblical event in (1) followed by forty years of wandering in the Sinai desert, during which the Jewish People received the Torah and became a nation. This is Judaism's story of redemption and the primary source of its religious laws. (3) The second book of the Torah.

Full price.   The money price of a good plus the value of time spent producing and/or consuming it.

Human capital.   Any personal characteristic created by people, not innate, that is beneficial for production or consumption activities. This includes knowledge, skills, memories, and relationships.

Human capital: general vs. specific.   General human capital affects a person's productivity in many different activities. Human capital is specific to a particular activity if it has no effect on productivity or consumption efficiency except in that activity.

Human capital: transferable vs. country-specific.   Country-specific human capital enhances productivity in only one country. Transferable human capital enhances productivity in more than one country. Common examples of country-specific human capital include knowledge of rare languages and unusual legal systems.

Human capital: religion-specific vs. secular.   Religious human capital enhances religious experience but has no effect on other activities. Secular human capital improves performance of non-religious activities.

Human capital: Jewish vs. other.   Jewish human capital enhances Jewish experience (religious or otherwise) but has no effect on other activities (religious or otherwise).

Jews-by-choice, Jews-by-birth.   Jews-by-choice are people who have converted from other religions (including "none"). Jews-by-birth are people born to a Jewish mother (or father for Reform Jews).

Labor Zionism.   A branch of political **Zionism** associated with the quasi-socialist Labor party in Israel.

Laissez-faire.   A system in which choices are left to the individual, without interference from government or communal authorities.

Law of Diminishing Returns.   An empirical observation that when an activity is continued long enough, the **marginal value** of an additional unit of that activity declines.

Marginal value.   The value of an additional unit; for example, the marginal value of time spent doing something is the additional benefit gained by spending one more unit of time on that activity.

Orthodox Judaism.   The **synagogue movement** formed in 1898 whose American **umbrella organization** is now the **Orthodox Union (OU)**.

Parareligious organizations.   Organizations associated with religious communities that are not religious institutions per se (for example, hospitals, schools, charities).

Rabbi. (lit., respected teacher)   Person ordained as Jewish clergy. The religious leader typically hired by Jewish congregation or community, often the leader of a synagogue service.

Reconstructionist Judaism.   The **synagogue movement**, once part of Conservative Judaism but independent since 1955, now represented by the **Reconstructionist Rabbinical College (RRC)**.

Reform Judaism.   The **synagogue movement** formed in 1873 whose American **umbrella organization** is now the **Union of Reform Judaism (URJ)**.

Relative price.   The price of a good expressed as its ratio to the price of another good.

Scarcity.   Multiple goals competing for limited resources.

Secular education.   Education in subjects other than religion.

Secular Jews.   Jews who identify as belonging the Jewish people but who distance themselves from religious belief.

Self-produced good (also, home-produced good).   A good that consumers cannot buy but rather must make by combining purchased items with their own time and effort. Examples of self-produced goods include family life, religious experience, and artistic expression.

Settlement House.   A center for education and social work aimed at helping immigrants and their children adjust to the American environment.

Substitutes.   Alternative items that are effectively interchangeable. (See **Trade-offs**)

Synagogue movements.   Subdivisions of Judaism, sometimes called "denominations" but with differences in practice and theology not great enough to cause a schism.

Time-intensity.   The importance of time as a component of the full price of a good.

Trade-off.   The amount of a good that must be given up in order to acquire more of another when resources are limited.

Ultra-Orthodox Judaism.   Independent congregations requiring strict observance of religious laws. Typically inspired by the teachings of a particular rabbi; often sectlike behavior.

Umbrella organizations.   Organizations whose members are congregations rather than individuals.

Zionism.   (1) A movement encouraging Jewish immigration to the Land of Israel. (2) A political movement supporting the establishment of a Jewish state in the Land of Israel. (3) The belief that the State of Israel is a homeland for all Jews regardless of nationality.

Glossary of Hebrew and Yiddish Terms

Author's notes:

Both languages are written in the Hebrew alphabet, and transliterations into the Latin alphabet can vary. Similarly, pronunciations can vary with the accent of the speaker, and in some accents the Hebrew pronunciation of a word is similar to the Yiddish. The transliterations and pronunciations used here are the ones I am most comfortable with but are not intended to be definitive. Alternative pronunciations are included when both are common among American Jews.

Hebrew and Yiddish have a guttural sound that has no English equivalent. It is usually written in English as "ch" and pronounced by many American Jews almost like an "h." It is *never* pronounced like the English "ch" (as in cheese). To forestall this confusion I have indicated its pronunciation as "kh."

Ashkenazi *(Ahsh-ken-ahz-ee)*.   Belonging to the Jewish Small Tradition of non-Mediterranean Europe, dating since about the tenth century.

Bar (m) or Bat (f) Mitzvah *(Bar Mitz-vah, Bat Mitz-vah)*.   The synagogue ceremony when a young person reads Torah publicly for the first time, usually at his or her thirteenth birthday.

Brit milah (Heb.), bris (Yid.) *(Breet Mee-la, Bris)*.   Ritual circumcision performed on infant Jewish boys, usually when they are eight days old.

Chanukah *(Khan-oo-kah; Ha-na-ka)*.   An eight-day holiday in winter, usually in December. Chanukah tells the story of the Maccabean revolt against Seleucid Greeks in 160 BCE and the subsequent rededication of the Temple in Jerusalem.

Chavura (pl. chavurot) *(Khah-voo-rah, khah-voo-rote)*.   A small affinity group of a dozen or so families sharing common interests.

Fleishig (Yid.) *(Flay-shig)*. (adj.)   Food prepared with meat or meat products and thus not served in the same meal as dairy products.

Gefilte fish (Yid.) *(Guh-fill-tuh fish)*.   Literally, stuffed fish. In America it is usually just the stuffing mixture shaped into patties.

Haftorah *(Haf-tore-ah)*. A portion from Prophets (books in the second part of the **Tanakh**) read in the synagogue after the **Torah** reading.

Haggadah *(Ha-ga-dah (Heb.), Ha-gaw-duh (Yid.))*. The book read during the Passover **Seder**.

Hamentashen (Yid.) *(Hah-men-tash-en)*. Special triangular pastry traditionally served on **Purim**.

Kashrut *(Kahsh-root)*. (n.) The Jewish dietary laws.

Kibbutz *(Kee-boots)*. A community organized as a collective, like an extended family, where everyone shares in the work and income is pooled so that everyone can also share in the consumption.

Klezmer *(Klehz-mehr)*. Ashkenazi folk music typically played at happy events, esp. for celebrations and dancing.

Kosher *(Koh-sher)*. (adj.) Describes something that meets requirements of the Jewish dietary laws. This can be the food itself, the kitchen in which it is prepared, or any utensils with which it comes in contact. Meat is kosher only if it comes from a kosher animal that is ritually slaughtered according to the laws of **kashrut**.

Landsmenshaften (Yid). *(Lants-men-shahf-ten)*. Societies of immigrants from the same town or region, typically formed to extend credit or mutual aid.

Latkes (Yid.) *(Laht-keez)*. Potato pancakes, especially when served during **Chanukah**.

Ma'abara (pl. Ma'abarot) *(Ma-ah-buh-rah; pl. Ma-ah-buh-rote)*. A temporary settlement for new immigrants, typically housed in tents, with services to facilitate their adjustment to life in Israel.

Matza *(Mah-tsa)*. A special crackerlike unleavened bread eaten during all eight days of the **Pesach** holiday.

Matza balls *(Mah-tsa balls)*. Spherical dumplings made from crushed matza, typically served in chicken soup.

M'chatanim *(Mih-kha-tahn-im)*. The parents of your daughter-in-law or son-in-law, people with whom you share common grandchildren.

Mezuzah *(Meh-zoo-zah)*. A small case attached to the doorpost of a Jewish home, containing a scroll with the biblical injunction to remember that Jews have only one God.

Mikva *(Mick-vuh)*. A facility for ritual baths.

Milchig (Yid.) *(Milkh-ig)*. (adj.) Food prepared with milk or with dairy products derived from milk and thus not served in the same meal as meat or meat products.

Minyan *(Min-yuhn)*. The quorum of ten adult Jews required for a synagogue service.

Mizrachi *(Mizz-rah-khee)*. Belonging to the Jewish Small Tradition of the Middle East, possibly dating back to ancient Jewish traditions in Babylonia and Persia.

Moshav *(Mow-shahv)*. A farming collective where families live and work separately but pool their products for sale.

Pareve (Heb., Yid.) *(Parv, Par-vuh)*. (adj.) Food that has neither meat nor milk products, including all fruits, vegetables, grains, and **kosher** fish. Pareve foods can be served in any meal, whether **fleishig** or **milchig**.

Pesach *(Pay-sakh)*. Passover, an eight-day holiday occurring in spring. Pesach observance includes telling the story of the **Exodus** from ancient Egypt.

Purim *(Poo-reem, Poor-um)*. A winter holiday, often occurring in early March. Purim observance includes telling the story of Esther, the Jewish queen of Persia, and how she saved Persian Jewry from impending genocide (probably about 425 BCE).

Rosh Hashanah *(Rawsh Ha-shah-nah)*. The Jewish New Year, occurring in autumn. Rosh Hashanah begins the solemn High Holy Days during which Jews affirm their identity with Judaism and the Jewish People.

Seder *(Say-der)*. The dinner and attendant ritual observed on the first two nights of Passover (one night for Reform Jews and Israelis).

Sephardi *(adj.) (Seh-far-dee)*. Belonging to the Jewish Small Tradition of Mediterranean Europe, dating from medieval Spain and spread widely to other countries after Spain expelled its Jews in 1492.

Shabbat (Heb.), Shabbos (Yid.) *(Shah-baht, Shah-buss)*. The seventh day of the week (sundown on Friday through sundown on Saturday), on which Jews are constrained from production activities.

Shavu'ot (Heb.), Shavuos (Yid.) *(Shah-voo-ote, Sha-voo-us)*. A spring holiday starting seven weeks after the beginning of Pesach. Shavu'ot commemorates receiving the Torah at Sinai and Shavu'ot observance includes telling the biblical story of Ruth. In ancient Israel Shavu'ot was also when offerings of the spring harvest's first fruits were brought to the Temple in Jerusalem. Also known as the Festival of Weeks or Pentecost.

Siddur *(See-dure [Heb.], Sidder [Yid.])*. The prayer book used for daily, **Shabbat**, and festival synagogue services.

Spiel *(Shpeel(Yid.))*. A short play, usually a satire or comedy, as in a **Purim** *spiel*.

Steibl *(Shtee-bull)*. Small Orthodox synagogue in the Jewish immigrant neighborhoods, often a storefront or the ground floor of someone's living quarters.

Sukkot (Heb.), Sukkos (Yid.) *(Soo-kote, Sook-us)*. A seven-day holiday occurring in the autumn, three days after **Yom Kippur**. Sukkot tells about the fall harvest in ancient Israel and commemorates the forty-year wandering in Sinai by building a temporary dwelling in which to eat. Also known as the Festival of Booths or the Festival of Tabernacles.

Tallit (Heb.), Tallis (Yid.) *(Ta-leet, Tal-us)*.   A special fringed shawl with **tsitsit** on its corners, worn during certain prayer services by Jewish men (and, in some American synagogues, by women).

Talmud *(Tahl-mood, Tal-muhd)*.   A collection of commentaries on **Torah** and discussions of its practical applications in daily life, begun in about the first century BCE and continuing through the seventeenth century. Talmud belongs to Judaism's Great Tradition.

Tanakh *(Tah-nakh)*.   The Hebrew Scriptures. This term is an acronym for the three parts of the Jewish bible: Torah, Nevi'im (Prophets), and K'tuvim (Writings).

Tefillin *(Teh-fill-in)*.   Two leather boxes with leather straps that a Jewish man wears, one bound to his forehead and the other to his arm, during the weekday morning prayers. Each box contains a scroll with the same biblical passage that is in the **mezuzah.**

Torah *(Toe-rah)*.   (1) Judaism's most fundamental religious text; (2) a parchment scroll on which (1) is written, in its original Hebrew, by a specially trained scribe. The contents of Torah are also known as the *Five Books of Moses*, or by the Greek term *Pentateuch*, and are the first five books of Christianity's *Old Testament*.

Tsitsit *(Tsit-tsit)*.   Special fringes on four corners of a garment, usually the **tallit**.

Ulpan *(Ool-pahn)*.   An intensive Hebrew language course that introduces students to daily life in Israel.

Yeshiva *(Yeh-shiv-ah)*.   A school for intensive religious studies, usually Orthodox or ultra-Orthodox.

Yid (Yid.) *(Yid)*.   Jew.

Yiddish *(Yid-ish)*.   The language of **Ashkenazi** Jewry written in the Hebrew alphabet. Yiddish is a Germanic language with a vocabulary rich in Hebrew and Slavic words.

Yiddishkeit *(Yid-ish-kite)*.   The secular culture of **Yiddish**-speaking Ashkenazi Jews.

Yom Kippur *(Yome Kee-poor, (alt. Yum-kipper))*.   Day of Atonement, occurring in autumn ten days after **Rosh Hahanah**. Yom Kippur ends the High Holy Day season with a day of complete fasting and collective prayer, atoning for the community's past sins and hoping for a good life in the coming year.

Notes

Chapter 2

1. The NJPS 2000–01 estimate is for adults under age fifty-five. These figures suggest that nonreligious Jews and non-Jews in Jewish households make up one-fourth to one-third of American Jewry when the community is broadly defined.

2. Although the Census figures include Jews, Jews are too small a fraction of the U.S. population to exert any influence on the statistics examined here.

3. These figures come from NJPS 2000 and refer to people age eighteen and over as adults. They would be somewhat higher if we focus on prime-age adults ages twenty-six to sixty-five (Jonathon Ament, "American Jewish Religious Denominations," Report 10, *United Jewish Communities Report Series on the National Jewish Population Survey 2000–01*, February 2005).

4. Jews include all persons over the age of thirty who were "born" Jewish (that is, who had Jewish parents). The U.S. Census figures include all persons over the age of twenty-five.

5. For the sake of comparison with the occupation data for 1948, the 2000 percentages in Figure 2.2 describe all Jewish men, whether or not they state their religion to be Judaism.

Chapter 3

1. Behavior is conditioned on the after-tax wage rate—that is, on the money you would actually get to spend if you were to work that extra hour. Here and elsewhere in this simplified discussion, the effects of taxes will be ignored.

2. Homemakers are stereotypically female, but the same logic applies to a husband who stays home with his children while his wife works in the labor force.

3. American Jews would also join other synagogue movements during the twentieth century, most notably the Reconstructionist (an offshoot of the Conservative movement) and several ultra-Orthodox groups. These attracted a much smaller number of adherents, however, and for reasons associated less with economic incentives than with theological and ideological preferences.

4. This theory is conventionally attributed to the sociologist Marshall Sklare. See M. Sklare, ed., *The Jews: Social Patterns of an American Group* (New York: The Free Press, 1958).

5. B. Lazerwitz, J. A. Winter, A. Dashefsky, and E. Tabory, *Jewish Choices: American Jewish Denominationalism* (Albany: SUNY Press, 1998).

Chapter 4

1. According to traditional religious Jewish law, any child born to a Jewish mother is a Jew, regardless of the father's religion.

2. The Jewish calendar has fifty-four weeks in a leap year with its "extra" month. In other years some of the portions are doubled up so that the annual cycle can be completed in fewer weeks.

3. Americans who identify themselves as "secular" Jews, or Jews who say they are "not religious," often celebrate at least some of the Jewish holidays. This ambivalence adds another dimension to our earlier discussion of the difficulty identifying Jews in our survey data.

Chapter 5

1. Measures of inequality that depend on rankings (for example, the richest 1 percent of the households) or ratios (such as the income of poor families as a fraction of the income of rich families) would remain the same even if all household incomes were doubled. The income gap between households at different levels would also double, however, and this is the sense in which inequality would increase.

Chapter 6

1. The statistics on occupation and education of Jews prior to 1970 do not permit distinguishing those who identify their religion as Judaism. Unlike the previous chapters, the data in this section therefore refer to all Jews.

2. Men born during WWII (1941–1945) would have been eligible for the military draft during the Vietnam War in the 1960s unless they had a student deferment, an incentive that probably contributed to the remarkably high educational attainment for men (but not women) in that birth cohort.

3. There was also a shift of high-level occupations from self-employment to salaried employment, in part because of trends in the American economy and in part because of a decline in employment discrimination against Jews.

4. Mordecai Kaplan's followers would eventually break off from Conservative Judaism and form the Jewish Reconstructionist Federation (JRF). This synagogue movement never attracted many members, possibly because Kaplan's most important ideas were so influential that they were already deeply embedded in American Jewish practice.

5. For an extensive treatment of this paradox, see J. Wertheimer, *A People Divided: Judaism in Contemporary America* (New York: Basic Books, 1993).

6. The Catholic Church is a partial exception to this rule, but the economic incentives leading to congregationalism are an ongoing source of tension between American Catholics and the Vatican.

Chapter 8

1. Surveys of American Jews during the first decade of the twenty-first century do not provide comprehensive information on their economic activities. Preliminary findings from these surveys confirm trends revealed by earlier surveys for changes in population size, intermarriage, and Jewish observance.

2. This combination of incentives has important precedents in Jewish history, leading simultaneously to a severe population decline and increased commitment within the Jewish community. For an economic analysis of this phenomenon during the first fourteen centuries after the destruction of the Temple in Jerusalem see Maristella Botticini and Zvi Eckstein, *The Chosen Few: How Education Shaped Jewish History, 70-–1492* (Princeton, NJ: Princeton University Press, 2012).

References

Economics

Becker, Gary S. (1975). *Human Capital: A Theoretical and Empirical Analysis, with Special Reference to Education,* 2nd ed. New York: NBER.

———. (1981). *A Treatise on the Family.* Cambridge, MA: Harvard University Press.

Chiswick, Barry R. (1978). "The Effect of Americanization on the Earnings of Foreign-born Men." *Journal of Political Economy* 86(5): 897–921.

———. (1988a). "Differences in Education and Earnings across Racial and Ethnic Groups: Tastes, Discrimination, and Investments in Child Quality." *Quarterly Journal of Economics* 103: 571–597.

———. (1988b). "Labor Supply and Investment in Child Quality: A Study of Jewish and Non-Jewish Women," *Contemporary Jewry* 9: 35–61.

Chiswick, Barry R. and Paul W. Miller (2005). "Do Enclaves Matter in Immigrant Adjustment?" *City and Community* 4(1): 5–35.

Michael, Robert T. (1973). "Education in Nonmarket Production." *Journal of Political Economy* 83: 306–327.

Mincer, Jacob. (1974). *Schooling, Experience and Earnings.* New York: Columbia University Press for the National Bureau of Economic Research.

———. (1984). "Human Capital and Economic Growth." *Economics of Education Review,* 3:195–205.

Schultz, T. Paul. (1981). *Economics of Population.* Englewood Cliffs, NJ: Prentice-Hall.

———. (1993). "Investments in the Schooling and Health of Women and Men: Quantities and Returns." *Journal of Human Resources* 28(4): 694–734.

———. (1997). "Assessing the Productive Benefits of Nutrition and Health: An Integrated Human Capital Approach." *Journal of Econometrics* 77: 141–158.

Schultz, Theodore W., ed. (1974). *Economics of the Family: Marriage, Children, and Human Capital.* Chicago: University of Chicago Press for the NBER.

Tommasi, Mariano, and Kathryn Ierulli, eds. (1995). *The New Economics of Human Behavior.* Cambridge, UK: Cambridge University Press.

U.S. Bureau of the Census, *U.S. Census of Population, 2000.* Various reports downloaded in August 2008 from http://pubdb3.census.gov/macro/03001.

Economics of Religion

Association for the Study of Religion, Economics and Culture. Available at www.thearda .com/asrec.

Azzi, Corry, and Ronald Ehrenberg (1975). "Household Allocation of Time and Church Attendance," *Journal of Political Economy* 83(1) 27–56.

Chiswick, Carmel U. (2006). "An Economic Perspective on Religious Education: Complements and Substitutes in a Human-Capital Portfolio." *Research in Labor Economics* 24: 429–467.

———. (2010a). "Egalitarian Religion and Economics." *The Lighthouse Economic Review* 1(1); available at http://egalitarianreligionandeconomics.blogspot.com.

Chiswick, Carmel U., and Evelyn L. Lehrer. (1991). "Religious Intermarriage: An Economic Perspective." *Contemporary Jewry* 12: 21–34.

Iannaccone, Laurence R. (1988). "A Formal Model of Church and Sect." *American Journal of Sociology* 94 (Supplement): S241–S268.

———. (1990). "Religious Participation: A Human Capital Approach." *Journal for the Scientific Study of Religion* 29(3): 297–314.

———. (1991). "The Consequences of Religious Market Regulation: Adam Smith and the Economics of Religion." *Rationality and Society* 3: 156–177.

———. (1992). "Sacrifice and Stigma: Reducing Free-Riding in Cults, Communes, and Other Collectives." *Journal of Political Economy,* 100(2): 271–292.

———. (1998). "Introduction to the Economics of Religion." *Journal of Economic Literature* 36: 1465–1496.

Lehrer, Evelyn L. (2004). "Religion as a Determinant of Economic and Demographic Behavior in the United States." *Population and Development Review* 30: 707–726.

———. (2009). *Religion, Economics, and Demography: The Effects of Religion on Education, Work, and the Family.* New York: Routledge.

Lehrer, Evelyn L., and Carmel U. Chiswick. 1993. "Religion as a Determinant of Marital Stability." *Demography,* 30(3):385–404.

Sociology of Religion

Gill, Anthony (moderator), *Research on Religion.* Podcast available at www.researchon religion.org.

Kelley, Dean M. (1972). *Why Conservative Churches Are Growing: A Study in Sociology of Religion.* New York: Harper & Row.

Kosmin, Barry. (1991). *National Survey of Religious Identity (NSRI) 1990.* Sponsored by Councl of Jewish Federations (now the Jewish Federation of North America). Available at www.jewishdatabank.org.

Kosmin, Barry R., and Ariela Keysar. (2006). *Religion in a Free Market: Religious and Non-Religious Americans, Who/What/Why/Where.* Ithaca, NY: Paramount Market Publishing.

Kosmin, Barry A., Egon Mayer, and Ariela Keysar. (2001). *American Religious Identification Survey 2001*. New York: The Graduate Center of CUNY. Available from the Berman Jewish Policy Archive at www.bjpa.org.

Schwartz, Jim, Vivian Klaff, and Frank Mott. (2002). *National Survey of Religion and Ethnicity (NSRE) 2000-01*. Sponsored by United Jewish Communities (now the Jewish Federation of North America). Available at www.jewishdatabank.org.

Stark, Rodney, and Roger Finke. (2000). *Acts of Faith: Explaining the Human Side of Religion*. Berkeley: University of California Press.

Warner, R. Stephen. (1993). "Work in Progress toward a New Paradigm for the Sociological Study of Religion in the United States." *American Journal of Sociology* 98(5): 1044–1093.

———. (1998). "Immigration and Religious Communities in the United States." In *Gatherings in Diaspora: Religious Communities and the New Immigration*, edited by R. Stephen Warner and Judith G. Wittner, 3–34. Philadelphia: Temple University Press.

Warner, R. Stephen, and Judith G. Wittner, eds. (1998). *Gatherings in Diaspora: Religious Communities and the New Immigration*. Philadelphia: Temple University Press.

Economics of Jews and Judaism

Botticini, Maristella, and Zvi Eckstein. (2012). *The Chosen Few: How Education Shaped Jewish History, 70–1492*. Princeton, NJ: Princeton University Press.

Chiswick, Barry R. (1983). "The Earnings and Human Capital of American Jews." *Journal of Human Resources* 18: 313–336.

———. (1986). "The Labor Market Status of American Jews: Patterns and Determinants." In *American Jewish Yearbook 1985*, 131–153. New York: American Jewish Committee.

———. (1991). "Jewish Immigrant Skill and Occupational Attainment at the Turn of the Century." *Explorations in Economic History 28*, 64–86.

———. (1997). "Working and Family Life: The Experiences of Jewish Women in America." *Papers in Jewish Demography*, 27: 277–287.

———. (1999). "The Occupational Attainment and Earnings of American Jewry, 1890–1990." *Contemporary Jewry* 20: 68–98.

———. (2007). "The Occupational Attainment of American Jewry: 1990 to 2000." *Contemporary Jewry*, 27, 112–136.

Chiswick, Barry R., and Carmel U. Chiswick. (2000). "The Cost of Living Jewishly and Jewish Continuity." *Contemporary Jewry*, 21, 78–90.

———. (2007). "Economic Transformation of American Jewry." *New Jewish Time: The Encyclopedia of Jewish Culture*. Jerusalem: Keter Publishing House (Hebrew). Reprinted in C. Chiswick (2008), *Economics of American Judaism*. New York: Routledge, 53–58 (English).

Chiswick, Carmel U. (1995). "The Economics of American Judaism," *Shofar* 13(4): 1–19.

———. (1996). "Israel and American Jewry in the Year 2020: An Economic Analysis." In *Israel and the Jewish People*, edited by Anat Gonen and Smadar Fogel, 257–272. *Israel 2020: Master Plan for Israel in the Twenty-First Century: The Macro Scenarios.* Haifa: Technion (Hebrew). Reprinted in C. Chiswick (2008). *Economics of American Judaism.* New York: Routledge (English).

———. (1997). "Determinants of Religious Intermarriage: Are Jews Really Different?" *Papers in Jewish Demography* 27: 247–257.

———. (1998). "The Economics of Contemporary American Jewish Family Life," in *Studies in Contemporary Jewry 14: Coping with Life and Death: Jewish Families in the Twentieth Century*, edited by Peter Y. Medding, 65–80. New York: Oxford University Press.

———. (1999). "The Economics of Jewish Continuity." *Contemporary Jewry*, 20:30–56.

———. (2001). "The Economics of Jewish Immigrants and Judaism in the United States." *Papers in Jewish Demography, 1997*, 331–344.

———. (2008). *Economics of American Judaism.* New York: Routledge.

———. (2010). "How Economics Helped Shape American Judaism." In *The Oxford Handbook of Judaism and Economics*, edited by Aaron Levine, 646–662. New York: Oxford University Press.

———. (2012). "Competition vs. Monopoly in the Religious Marketplace: Judaism in the United States and Israel." Paper presented to the Conference on Religion and Economic Liberty: A Match Made in Heaven? Jerusalem, Israel: Jerusalem Institute for Market Studies. Available at http://jimsisrael.org/pdf/Conference 2012/CarmelChiswick.pdf.

Chiswick, Carmel U., Tikva Lecker, and Nava Kahana, eds. (2007). *Jewish Society and Culture: An Economic Perspective.* Ramat Gan: Bar-Ilan University Press.

Godley, Andrew. (2001). *Jewish Immigrant Entrepreneurship in New York and London 1880–1914: Enterprise and Culture.* New York: Palgrave, 2001.

Hollander, Gideon, Nava Kahana, and Tikva Lecker. (2007). "Human Capital and the Economics of Religion." In Carmel U. Chiswick, Tikva Lecker, and Nava Kahana, eds., *Jewish Society and Culture: An Economic Perspective*, 87–102. Ramat Gan: Bar-Ilan University Press.

Lo, Stephanie, and E. Glen Weyl, eds. (2011). *Jewish Economies: Development and Migration in America and Beyond. Vol. II: The Economic Life of American Jewry.* New Brunswick, NJ: Transaction Publishers.

———. (2012). *Jewish Economies: Development and Migration in America and Beyond. Vol. I: Comparative Perspectives on Jewish Migrations.* New Brunswick, NJ: Transaction Publishers.

Lytton, Timothy D. (2013). *Kosher: Private Regulation in the Age of Industrial Food.* Cambridge, MA: Harvard University Press.

Roberts, Helen. (1999). "American Jewish Donations to Israel." *Contemporary Jewry* 20: 201–213.

American Jewry

Ament, Jonathon (2005). "American Jewish Religious Denominations," Report 10, *United Jewish Communities Report Series on the National Jewish Population Survey 2000–01*, February 2005.

Birmingham, Stephen. (1996). *Our Crowd: The Great Jewish Families of New York*. Syracuse, NY: Syracuse University Press.

———. (1997). *The Grandees: America's Sephardic Elite*. Syracuse, NY: Syracuse University Press.

———. (1999). *The Rest of Us: The Rise of America's Eastern European Jews (Modern Jewish History)*. Syracuse, NY: Syracuse University Press.

DellaPergola, Sergio. (2000). "World Jewish Population, 2000." In *American Jewish Yearbook 2000*, edited by D. Singer and L. Grossman, 484–495, New York: American Jewish Committee.

Hasia, R. Diner. (2004). *The Jews of the United States, 1654 to 2000*. Berkeley: University of California Press.

Elazar, Daniel J., and Rela Mintz Geffen. (2000). *The Conservative Movement in Judaism: Dilemmas and Opportunities*. Albany: SUNY Press.

Farber, Roberta Rosenberg, and Waxman, Chaim I., eds. (1999). *Jews in America: A Contemporary Reader*. Waltham, MA: Brandeis University Press.

Goldstein, Sidney. (1992). "Profile of American Jewry: Insights from the 1990 National Jewish Population Survey." *American Jewish Yearbook 1992*: 77–173 New York: American Jewish Committee.

Goldstein, Sidney & Alice Goldstein (1998). *Conservative Jewry in the United States: A Sociodemographic Profile*. New York: Jewish Theological Seminary.

Gordis, David M., and Dorit P. Gary, eds. (1997). *American Jewry: Portrait and Prognosis*. West Orange, NJ: Behrman House.

Joselit, Jenna Weissman. (1994). *The Wonders of America: Reinventing Jewish Culture 1880–1950*. New York: Hill and Wang, 1994.

Kaplan, Dana Evan, ed. (2013). *Contemporary Debates in American Reform Judaism: Conflicting Visions*. New York: Routledge.

Kobrin, Rebecca, ed. (2012). *Chosen Capital: The Jewish Encounter with American Capitalism*. New Brunswick, NJ: Rutgers University Press.

Kosmin, Barry (1991). *National Jewish Population Survey (NJPS) 1990*. Sponsored by Councl of Jewish Federations (now the Jewish Federation of North America). Available at www.jewishdatabank.org.

Kosmin, Barry A., N. Lerer, and E. Mayer. (1989). "Intermarriage, Divorce and Remarriage among American Jews: 1982–87." *Family Research Series*, No. 1. New York: CUNY, North American Jewish Data Bank.

Kosmin, Barry A., and Paul Ritterband, eds. (1991). *Contemporary Jewish Philanthropy in America*. Savage, MD: Rowman & Littlefield.

Kuznets, Simon S. (1975). "Immigration of Russian Jews to the United States: Background and Structure." *Perspectives in American History* 9: 35–126.

Lazerwitz, Bernard, J. Alan Winter, Arnold Dashefsky, and Ephraim Tabory (1998). *Jewish Choices: American Jewish Denominationalsim*. Albany: SUNY Press.

Lipset, Seymour Martin, and Earl Raab (1995). *Jews and the New American Scene*. Cambridge, MA: Harvard University Press.

Manners, Ande. (1972). *Poor Cousins*. New York: Coward, McCann & Geoghegan.

Mayer, Egon, Barry Kosmin, and Ariela Keysar. (2001). *American Jewish Identity Survey 2001*. Sponsored by Posen Foundation. Available at www.jewishdatabank.org.

Metzker, Isaac, ed. (1971). *A Bintel Brief: Sixty Years of Letters From the Lower East Side to the Jewish Daily Forward*. Garden City, NY: Doubleday.

Meyerhoff, Barbara (1979). *Number Our Days*. New York: E. P. Dutton.

Rebhun, Uzi. (1993). "Trends in the Size of American Jewish Denominations: A Renewed Evaluation." *CCAR Journal: A Reform Jewish Quarterly* (Winter):1–11.

Sarna, Jonathan D. (2004a). *American Judaism: A History*. New Haven, CT: Yale University Press.

———. (2004b). "New Paradigms for the Study of American Jewish Life." *Contemporary Jewry* 28: 157–169.

Schwartz, Jim, Vivian Klaff, and Frank Mott. (2004). *National Jewish Population Survey (NJPS) 2000–01*. Sponsored by United Jewish Communities (now the Jewish Federation of North America). Available at www.jewishdatabank.org/NJPS2000.asp.

Schwartz, Jim, and Jeffrey Scheckner. (2001). "Jewish Population in the United States, 2000." *American Jewish Yearbook 2000*, 253–278. New York: American Jewish Committee.

Silberman, Charles E. (1985). *A Certain People: American Jews and Their Lives Today*. New York: Summit Books.

Silverstein, Alan. (1994). *Alternatives to Assimilation: The Response of Reform Judaism to American Culture 1840–1930*. Hanover, NH: University Press of New England.

Sklare, Marshall, ed. (1958). *The Jews: Social Patterns of an American Group*. New York: The Free Press.

———. (1993). *Observing America's Jews*. Waltham, MA: Brandeis University Press.

Smith, Tom W. (2005). *Jewish Distinctiveness in America: A Statistical Portrait*. New York: American Jewish Committee.

Waxman, Chaim I. (1983). *America's Jews in Transition*. Philadelphia: Temple University Press.

Wertheimer, Jack. (1993). *A People Divided: Judaism in Contemporary America*. New York: Basic Books.

———. (1996). *Conservative Synagogues and Their Members: Highlights of the North American Study of 1995–96*. New York: Jewish Theological Seminary of America.

———. (1997). "Current Trends in American Jewish Philanthropy." In *American Jewish Year Book 1997*, 3–92. New York: American Jewish Committee.

———. (1999). "Jewish Education in the United States: Recent Trends and Issues," in *American Jewish Year Book 1999*, 3–115. New York: American Jewish Committee.

Index

Abraham, 90
adult singles, 122, 123–24, 125
aging of American Jewry, 190–92,
    195–96
AJIS. *See* American Jewish Identity
    Survey
Allen, Woody, 89
American Community Survey, 27
Americanism Commission, 151
Americanization. *See* Small Traditions,
    American Judaism
American Jewish Committee, 151
American Jewish Identity Survey (AJIS),
    31–33
American Religious Identification Sur-
    vey (ARIS), 31
Amsterdam Haggadah, 99
Anticomplementary skills. *See* human
    capital
Anti-Defamation League (ADL), 151
anti-Semitism, 3, 91, 111, 150–51, 172,
    178, 179. *See also* Holocaust
Aramaic, 77
Ashkenazi Judaism. *See* Small Tradi-
    tions, Ashkenazi Judaism

Bar Mitzvah ceremony, 16, 83, 84, 86,
    123, 125, 146; Haftorah reading in,
    82, 147; as new tradition, 15, 144
Bat Mitzvah ceremony, 83, 86, 123, 125;
    Haftorah reading in, 82; as new tradi-
    tion, 15, 144, 147

Berlin, Irving: "Easter Parade," 94;
    "White Christmas," 94
Birthright Israel, 86–87
B'nai Brith, 151
Botticini, Maristella, 217n2
British Mandate Palestine, 151, 161, 164;
    economic conditions in, 162–63,
    172
brit milah, 12, 13, 178

Catholicism, 111, 217n.5
Chanukah, 12, 14, 88, 90–91, 92, 93–95
chavurot, 199–200
chicken soup, 14
children: cost of, 115–17; economics of
    parenting, 23, 113–17, 118; invest-
    ments regarding, 106, 107, 115–17;
    Jewish fertility rate, 113–16, 118–21,
    124–25, 190, 191, 193, 197; large ver-
    sus small families, 118, 119–21; and
    marriage, 23, 38, 40, 41, 49, 105–6,
    111, 112, 113–21, 122, 136, 153, 181,
    190, 195; medical care for, 116, 117;
    parental legacy for, 118–21; quantity-
    quality trade-off regarding, 117–18;
    of two-career couples, 118. *See also*
    Bar Mitzvah; Bat Mitzvah; Jewish
    education
Christianity, 3, 10, 93, 111
Christmas, 3, 93–96
circumcision, 12, 13, 178
cohabitation, 122

Complementary skills. *See* human capital
congregationalism, 166–67, 168, 217n5
Conservative Judaism, 33, 63, 70, 145;
and Israel, 175, 176–77; Jewish education in, 16, 53–54, 80, 83; Passover
celebration in, 96, 99–100; and Reconstructionist Judaism, 69, 196–97,
215n3, 216n4; siddur (prayer book)
in, 78–79; synagogue members, 32,
68; synagogue services in, 76, 78–79,
81, 146, 199; United Synagogue of
Conservative Judaism (USCJ), 65,
143, 167; USCJ, 65, 143, 167; and
value of time, 22, 66, 157, 168
continuity, 195, 196
cost: direct versus indirect 7, 8; money
versus time, 19, 22, 56–58, 61–65,
67, 71, 75, 92, 108, 115–16, 117, 138,
141, 144, 146, 153–54, 168–69, 185,
192, 196; marginal, 59–61; full, 8,
19, 57–58, 62–63, 64–65, 71, 75, 153,
154, 192, 193, 198. *See also* full price.
Council of Jewish Federations and Welfare Funds (CJF), 31, 152

democracy, 5, 8, 53, 93
dietary laws. *See* kashrut
diversity among Jews, 21–22, 25–26, 27,
28, 31, 192, 200
divorce, 113, 121, 122, 168, 189

Eckstein, Zvi, 217n2
earnings: by education level, 43–45,
61–62, 156–57; by occupation, 43,
45–46, 48, 61–63, 67, 115, 138, 153.
See also income; wage rates
economic incentives: in the future,
192–94; in Israel versus United
States, 169–70, 171; regarding Jewish education, 75, 76, 77; regarding
parenting activities, 23, 113–17, 118;
relationship to religious observance,
7–8, 9–10, 20–21, 24, 29, 64–65,
66–71, 156–57, 168, 180–82, 195–96,

198, 215n3, 217n2; relationship to
technological innovation, 183, 189.
See also value of time
economic inequality, 110, 193, 216n1;
poverty, 47–48, 115, 127, 128,
133–34. *See also* wealth
economics: economic principles, 24,
59, 66, 181; Economics of Religion,
6, 20; labor economics, 17–20, 22,
56–57; and scarcity, 5–6; and self-
produced/home-produced goods,
5–6; and spending patterns, 5. *See
also* full price; human capital; value
of time
economies of scale, 117–18
education: advanced degrees, 33, 34,
35–36, 37, 40, 42, 43–44, 66, 70,
116, 117, 137–38, 183, 184, 186, 193;
attainment, 22, 32, 33–36, 50, 102,
125, 146, 155, 171, 181, 198; high
school graduation, 33, 34–35, 66, 184;
as investment, 26, 74, 116, 117, 122,
138, 193; of Jews versus non-Jews,
33, 34, 38, 112, 138, 189, 193–94; of
parents, 49, 116, 119, 120; relationship to health, 48–49; relationship
to income, 43–45, 61–62, 109, 110,
117, 156–57, 197; relationship to
Jewish education, 101; relationship
to marriage, 45, 108–10, 116, 189;
relationship to problem solving, 48,
49; relationship to synagogue movements, 65–66, 67–71, 76, 156; women
versus men regarding, 33–35, 36,
43–44, 48, 109–10, 116, 120, 136–38,
153–54, 184, 216n2. *See also* Jewish
education
elderly parents, 36, 42, 47–48, 113, 119,
184, 191; care for, 41, 44, 48
Ellis Island, 127–28, 131
empty nesters, 124, 125–26, 187, 191
enclave communities, 157, 165; of Jewish
immigrants, 25, 129, 133–34, 137,
145, 148, 149, 152

English language: learning of, 14, 128,
129, 131, 134, 144; in synagogue
services, 76, 78–79, 80, 83, 142;
translations from Hebrew, 70, 75–76,
78, 79, 80, 83, 87–88, 92, 99, 142
Enlightenment, 15
entrepreneurship, 25, 129, 132, 134, 136,
185–86
Esther, Book of, 11, 12, 95
ethnicity: ethnic goods, 133; and Jewish
identity, 28, 29, 31, 32, 36, 72, 146
Exodus from Egypt, 90, 96, 97, 98–99,
100, 106. *See also* Passover (Pesach)
extended families, 112, 113, 118, 125,
161, 176, 192

full price: defined, 22, 55, 56–58, 153; of
Jewish education, 54–64, 75, 116–17;
relationship to value of time, 22, 55,
56–58, 65–66, 69, 70, 153, 181; of religious observance, 64–66, 68, 69–71,
181, 198; of self-produced goods, 181

garment industry, 14, 25, 38, 64, 128,
132, 148
gefilte fish, 14, 16
Gemara, 10
globalization, 186–87, 189
Great Depression, 34, 155
Great Recession, 187–88, 194
Great Tradition: Haggadot, 98–100; and
innovations, 15, 23; versus Small Traditions, 8–9, 11, 13, 14–15, 92, 201;
Talmud, 10–11, 94, 98, 101; Torah,
10–13, 75, 78–82, 88, 89, 90, 93, 96,
97–98, 101, 106, 142, 147, 148, 169,
184; in United States, 10–13. *See also*
Hebrew language; Hebrew Scriptures; kashrut

Hadassah, 151, 166
Haftorah, 80–81, 82, 147
Haggadot, 98–100
hamentashen, 14, 95

Hanukah. *See* Chanukah
Hebrew Immigrant Aid Society (HIAS),
150
Hebrew language, 14, 64, 70, 77, 85,
148; English translations, 76, 78–79,
80, 83, 99, 100, 142; and Hebrew
schools, 83, 84, 170–71; modern
Hebrew, 75, 80, 87, 156, 162, 163,
164, 165, 169, 170–71; reading from
Torah, 10, 12–13, 78–82, 89, 90, 147,
169; *ulpan* method, 87, 165; and value
of time, 75–76, 92
Hebrew Scriptures, 75, 162, 163;
Prophets, 11, 80–81; Torah, 10–13,
75, 78–82, 88, 89, 90, 93, 96, 97–98,
101, 106, 142, 147, 148, 169, 184;
Writings, 11
High Holy Days. *See* Rosh Hashanah;
Yom Kippur
Hillel Foundation, 123, 151
Holocaust, 15, 23, 86, 132, 155, 157, 161,
164; Remembrance Day, 91
homemakers, full-time, 38, 40, 41, 42,
60, 61, 136, 153, 215n2
homogamy, 109–10
homosexuality, 121
honey cake, 14
human capital: anticomplementary
skills, 93–96, 181; complementary
skills, 92–93, 95, 96–102, 129, 132,
181, 190; as country-specific, 76,
128–29, 131–32, 134, 140, 141, 146,
162, 163–65, 170; defined, 22, 73,
181; general versus specific skills,
73–74, 76; investment in, 22, 74–75,
92, 101–2, 108–10, 132–33, 135, 140,
141, 146–47, 148, 150, 153, 162, 163,
164–65, 181, 184, 190, 192–93; and
Jewish education, 22, 73–76, 77,
92–93, 110, 111, 116–17, 146; Jewish human capital, 22–23, 74–102,
108–10, 111, 112, 116–17, 119, 120,
129, 145–48, 156, 162, 163–64,
169, 170–71, 181, 190, 195, 196;

human capital (*continued*)
of Jewish immigrants, 127–34,
145–48; and marriage, 108–10, 111;
as parental legacy, 118–20; secular
versus Jewish, 22–23, 73–74; as transferable, 128–29, 131, 140, 165, 170;
universal versus parochial aspects of
Judaism, 76, 92–102
Humanistic Judaism, 197

immigrants. *See* Jewish immigrants,
American
income, 5, 22, 27, 42–48, 171, 181;
versus earnings, 46–48, 68, 69, 71,
183–84, 185, 187, 192, 198; preferences and income levels, 62–63, 69;
relationship to religious observance,
7, 8, 66–70, 157; relationship to synagogue movements, 54, 66–70; women
versus men regarding, 43–44, 45–46,
109. *See also* earnings; wage rates
intermarriage. *See* marriage, intermarriage between Jews and non-Jews
investment: in children, 106, 107,
115–17; defined, 74, 106, 181; in
human capital, 22, 73, 74–75, 92,
101–2, 108–10, 132–33, 135, 140,
141, 146–47, 148, 150, 153, 162, 163,
164–65, 181, 184, 190, 192–93; Jewish education as, 26, 72–73, 74–75,
76, 92–93, 101, 116–17; marriage
as, 106, 107–8, 109, 113; secular
education as, 26, 74, 116, 117, 122,
138, 193. *See also* education; Jewish
education
Islam, 3
Israeli Jews, 75, 80; celebration of
holidays by, 88, 89, 96; celebration of
Passover by, 96; relations with American Jews, 20, 23–24, 86–87, 161–62,
166, 170–79, 182
Israel, State of: Board of Rabbis, 167–68,
169–70, 176–77; economic condi-

tions in, 155, 157, 161–62, 164, 168,
171–73, 175, 177, 182; founding of,
23–24, 100, 152, 156, 161, 175; Independence Day, 91; Jewish immigration to, 161–66, 171, 172, 175–76;
Jewish observance in, 166–77, 182;
Jewish population in, 4, 5; kibbutz
life in, 86; Ministry of Religious Services, 167; religious political parties
in, 170; and security, 178–79; Six-
Day War, 173–75; trips to, 22, 86–87,
102, 123, 148, 155, 161–62, 170, 171,
172–73, 174, 175, 195; Western Wall,
174, 177. *See also* Land of Israel

Jewish Agency for Israel, 166
Jewish calendar, 87–89, 106, 216n2
Jewish camping, 22, 73, 84–86, 102, 123,
171, 195
Jewish clergy, 6, 7, 15, 20, 67, 121, 142,
147, 195, 199; Rabbinate in Israel,
167–68, 169–70, 176–77
Jewish Community Center (JCC), 150,
155
Jewish education: day schools, 16,
17–19, 53–56, 57–58, 61–63, 83, 116;
defined, 72; economic incentives
regarding, 75, 76, 77; full cost of,
54–64, 75, 116–17; Hebrew schools,
13, 53, 54, 55–56, 57–58, 61–63,
76, 77, 83–84, 101, 102, 117, 120,
123, 146, 147, 167, 170–71, 195;
during holiday celebrations, 22, 87,
90–91, 98–100, 105–6; and human
capital, 22, 73–76, 77, 92–93, 110,
111, 116–17, 119, 171; as investment,
26, 72–73, 74–75, 76, 92–93, 101,
116–17; money price of, 54–55, 56,
74–75; relationship to State of Israel,
24; relationship to wage rates, 57–59,
61–63; role in Jewish identity, 72–73,
93, 102, 112, 195, 196; versus secular
education, 53–54, 101; and value

of time, 55–56, 57–58, 71, 74–76,
117; women versus men regarding,
120–21
Jewish Federation, 152
Jewish Federations of North America
(JFNA), 152
Jewish holidays: abstention from work
on, 11, 89, 90, 92, 96; as conflicting
with larger society, 93–96; as education, 22, 87, 90–91, 98–100, 105–6;
and Jewish human capital formation,
87–102; observance of, 3, 7, 8, 10, 11,
13, 14, 17, 22, 23, 64, 77, 81, 87–100,
101, 102, 112, 116, 118, 124, 140,
141, 147, 179, 195, 216n3; role of
food in, 14; and value of time, 92,
96–97
Jewish identity: by conversion, 72, 112,
168, 189; and ethnicity, 28, 29, 31,
32, 36, 72, 146; and intermarriage,
112, 190; and marriage, 112, 190,
194, 195, 201; by parentage, 30, 31,
32, 72, 112, 145–46, 189, 215n4,
216n1; role of Israel in, 173; role of
Jewish education in, 72–73, 93, 102,
112, 195, 196; role of Jewish human
capital in, 91, 93, 102, 112, 129, 190,
195; role of Jewish immigrant experience in, 127; role of parareligious organizations in, 155, 156, 189–90; role
of religion in, 29–30, 32–33, 35–36,
41, 69, 72, 152, 190, 194, 195, 201;
self-identification, 22, 28–30, 32–33,
41, 69, 72; and trips to Israel, 87, 155
Jewish immigrants, American, 9, 12,
127–57; assimilation of, 21, 29, 94,
102, 129, 131–32, 134–41, 144, 145,
148–49, 152–54, 155–56, 166, 176,
181, 200; economic conditions for,
23, 64–65, 127–28, 130–39, 140,
142, 150, 153, 155, 156–57, 168, 171,
181, 200; enclave communities of,
25, 129, 133–34, 137, 145, 148, 149,

152; family size among, 114–15; from
Germany, 13–14, 64, 127, 130–31,
141–43, 145, 151, 154; human capital
of, 127–34, 145–48; versus immigrants to Israel, 162, 164; Jewish
education among, 145–48; Jewish
human capital of, 145–48; Jewish
observance among, 139–44, 147,
149, 152; from Middle East, 132, 145;
occupations of, 14, 25, 27–28, 35,
38, 47, 64, 128, 129, 130–33, 135–36;
parareligious organizations for, 149,
150–55, 156; from Russia and Eastern
Europe, 13–15, 23, 27, 64, 100, 127,
128, 130–32, 133–34, 135, 139–41,
143, 145, 146, 150–51, 156, 192;
the siddur among, 79; from Soviet
Union, 132, 145
Jewish National Fund (JNF), 151
Jewish observance: by adult singles,
123–24; cost of, 7–8, 19, 89; by
empty nesters, 124; full price of,
64–66, 68, 69–71, 198; innovations in, 194; by Israeli Jews, 23–24,
166–75; in Israel versus United States,
166–77, 182; by Jewish immigrants
to America, 139–44, 147, 149, 152;
in large versus small families, 118;
relationship to economic incentives,
7–8, 9–10, 20–21, 24, 29, 64–65,
66–71, 156–57, 168, 180–82, 195–96,
198, 215n3, 217n2; relationship to
occupational attainment, 49, 66,
71; relationship to scarcity, 5–6, 17,
19; relationship to value of time, 22,
63–66, 68, 70–71, 141, 142, 143, 144,
146, 147–48, 156–57, 168–69, 177,
184, 197–98; relationship to wage
rates, 64, 65–70, 71, 76, 157, 177, 197,
198; rules of observance, 7–8, 10–11,
12, 13; time-intensity of, 64, 65–66,
67, 68, 69, 70, 83, 141, 142, 147, 152,
157, 168–69, 171, 195–96, 197–98.

Jewish observance (*continued*)
   See also dietary laws; Jewish holidays;
   Sabbath observance
Jewish parareligious organizations, 123,
   125, 166, 169, 182, 192, 194, 200; and
   Jewish identity, 155, 156, 189–90; and
   Jewish immigrants, 149, 150–55, 156
Jewish population: in Israel, 4, 5; by
   metropolitan area, 4, 25–26, 30; in
   United States, 4, 5, 9, 12, 13–15,
   25–26, 27–28, 30–31, 32, 38, 113–14,
   124–26, 189–92, 217n1; in world,
   3–4
Jewish Renewal, 197
Jewish Theological Seminary, 144
Joint Distribution Committee (JDC),
   151, 166

Kaplan, Mordecai, 143–44, 216n4
kashrut: defined, 12; holiday cuisine, 14,
   16; observance of, 7, 13, 70, 85, 97,
   133, 140, 141, 150, 195
klezmer bands, 133
kosher foods. *See* kashrut

Lag B'Omer, 88, 91
Land of Israel, 11, 90
landsmenshaften, 133
latkes, 14
law of diminishing returns, 58–59, 67
laws of Noah, 106
lay leaders, 125–26
Lent, 95
life-cycle ceremonies, 15, 16, 77, 82, 83,
   84, 86, 105
lox and bagels, 16

ma'abarot, 165, 166
Maccabees, Book of, 12, 94
Mardi Gras, 95
marriage: age at, 121–23; and children,
   23, 38, 40, 41, 49, 105–6, 111, 112,
   113–21, 122, 136, 153, 181, 190, 195;
and continuity, 195, 196; as contract,
   107–8; divorce, 113, 121, 122, 168,
   189; economics of marriage, 107–12;
   economics of parenting, 113–17; and
   extended families, 112, 113, 118;
   full-time homemakers, 38, 40, 41, 42,
   60, 61, 136, 153, 215n2; homogamy,
   109–10; and human capital, 108–10,
   111; intermarriage between Jews and
   non-Jews, 15, 29–30, 36, 110–12, 114,
   121, 189, 190, 191, 194, 196, 201,
   217n1; as investment, 106, 107–8,
   109, 113; and Jewish human capital,
   108–10, 111; partner selection, 8, 23,
   45, 106, 107–8, 109–10, 111, 121,
   189, 194; positive assortative mating,
   109–10; relationship to educational
   attainment, 45, 108–10, 116, 189;
   relationship to Jewish identity,
   112, 190, 194, 195, 201; two-career
   couples, 40–42, 43, 44–45, 46, 63,
   110, 115, 116, 118, 125, 193, 195, 196
matza, 14, 16, 96, 98
Maxwell House Haggadah, 99
mezuzah, 12, 13
Mishna, 10, 98
Mizrachi, 164
Modern Orthodox Judaism. *See* Orthodox Judaism
money price, 22, 181; of Jewish education, 54–55, 56, 74–75. *See also* full
   price.
morning prayers, 70

National Farm School, 150
National Jewish Hospital, 151
National Jewish Population Survey
   (NJPS), 29–30, 31–36, 37–38, 39, 41,
   42–43, 47, 215nn1,3,5
National Survey of Religion and Ethnic-
   ity (NSRE), 31
National Survey of Religious Identity
   (NSRI), 31

New Age Judaism, 197

NJPS. *See* National Jewish Population Survey

occupational attainment, 22, 32, 37–42, 74, 76, 181; among Jewish immigrants, 14, 25, 35, 38, 47, 64, 128, 129, 130–33, 135–36; lawyers, 33, 37, 38, 39, 46, 57–58, 61, 110, 136, 184, 192–93; managerial occupations, 37, 38, 39, 41–42, 45, 46, 49, 135, 136, 139, 146, 185–86, 192–93; medical doctors, 33, 37, 38, 39, 45–46, 110, 119–20, 135, 136, 151, 184, 192–93; paraprofessional occupations, 193; professional occupations, 37, 38, 39, 40–42, 43–44, 45–46, 48, 49–50, 112, 135, 136, 139, 146, 162, 183, 184, 188, 192–93, 196, 197, 200; relationship to earnings, 26–27, 43, 45–46, 48, 67, 115, 117, 138, 192–93; sales occupations, 37–38, 40, 41, 42, 131, 135; STEM occupations, 185, 192–93; teachers, 37, 38, 40, 46, 135, 136, 184; two-career couples, 40–42, 43, 44–45, 46, 63, 110, 115, 116, 118, 125, 193, 195, 196; white-collar versus blue-collar occupations, 37–38, 39, 131, 135, 136, 182–83, 185–86, 188; women versus men regarding, 38, 40, 118–19, 120–21, 136–37, 153–54, 183

Orthodox Judaism, 63, 68–69, 196–97; in Israel, 167–68, 171, 176; Jewish education in, 83, 120; among Jewish immigrants, 144–45, 147; as Modern Orthodox, 35, 69, 143; Passover celebration in, 96; synagogue members, 32–33; synagogue services in, 76, 79–80, 81, 82, 144; time-intensity in, 83; and value of time, 65–66, 67, 70. *See also* ultra-Orthodox Judaism

Orthodox Union (OU), 65, 143, 167

parareligious organizations: *See* Jewish parareligious organizations.

parentage, 30, 31, 32, 72

Passover (Pesach), 11–12, 14, 88, 89, 90, 92; Haggadot, 98–100; Seder, 96, 97–100, 118, 147; and value of time, 96–97

Pilgrimage Festivals, 11–12

population cylinder versus population pyramid, 124–25, 190, 195–96

positive assortative mating, 109–10

poverty, 47–48, 115, 127, 128, 133–34

prices. *See* full price; money price

Prophets (in Hebrew Scriptures), 11, 80–81

Protestantism, 111

Purim, 12, 14, 88, 90–91, 95–96

Reconstructionist Judaism, 22, 69, 175, 176–77, 196–97, 215n3, 216n4

Reform Judaism, 25, 63, 68–70, 144, 196–97; celebration of holidays in, 88, 89, 96, 97; and German Reform movement, 64–65, 76, 142, 143; and Israel, 175, 176–77; Jewish education in, 83; Passover celebration in, 96; synagogue members, 32, 68; synagogue services in, 80, 81, 83, 142, 143, 146; time-intensity in, 67; and value of time, 22, 65–66, 97, 142–44, 157, 168

retail industry, 25, 130, 142

ritual baths (mikva), 150, 168

Rosh Hashanah, 11, 14, 88, 89, 90, 92, 141

Sabbath. *See* Shabbat (Sabbath)

scarcity: relationship to religious behavior, 5–6, 17, 19; of time, 22, 74–75

Schechter, Solomon, 144. *See also* Solomon Schechter schools.

secular Jews, 30, 116–17, 190, 198, 216n3

self-employment, 25, 129, 136, 216n3
self-produced goods, 5–6, 181
Senior citizens (demography, population cylinder, retirees, etc.), 41, 60–61, 125, 134, 184, 185, 191–92, 195, 196
Sephardi Judaism, 9, 25, 80, 130, 145, 154, 164, 167, 170
Shabbat (Sabbath): and God's creation, 90, 106; observance of, 7, 11, 70, 85, 88, 92, 105, 116, 118, 140, 141, 147, 195; at sundown, 13, 18, 142; synagogue services on, 10, 18–19, 64, 80, 81, 89, 142, 199
Shavuot (Feast of Weeks/Pentecost), 11–12, 88, 90
Shmini Azeret, 88, 89
siddur (prayer book), 78–79
Simhat Torah, 88, 89
Six-Day War, 173–75
Skare, Marshall, 216n4
Small Traditions: American Judaism, 15–21, 24, 144, 156–57, 200–201; Ashkenazi Judaism, 9, 12, 13–15, 16, 25, 80, 130–33, 145, 156, 164, 167, 170, 201; cuisine in, 13, 14, 16; versus Great Traditions, 8–10, 11, 13, 14–15, 201; relationship to economic conditions, 9–10; Sephardi Judaism, 9, 25, 80, 130, 145, 154, 164, 167, 170
Solomon Schechter schools, 53–54. See also Schechter, Solomon
stereotypes, 21–22, 25, 26, 38, 45, 50, 53, 134, 175
Sukkot, 11–12, 88, 89
surveys of American Jews, 28, 40, 217n1; American Jewish Identity Survey (AJIS), 31–33; National Jewish Population Survey (NJPS), 29–30, 31–36, 37–38, 39, 41, 42–43, 47, 215nn1,3,5
synagogue movements, 63–71, 149, 155, 201; and Hebrew schools, 77, 83–84; and Israel, 176–77; and Jewish camping, 85; and Jewish human capital, 76, 156, 190; relationship to educa-

tional attainment, 65–66, 67–71, 76, 156; relationship to income, 54, 66–70; relationship to value of time, 22, 63–66, 67, 70, 97, 141–44, 157, 168; relationship to wage rates, 66–70, 157; splintering of, 196–97; umbrella organizations, 65, 142, 143, 152, 167, 182, 197. See also Conservative Judaism; Orthodox Judaism; Reconstructionist Judaism; Reform Judaism
synagogue services: attendance at, 8, 17, 55–56, 92, 140, 141, 142, 144, 147, 148, 169; choice of synagogue, 69–70; in Conservative synagogues, 76, 78–79, 81, 146, 199; English language in, 76, 78–79, 80, 83, 142; and Jewish human capital, 22, 78–82, 101, 195; music in, 78, 79, 80; in Orthodox synagogues, 76, 79–80, 81, 82; Purim celebrations, 95–96; reading of Haftorah in, 80–81, 82; reading of Torah in, 10, 11, 12–13, 78–82, 89, 90, 147, 169; in Reform synagogues, 80, 81, 83, 142, 143, 146; scheduling of, 15, 18, 142; and State of Israel, 175; in storefront synagogues (steibls), 140–41, 144; for teenagers, 123; time-intensity of, 64, 65–66, 68, 142; women during, 15, 81–82, 121

tallit, 13
Talmud, 10–11, 94, 98, 101
Tanakh, 11
technological innovation, 182–83, 185–87, 188–89, 190, 191, 197–98
teenagers, 19, 60, 84, 85, 86, 123
tefillin, 12, 139
Temple in Jerusalem: destruction of, 91, 98, 217n2; pilgrimages to, 12, 97–98
Ten Commandments, 106
time: allocation of, 17–20, 55–57, 58–61, 63–65; in direct and indirect costs,

7, 8; leisure time, 58–59, 67, 68; marginal value of, 59, 60–61; monetary value of, 56–57, 58; nonmarket time, 59–61; scarcity of, 22, 74–75. *See also* time-intensity; value of time
time-intensity, 56, 61, 138, 192; defined, 55; of Jewish education, 63, 77; of Jewish observance, 64, 65–66, 67, 68, 69, 70, 83, 141, 142, 147, 152, 157, 168–69, 171, 195–96, 197–98; of language learning, 74, 75; of parenting activities, 118; of self-produced goods, 181; of synagogue services, 64, 65–66, 68, 142. *See also* value of time
Tisha B'Av, 88, 91
Torah, 10–13, 75, 93, 101, 106, 142, 148, 184; holidays designated in, 11–12, 88, 96, 97–98; reading from, 10, 12–13, 78–82, 89, 90, 147, 169
tsitsit, 12

ultra-Orthodox Judaism, 6, 33, 69, 143, 148, 149, 169, 184, 215n3; and educational attainment, 35, 36, 48; and family size, 115, 119, 197–98; Jewish education in, 35, 48; and poverty, 48; time-intensity in, 198
umbrella organizations; *See* synagogue movements, umbrella organizations
Union of American Hebrew Congregations (UAHC), 65, 142–43, 167
Union of Orthodox Jewish Congregations of America (OU), 143
Union of Reform Judaism (URJ), 142, 167
United Jewish Appeal (UJA), 152, 166
United Jewish Communities, 31
United Palestine Appeal, 152
United States: future of Judaism in, 194–201; Jewish-Christian relations in, 3, 14; Jewish fertility rate in, 113–16, 118–21, 124–25, 190, 191, 193, 197; Jewish population in, 4, 5, 9, 12, 13–15, 25–26, 27–28, 30–31,

32, 38, 113–14, 124–26, 189–92, 217n1; relations between American and Israeli Jews, 20, 23–24, 86–87, 161–62, 166, 170–79, 182; technological innovation in, 182–83, 185–87, 188–89, 190, 191, 197–98. *See also* Jewish immigrants, American
United Synagogue of America (USA), 65, 143, 167
United Synagogue of Conservative Judaism (USCJ), 65, 143, 167
upward mobility, 26, 67, 134, 153, 161, 164, 183
U.S. Census, 27, 31, 215nn2,4; 2000 Census, 32, 33, 43–44, 137–38

value of time, 55–61, 62–67, 138, 153–54, 196; and Conservative Judaism, 22, 66, 157, 168; and Hebrew language, 75–76, 92; and Jewish education, 55–56, 57–58, 71, 74–76, 117; and Jewish holidays, 92, 96–97; and Orthodox Judaism, 65–66, 67, 70; and Reform Judaism, 22, 97, 142–44, 157, 168; relationship to full price, 22, 55, 56–58, 65–66, 69, 70, 153, 181; relationship to Jewish observance, 22, 63–66, 68, 70–71, 141, 142, 143, 144, 146, 147–48, 156–57, 168–69, 177, 184, 197–98; relationship to synagogue movements, 22, 63–66, 67, 70, 97, 141–44, 157, 168; relationship to wage rates, 56–58, 59, 60, 62–63, 64, 65–66, 67, 68, 69, 115–16, 140–41, 143, 144, 168–69, 177, 181, 184; for senior citizens, 184–85. *See also* time-intensity
Vocational Service Bureau, 151
volunteers, 40, 153–54

wage rates, 74, 153, 157, 182–85, 187, 192, 195; high versus low, 58, 60, 61–63, 181, 183; relationship to Jewish education, 57–59, 61–63;

wage rates (*continued*)
    relationship to Jewish observance, 64,
      65–70, 71, 76, 157, 177, 197, 198; re-
      lationship to synagogue movements,
      66–70, 157; relationship to value
      of time, 56–58, 59, 60, 62–63, 64,
      65–66, 67, 68, 71, 140–41, 168–69,
      181, 197; and taxation, 215n1; in
      United States versus Israel, 171. *See
      also* earnings, income
wealth, 5–6, 62, 63, 66–67, 68, 110, 157
Wertheimer, Jack: on paradox of apathy
    and renewal, 148
Wise, Isaac Mayer, 142
Writings (in Hebrew Scriptures), 11

yeshivas, 87
Yiddish, 13–14, 15–16, 25, 27–28, 79,
    140, 149, 150, 154; Yiddish press,
    133, 134, 136, 148; Yiddish theater,
    133, 148
Yom Kippur, 11, 88, 89, 90, 92, 141
Young Men's Hebrew Association
    (YMHA), 151

Zionism, 163–64, 166, 169; Labor Zion-
    ism, 85–86; in United States, 151,
    166, 172, 173–74
Zionist Organization of America, 151